THE GOLD OF TUTANKHAMEN

THE GOLD OF TUTANKHAMEN

Kamal El Mallakh / Arnold C. Brackman

Preface by WILLIAM KELLY SIMPSON
Curator of Egyptian and Near Eastern Art
Museum of Fine Arts, Boston and
Professor of Egyptology, Yale University

Newsweek Books, New York

1978 First English Language Edition

Introduction, preface, illustrations and
captions ©1978 Kodansha Ltd. Tokyo

Text ©1976 Arnold C. Brackman
The Search for the Gold of Tutankhamen.

Library of Congress Cataloging in Publication Data

el-MALLĀKH, KAMĀL.
    The Gold of Tutankhamen.

    Includes index.
    1. Tutankhamen, King of Egypt-Tomb.
    2. Excavations (Archaeology)-Egypt.   3. Egypt-
    Antiquities.   I. Brackman, Arnold C., joint
    author.   II. Title.
    DT87.5.M24 1978   932'.01'0924   78-7184

el-Mallākh, Kamāl.

ISBN 0-88225-264-X

Printed and bound in Japan by
Dai Nippon Printing Company, Tokyo

CONTENTS

Preface

In the chapel paintings of the tombs of the officials of the New Kingdom at Thebes are scenes of the inspection of the royal and temple workshops. These representations, which have a tradition in the earlier Old and Middle Kingdoms, show craftsmen at work producing elaborate jewelry, intricate pieces of state furniture, vessels of alabaster, hard stone, and precious metals, and a wide selection of statues in wood and stone. There are also extraordinary scenes of gifts and tribute from the neighboring nations and regions, elaborate textiles, gold, ebony, leather goods, and ivory from the south, and drinking vessels of foreign shapes and ornamentation from the northeast. These processions of tribute bearers even include live animals and plants, the apes, monkeys, and giraffes from the south, and bears from Syria. In the Amarna correspondence there is a record of the king of Egypt sending ten ebony chests inlaid with ivory and lapis-lazuli to a ruler in Asia Minor, and many other gifts of this nature were dispatched to Assyrian and Palestinian potentates. Intensive excavations of modern times seemed to prove again and again that the royal tombs had been quite completely plundered in ancient times and their contents melted down, burnt, or reused. Nevertheless, the excavations of Theodore Davis and others revealed traces and battered fragments which suggested that the representations in the painting corresponded to real objects and were not fanciful at all. Confirmation for this existed in the occasional find of intact or fragmentary furniture and jewelry from the burial equipment of the royal officials.

Then in 1922 Carter and Carnarvon discovered the long missing burial of the relatively obscure Tutankhamen, a king whose reign lasted only ten years. Although there were abundant traces of plundering, the greater part of the contents had not been stolen, the actual burial in its coffins, sarcophagus, and enclosing shrines was indeed intact, and an unbelievable wealth of funerary equipment in its original context was miraculously preserved. A curious combination of circumstances seems to have made the preservation of the tomb possible. Tutankhamen was a minor ruler at the end of a period which saw a major change in the kingship, the age of Akhenaten and Nefertiti known as the Amarna age. The official king lists pass directly from Amenhotep III to Horemheb and simply omit the Amarna kings as if they had never ruled. Many of their monuments were dismantled for use in the foundation of other buildings. The initial plundering of the tomb and the subsequent re-sealing of its entrance alerted the officials of the time to the ever-present danger of violation. The entrance of the tomb was located in the floor of the Valley near the well-guarded gateway to the area. Several years after it was re-sealed, work commenced on the tomb of Horemheb, the roadway was raised by limestone chips and rock falls, and construction workers built their houses above the area. By incredible chance the secret of the site of the tomb of this little-known ruler must have been carefully guarded by those who knew it and forgotten by the ever-present malefactors. Generations of tomb robbers walked over the site of the entrance in ignorance of its location as did the archaeologists of modern times.

As we marvel at the beauty and strangeness of the contents, we should be aware of several factors. First of all, each of the objects served a functional purpose in the funerary arrangements of the king. Some of these purposes are not yet clearly understood, but there was a reason for the inclusion of each object. We must have a grasp of the symbolism of the objects and a basic knowledge or acquaintance with Egyptian religion and artistic conventions. Second, we should be able to place the objects in the context of their development in Egyptian art, their relation to the change of style seen in the Amarna period, and their real aesthetic value. An eminent Egyptologist has in fact described some of the objects as "pretentious set-pieces which strain hard for effect with their heavily overloaded ornament." And his judgment is correct; the artistic level of the contents is uneven, ranging from the finest achievements of the Egyptian artist-craftsman to the pretentious. Yet the level of competence is consistently high, whether the object reflects the achievement of a master sculptor or a professional craftsman.

Inscriptions abound on the objects, identifying their owner, their use, and some of the rites. Yet modern scholars have always been bemused that the young king did not take part of his library with him. The recorded contents of the tomb do not include any inscribed papyrus or leather rolls with religious texts or even the wisdom literature, narratives, or love poetry of the times. His age was a turbulent one, which may, as suggested, account for the preservation of the tomb. Yet his successor and the officials in charge of his burial do not appear to have included any historical record of it in the tomb, leaving the myriad of objects and burial trappings to speak for themselves. And as we look at the magnificent photographic record of these marvels, they do speak to us in a universal language.

WILLIAM KELLY SIMPSON
Professor of Egyptology, Yale University

Curator of Egyptian and Ancient Near Eastern Art
Museum of Fine Arts, Boston

Introduction

The first desire of any visitor to Egypt surely is to see the Nile and the Great Pyramid, to gaze upon the Sphinx, and then to view the treasures of Tutankhamen. The Great Pyramid, the largest tomb in the world, represents the greatest surviving evidence of the architectural achievement of ancient Egyptian civilization. Some 465 miles to the south, visitors may wander about the great temples of Luxor and the Valley of the Kings, and descend into the darkness of Tutankhamen's tomb.

Tutankhamen was one of the least effective of the pharaohs. In contrast to Akhenaten, his immediate predecessor, who holds a well deserved place in the history of civilization, Tutankhamen was not distinguished by any innovations in thought or science, nor in political or military achievements. Yet this minor ruler, called the "Boy Pharaoh," is known far and wide, not because of what he did or inspired—although he lived through a most ferocious conflict between two faiths—but because his final resting place was the only one to have remained undisturbed into this century.

When Howard Carter opened Tutankhamen's tomb little more than fifty years ago, the grandeur of Pharaonic Egypt overwhelmed him. Imagination runs wild when conjecturing what must have filled the tombs of more powerful pharaohs, such as a Rameses, or a Cheops, or a Seti. Nonetheless, Tutankhamen today is a mighty conqueror: he has captured the minds and imaginations of countless millions around the world who have gazed upon his images and possessions.

Inside his tomb in the Valley of the Kings, the visitor may look at the murals; but the royal mummy, now enclosed in the outermost gilded coffin lying inside the stone sarcophagus in the Burial Chamber will not be visible. Should the viewer wish to see the other two coffins in the likeness of the king, one of which is of solid gold, he will have to return to Cairo to the Museum of Egyptian Antiquities. There can be seen the dazzling gold coffin, together with a collection of 2,250 funerary objects found in the boy-king's tomb. These objects tell a story and bring a pathos and reality to this long-ago being—his toys, his much worn and obviously favorite ornaments, his trappings of power as Pharaoh of the Land of the Nile, over which he ruled towards the end of the Eighteenth Dynasty (c. 1361–1352 B.C.), more than a thousand years after Cheops.

Tutankhamen died before he was twenty, at the very same age when Alexander the Great, a thousand years later, embarked on his conquest of the world. But, you may ask, where is the tomb of Alexander, who brought civilization and terror to multitudes of people, numbering hundreds of times more than the population of his native Macedonia? The world has lost all trace of his tomb, of his favorite objects, of his furniture. Yet Tutankhamen, whose everyday possessions were found together with his mummified remains, has found immortality.

With the number of volumes already published on Ancient Egypt, why then another? Many elements figured in the conception and implementation of this project. As an archaeologist who worked with the Department of Antiquities (and as a current member of the Egyptian Supreme Council of Archaeology), I identify with and am still moved by that extraordinary adventure in 1922, when the tomb was first discovered by Howard Carter and Lord Carnarvon. This association has been reinforced perhaps by my own fortunate discovery thirty-two years later of the Solar Boats beside the Great Pyramid, vessels 1,600 years older than the treasures of Tutankhamen. Yet, there still remains the excitement and the controversy surrounding the Tutankhamen find, of which Arnold Brackman's text offers a most readable, insightful, and sound narration of this real-life adventure. Hopefully, this volume will allow you to share in the excitement which accompanied this achievement.

The overwhelming public response generated by the Tutankhamen traveling exhibition provided still another important impetus for the creation of this book. It is only recently that Egypt began to allow some of its ancient masterpieces to leave the country for display in other nations. A selection from the Tutankhamen treasures went first on loan to the British Museum in London, where the crowds it drew were the largest in that museum's history for any single exhibition. Fifty-five of the most precious items in the collection have subsequently been sent by the Egyptian government for viewing in the principal cities of the United States: Washington, D.C., Chicago, New Orleans, Los Angeles, Seattle, New York, and San Francisco. This was a gesture of international friendship on the occasion of the bicentenary of the United States. After this tour, these objects will be exhibited in Canada and West Germany. The choice of fifty-five items is itself a symbolic tribute to the fifty-five years which have elapsed since this stupendous discovery first opened these treasures to the light of day.

It has been my deep pleasure and privilege to assist in the selection of the items for these exhibitions and to participate in the opening ceremonies.

The pieces which I have chosen for inclusion in this volume were especially positioned for photographs at the Cairo Museum. The result, as you will see in this volume, are unique views of these fabulous treasures. The captions, which I and my staff have prepared, inform the reader in detail of the function and meaning of each object.

I would like to express my appreciation to Dr. Rowland Ellis, Dr. Magdi Wahba, Dr. Labib Habachi, Dr. Dorothea El Mallakh, Dr. Robert Bianchi, Mr. James F. Romano, Mr. Henry A. La Farge, Ms. Catherine Bernard, and the Antiquities Organization, without whose help this project would not have been possible.

The meaning of the young king's name is "He who spends his life making images of Amen." Time seems to have transformed his name into a living truth. His remains and his treasures will continue to dazzle generations long after we ourselves are gone. May you find on these pages a pictorial feast, and may you re-live as well the true detective story ending in the discovery of Tutankhamen's tomb.

Cairo,
May 1978

KAMAL EL MALLAKH
Deputy Editor-in-Chief, *Al-Ahram*

Member, Supreme Council of
Archaeology of Egypt

THE GOLD OF TUTANKHAMEN

Decision at Highclere

In 1922, as summer waned in England, George Edward Stanhope Molyneux Herbert, fifth earl of Carnarvon, came to a painful decision. For eighteen years he had underwritten annual expeditions in desolate Upper Egypt in search of an archaeological will-o'-the-wisp: the lost, but perhaps intact, tomb of an Egyptian pharaoh. Carnarvon decided to abandon the quest.

Although his expeditions, field-marshaled by Howard Carter, a self-taught Egyptologist, had turned up an occasional bush-league trophy—for example, a stele overlaid with hieroglyphics, the so-called Carnarvon Tablet—the search no longer seemed worth continuing. Fifty thousand pounds ($250,000) had so far been gambled on the venture.

Except for the war years, 1914–1918, when he converted his picturesque family seat of Highclere Castle—built in the twelfth and thirteenth centuries—into a military rest and rehabilitation center, Carnarvon spent half a year or more annually in the cramped, depressing bungalow he had built for himself in Upper Egypt. It was at a point directly across the Nile from the site of ancient Karnak. Perched on a lonely hill, the house was situated at the entrance to Biban-el-Moluk—variously spelled Biban-el-Molok, Biban-el-Muluk and Biban-el-Melok—the Arabic name for "Gate of the Kings," or for what foreigners called the Valley of the Tombs of the Kings.

Like the Libyan mountains in which the Valley nestled and like the ground on which his bungalow was erected, Carnarvon's house was the color of burnt sienna, the hue that, with the exception of the green fields astride both banks of the Nile, is the dominant color of Egypt. Unlike the cared-for lawns, pastures, and woodlands of Highclere, Carnarvon's cottage here had not a tree, not a shrub, not a blade of grass anywhere near it. The sun beat down unmercifully. At a distance, as one approached the house from the luxuriant village of El Gournah, on the western bank of the Nile, his double-domed house, fashioned from clay and compacted sand, gave the appearance of a mosque or tomb. Yet the architectural style was strangely appropriate. Indeed, present-day Egyptians say that Carnarvon's bungalow (and, nearby, Carter's, for that matter) remind them of the Aga Khan's mausoleum at Aswan. In a manner of speaking, Carnarvon had buried himself alive in Upper Egypt.

Carnarvon's house provided a panoramic view of the Valley of the Tombs of the Kings; of its brooding, somber precipices and escarpments in different shades of raw and burnt umber; of its bleak, lifeless peaks, some rising 1,800 feet above the surface of the blue Nile.

A terrifyingly lonely and inhospitable place, the area west of Carnarvon's house bore a striking resemblance to the terrain of the moon, which was photographed for the first time in 1839, only thirty-three years before Carnarvon's birth at Highclere.

In this remote setting, the pharaohs built their hypogea: rock tombs or sepulchers cut directly into the rock, often replete with hidden passages, secret chambers, stairwells, and annexes. Since the beginning of the last century, sixty-four tombs had been discovered in the Valley. Some almost defied description. The largest, for example, designed to house the mummy of Seti (Sethos) I and built more than thirty centuries ago, was 470 feet long and plunged 180 feet below the earth's surface. "The atmosphere is suffocating," wrote a traveler who descended into its depths almost a hundred years ago. "The place is ghostly and peopled with nightmares." It still is.

The traveler was not the first to render this judgment. In 1843, the Reverend Stephen Olin, the president of Wesleyan University, visited the Valley and recorded a corresponding sentiment. "Our way led us for more than an hour through a region of sterility and desolation," he wrote. Not a shrub, not a bird, not an insect, enlivened the "gloomy, dreary retreat." And he added as an afterthought: "It is a singular fact that when first explored by modern [sic] travellers, all the royal tombs had been broken open and rifled of their contents."

Ten years later, S. G. Goodrich, the author of the popular *Universal History*, described the Valley as a place of "gloomy solitude, presenting the arid and desolate aspect of the most frightful desert." After entering the Valley, Goodrich looked in vain on all sides for the narrow track along which he had wound his way into the gorge by donkey. He could not find it. The heat was stifling—violent enough, he said, to kill people (as it has, indeed, on occasion). "In this awful solitude, the ancient Egyptians sought to seclude from every human eye the magnificent tombs of the kings," Goodrich wrote. "Avarice and curiosity, however, have triumphed over every precaution."

Manifestly, this was an odd place for an English lord to spend most of the year, much less the autumn and winter of his life.

Lord Carnarvon's daily pattern had always been much the same. He rose just before daybreak, around 5:30, to avoid the heat of the day; and after a breakfast of tea and *totleh*, an Egyptian jelly encrusted with blanched almonds, he set out for the Valley. He rode by donkey over the rock-strewn trail, covered with chips of limestone and white and black flint, which led by his house and into the core of Biban-el-Moluk. At the dig, he joined his ringmaster, Howard Carter, who actively supervised crews of as many as 175 men, clad in their traditional gallabiyas (long, loose, and billowing white robes), painstakingly removing more than 200,000 tons of debris by wicker basket in search of a clue to that prize of prizes, the inviolate, treasure-filled tomb of a pharaoh. The men, fellahin from neighboring villages, worked for as little as three piasters (fifteen cents) a day. They worked every day except Tuesday (by tradition, no digging was done on this day) and for only a half day on Friday, the Moslem Sabbath.

At the end of the work day, Carnarvon remounted his donkey for the trek back to his double-domed bungalow, which the impoverished Egyptians dubbed "Castle Carnarvon." At sundown, he sat on the second story terrace, a whiskey in hand, and gazed out on the forbidding landscape. At that latitude (20°N), the sun sets rapidly, leaving a crimson line along the horizon for only a few minutes. The countryside is plunged into darkness. Carnarvon dined lightly either on canned goods imported from England or on local mutton. A bottle of red wine was always on the table. Exhausted by the day's work, he usually retired early.

For years, Carnarvon almost unfailingly followed this pattern. By 1922, however, he felt there was no longer any chance of his and Carter's discovering an intact king's tomb.

In point of fact, no such tomb had ever been found. Indeed, there was a spreading conviction among Egyptologists that one never would be found. Sir Gaston Maspero, who served as Egypt's director general of excavations and antiquities, was convinced that Carnarvon's great enterprise, however worthy, was a futile one. The American millionaire, Theodore M. Davis, like Carnarvon an amateur archaeologist, had also spent a fortune in the same pursuit without success. In 1912, after more than a dozen years in the field, Davis quit. "I fear," he concluded, "that the Valley of the Tombs is now exhausted."

That, to the mind of Carnarvon (and Carter), was precisely the trouble. Every time somebody declared the Valley exhausted, something else was later found: a despoiled tomb or a clue to the existence of other tombs. For example, in 1815 Giovanni Belzoni, the first modern excavator of the Valley, uncovered the plundered tombs of Seti I, Rameses I, and other great pharaohs. When he left the field, he expressed the "firm conviction" that he had found everything there was to find. "I exerted all my humble abilities in endeavoring to find another tomb," he wrote five years later, "but [did] not succeed."

Twenty-four years later, a Berlin expedition led by the celebrated Karl Richard Lepsius took the first detailed measurements of the Valley. Archaeologically speaking, Lepsius announced the place was "exhausted." Yet in 1898 Victor Loret, a Frenchman, stumbled on several new tombs. But, as with all twenty-nine hypogea found in the Valley since Belzoni's days, each tomb had been rifled and ravaged in antiquity. In some cases, the cream-colored linen wrappings of the mummies were shredded by thieves in their frenzied search for treasure. In other cases, the tombs were stripped of everything except immovable wall paintings, annotated with hieroglyphics, works of inestimable historic and artistic value. Yet Loret's find generated new hope that more tombs, possibly an untouched tomb, might yet be found.

Amelia Edwards, the intrepid traveler and commentator who deserves the title of first woman Egyptologist, was among those who thought so. "Fresh wonders are disclosed wherever the spade of the diggers strikes new ground," she wrote enthusiastically. "The interest never flags, the subject never palls upon us, the mine is never exhausted. I will go yet further," she added, "and say that this mine is practically inexhaustible."

For Carnarvon and Carter, during their annual winter campaigns in Egypt, usually between October and April, their occasional discoveries served to whet their appetites. But as the years swept by, as one decade slipped into another and the grand prize still eluded them, the Valley took its terrible psychological toll. The harsh heat and the grim reality of the terrain eventually drained Carnarvon, if not yet Carter, of ambition, energy, and hope.

Although Carnarvon wearied of his own endless search, he did gradually amass the world's finest private collection of Egyptian antiquities. He not only scoured the Valley of the Tombs of the Kings and other sites for finds—Luxor, Thebes, Karnak— but he combed the thieves' market in Cairo and maintained regular contact with antiquity dealers throughout the Near East. The clou of his collection was a solid gold statue, about a foot high, of Amen-Re, who had emerged by the beginning of the Eighteenth Dynasty as the supreme god of Egypt, a melding of Amen, the ram-headed god of Thebes, and Re, the sun god of Memphis. Neither Carnarvon nor Carter actually found the figure. It was recovered from the sand amid the ruins of the fabulous temple complex at Karnak like so many other objects of art by a nameless Egyptian fellah. In those days, the gold alone was worth almost £10,000 ($50,000). Today, on the wildly fluctuating Zurich gold market, it is probably worth many times that figure, exclusive of its artistic value.

In any event, by the summer of 1922, the fifty-six-year-old Carnarvon concluded that the archaeological establishment was probably right: another pharaoh's tomb would never be found. Even if it were, it would most assuredly be empty, looted in antiquity.

It was equally assured that an inviolate tomb would contain a treasure trove. The ravaged tombs were evidence of that—and so was Egyptian tradition. For thousands of years, in accordance with their religious beliefs about the existence of a hereafter, the Egyptians buried with their monarchs gilded chariots and funerary statues, weapons, furniture, and urns filled with food. The coffins of the dead were made of solid gold, it was said, and the mummy wore a mask of gold inlaid with semiprecious stones. Within the folds of the mummy's wrappings, the high priests tucked jeweled amulets and charms. "That the body should not waste or decay was an object of anxious solicitude," explained Samuel Birch, curator of Egyptology at the British Museum, as early as 1867, "and for this purpose various bandlets and amulets, prepared with certain magical preparations, and sanctified with certain spells or prayers, or even offerings and small sacrifices, were distributed over various parts of the mummy." Thus, gold rings adorned the mummy's fingers; gold bracelets, the wrists; gold necklaces, the throat; and gold pendants, the chest. Even the fingernails and toes were sheathed in gold. A papyrus of the Middle Kingdom, written four thousand years ago, during the classic period of Egyptian prose and poetry, provided convincing proof that a pharaoh's tomb was literally worth its weight in gold. The papyrus described the moment of a pharaoh's burial as "the night devoted to oils with bandages [when] thou art reunited with the earth in the mummy case of gold with head of lapis-lazuli."

Obviously, such descriptive passages in the funerary rites of the day were an open invitation to the local mafia. The Amherst Papyrus, a portion of a roll containing three and one-half columns of hieroglyphics, which was acquired shortly before the turn of the last century by Lord Hackney—like Carnarvon, a "collector"—astonishingly contained the court record of the prosecution of a band of tomb robbers in the time of Rameses IX, who lived and died more than a millennium before the appearance of Christ. Here was the world's first account of organized crime. The despoilers, the papyrus reported, consisted of a gang of thirty-nine grave robbers, about half of whom were "insiders," members of the Establishment, including eight sacred scribes and seven high priests. The latter knew the secret location of the royal tombs. For good measure, they had access to the offices of the royal architect and stole floor plans. The papyrus provides hard evidence that, the authoritarianism of a system notwithstanding, the Establishment had neither faith nor respect for the system and bent that system towards its own ends. Thus, as some of the high priests solemnly went about the business of preparing the pharaoh's mummy for the Valley of the Tombs, for the journey into immortality, they were also deviously plotting to plunder the pharaoh's august body and rob it of the chance of obtaining immortality.

"We opened their coffins and unwrapped their mummies," a ringleader confessed in court. ". . . There were numerous amulets and ornaments at the mummy's throat. Its head had a mask of gold upon it. The august mummy of the king was overlaid with gold throughout. Its coverings were wrought of gold and silver within and without.

. . . We found the king's wife likewise. We stripped off all that we found. . . . We set fire to their wrappings. We stole their furniture, which we found with them, and vases of gold, silver and bronze."

But however attractive the thought of gold, Lord Carnarvon was forced to abandon the search in 1922 for sound financial reasons. Although the pound, like Britain herself, ruled the world, England was caught up in the inflationary squeeze that followed World War I. Lord Carnarvon felt the pinch as he struggled to maintain the standard of living to which he was accustomed after inheriting his father's title and estate, which included 36,000 acres of land.

No question about it. The string had run out on his expensive hobby, Egyptology.

The Valley Beckons

As was their autumnal custom, Carnarvon and Howard Carter were to confer at Highclere—a setting of crenellated walls and towers, formal gardens and hunting preserves —to review the year's work in Upper Egypt and map their upcoming winter campaign. In 1922, Carnarvon dreaded the interview.

An extrovert who made and kept friends easily, an attractive personality, in many ways a free soul despite his overlay of British reserve, Carnarvon realized that his decision to abandon the quest would crush Carter, a lonely bachelor whose entire life was given over to Egyptology. Carnarvon feared that quitting the pursuit at so late a date was not quite the gentlemanly thing to do.

Carnarvon's blood was blue to the last cubic centimeter, and the concept of honor was deeply ingrained. His father had been the fourth earl of Carnarvon; his mother was sired by the earl of Chesterfield. He was a first cousin to the Barons Lucas and Dingwall. He had access to the king at Buckingham Palace.

In many ways, Carnarvon was like his father. He dabbled in spiritualism and enjoyed travel.

For a time, the father was interested in spiritualism, which was to Victorian England what Freudian analysis is to the witty and clever New York set today. The interest got the fourth earl as far as a séance in 1876, but, as his father remarked later, "I was not impressed." At the séance he was invited to ask for anything he liked, and, the Carnarvon pixy surfacing, he called for a piebald rabbit—without success. The son likewise potted in the occult, was a member of the Spiritualist Alliance of London, and subscribed to *Occult Review*. Doubtless, this speculation in the hereafter was intensified by his later association with Egyptology and its great literary classics, the Coffin Texts and the Book of the Dead. For example, he often arranged for séances to be conducted in Highclere's East Anglican Room, and on one occasion a bemused Carter attended. At that session, a woman went into a trance and uttered unintelligible words, which Carter thought he recognized as Coptic, the tongue of the present-day descendants of the ancient Egyptians. With Carter's Egyptological bent, he must have thought the exercise was a put-on. If he did, he was too polite a guest to say so. Thereafter, he politely avoided those sessions.

Inexplicably, both father and son also were drawn to Egypt's no-man's-land, the Valley of the Tombs of the Kings.

Early in life, the fourth earl became interested in "antiquities," as archaeology was called in the Victorian period, and he was elected president of London's prestigious

Society of Antiquarians. In 1861, five years before his son's birth, he visited Egypt and toured the Valley. In a letter addressed to Highclere, February 9, 1861, the fourth earl described the gorge as a "bare, rocky mountain pass which grows wilder and more desolate at every step." Like others before and since him, he was overcome by its heat and morbid grandeur. In the Valley, he shuddered, "the silence is complete." He was troubled by what he saw in the light of the pharaohs' desire to rest in peace throughout eternity. "The hand of the spoiler has been everywhere," he wrote, "and it is sad to see how vain has been the attempt to preserve an eternal silence and repose in the tomb." More than a half century later, his son would cast himself in the role of the most celebrated body snatcher in the Valley's history.

Although father and son shared much in common superficially, their basic characters were dissimilar. Unlike his father, who was serious-minded and intensely political, Lord Porchester, as the fifth earl was called during his father's lifetime, was an apolitical playboy.

The fourth earl, on the other hand, was an activist leader of the liberal wing of the Conservative party. He served briefly as secretary of state for the colonies; opposed Disraeli's imperialist, expansionist policies; introduced legislation that led to Canadian independence; fought against the abuses of English shipping companies that trafficked in Chinese coolie labor; and, as an open sympathizer with the Irish nationalists, favored home rule for Ireland.

He also fought for civil rights at home. In 1847, for example, Baron Rothschild was the first Jew elected to Parliament. When he refused to repeat the words "on the true faith of a Christian" in the parliamentary oath, he was unable to take his seat in the House of Commons. The issue occasioned an uproar—which Lord Carnarvon ingeniously quieted by suggesting that Commons simply abrogate by resolution any disqualification against an individual elected to Parliament. The enabling legislation was quickly steered through the house, and thereafter a strong bond of friendship developed between the houses of Herbert (Carnarvon) and Rothschild.

As a child, Porchy, as Lord Porchester was called, lost his mother when he was only nine. His lovable, mindless aunt, Lady Gwendolen, tried to take over by pampering the attractive, curly-haired lad. If he smashed a library window with a cricket ball or golf ball (Highclere boasted its own private golf links), his aunt rewarded him with a crown as a consolation.

Porchy attended Eton briefly and failed to graduate. After much tutoring, he later got through Cambridge's Trinity College. The young man's principal distraction was sports. He had a passion for the outdoors, especially for fishing and hunting, both of which required the patience, keen sense of observation, and self-discipline that he declined to apply in the study hall. "He is one of these men who must ever be on the move," a close friend said of him later. "He cannot sit still."

When Porchy's father acquired a villa that was accessible only by boat at Portofino on the Italian Riviera, the young man developed a lifelong affection for the sea. He no sooner slipped through Trinity than he embarked on a round-the-world journey under sail. At Rio de Janeiro, the admiral commanding His Britannic Majesty's South Atlantic Squadron dissuaded the youth from continuing his venture around the Horn because it was the wrong time of year and he had the wrong type of sailing rig. "Suicidal," the admiral insisted.

Until he was thirty-five, Porchy was little more than a drifter, a man without a focal point of interest. After South America and an African safari, he toured Australia and Japan. In addition to yachting and aimless travel, he raced a stable of thoroughbreds and his colors—scarlet jacket, blue sleeves, scarlet cap, black and white cross belts—were among the most popular at Ascot.

A slender figure of medium height, appealing to women, with roguish eyes and a Ronald Colmanesque moustache, his handsome face unlined by a day's worry or a day's work, the fifth earl dressed conventionally in checks and bow ties. His trademark was a porkpie white hat, a hybrid boater, which he wore at a Maurice Chevalier jaunty angle. In 1895, five years after he acquired the title at his father's death, his thoughts turned to preserving the Carnarvon line. He married the beautiful Almina Victoria Marie Alexandra, daughter of Frederick Charles Wombwell, the son of Sir George Wombwell, third baronet. A scintillating affair that made *The Times* of London, the wedding was attended by royalty and society, including close friends Alfred and Alice de Rothschild.

The union produced two offspring. The son is today the sixth earl of Carnarvon. Now seventy-seven, he was a career army officer who served in both world wars and married an American woman. Porchy's daughter, Lady Evelyn Herbert, was the apple of his eye, almost always a companion to him on his Egyptian journeys.

Carnarvon's love of adventure also drew him to the flying machine and the motorized carriage. With Carnarvon's encouragement, Captain Geoffrey de Havilland, later Sir Geoffrey, built and flew Britain's first plane from the fields of Highclere. As for himself, Carnarvon owned motor cars on the Continent before they were permitted in England. When the ban was lifted, one of his vehicles was the third automobile registered in the United Kingdom.

Given this sketch, there emerges in the fifth earl of Carnarvon a shiftless member of the idle rich, a gay blade of Edwardian England, which, in Alistair Cooke's words was "an affluent, carefree, festive time." Like his sometime companion, the loose-living Prince of Wales, later Edward VII, Carnarvon frittered away the days, shooting and hunting with the sporty crowd, whizzing through the streets in the alarming new horseless carriage, leading his horses into the winner's circle at the track, and making periodic junkets to the French and Italian Rivieras.

Then in 1903, at the age of thirty-four, Carnarvon changed his life-style abruptly—and radically. Chance pointed him in the direction of the Valley of the Tombs of the Kings.

Carnarvon in Egypt

That year, motoring in rural Germany, Carnarvon crashed while trying to avoid two bullock carts blocking the road. He sustained serious injuries, including a concussion, a broken wrist, damage to the mouth, first and second degree burns across parts of his body, and temporary blindness. As he returned briefly to consciousness, the mettle of the man emerged: "Have I killed anyone?" he asked. Miraculously, he had not; he himself never fully regained his health.

Carnarvon's life hung in the balance for weeks. A long period of rest and rehabilitation, under the constant supervision of doctors and nurses, followed and, as often happens in a confrontation with death—the reality of life—Carnarvon took stock of his aimless existence.

Heinrich Schliemann's discovery of Troy was the conversation piece of the late nineteenth century. A self-made millionaire, Schliemann, the son of an impoverished German minister, abandoned the countinghouse in mid-life and devoted his fortune and the remainder of his life to archaeology. His action roused such formidable British scholars as Professor A. H. Sayce of Oxford, the philologist, to denounce publicly the sporting buffs of Victorian and Edwardian England. "Why is it that Dr. Schliemann's example has not been followed by some of the rich men of whom England is full?" Sayce asked angrily. "Why cannot they spare for science a little of the wealth that is now lavished upon the breeding of horses or the maintenance of a dog kennel? Surely, England must contain one or two, at least, who would be willing to help in recovering the earlier history of our civilization."

At a time when such sentiments were a topic of the times, Carnarvon's physicians warned him that with his difficulty in breathing, as a result of the motor accident, a serious attack of influenza would prove fatal. He must avoid the damp and dank English winters. They suggested a hot, dry climate. Naturally, since Carnarvon was a member of high society, they suggested Upper Egypt.

The word *naturally* is used with deliberation. For reasons that continue to confound contemporary historians, Upper Egypt emerged in the latter half of the last century into what British scholar H. S. Deighton described as "a winter resort for well-to-do English people." More likely than not, this remarkable development was inspired by the iconoclastic Lady Lucie Duff-Gordon, who went to live at Luxor amid the ruins of Karnak and Thebes in the hope of curing herself of tuberculosis, which, like the flu, was rampant in England at that time.

Lady Lucie was a courageous woman, radiantly beautiful, with dark brows on a brilliant complexion. When her physician hinted that whiffs of tobacco might soothe an irritated throat, she tried a cigar, liked it, and smoked from that day on—in her armchair and on horseback. Prim Victorians were horrified, and she was roundly criticized. The criticism did not faze her. It made her more determined to liberate her sex.

On March 22, 1864, in a letter to her husband, "Dearest Aleck," with whom she was deeply in love, Lady Lucie told of her first visit to the Valley of the Tombs of the Kings. "The mountains were red-hot, and the sun went down into Amenti [the Egyptian nether world] all on fire," she wrote. "The road was long and [a] most wild one—truly through the valley of the shadow of death." The day she selected for the trek was pleasant, only 84°F in the tombs, but a tremendous wind blew up a sandstorm. "The dust is horrid with this high wind," she wrote. "Everything is gritty, and it obscures the sun."

A year later, her *Letters from Egypt* was published. She characterized Egypt as an enchanting Biblical land, the land of pharaohs, Moses, and Exodus. The book, favorably reviewed by such influential journals as *The Edinburg Review*, became a minor classic overnight, and, in the process of several new editions of the book, Upper Egypt became the "in" resort of the carriage trade. To accommodate the influx, a magnificent hostelry was built at Luxor: the Winter Palace Hotel, the Hilton-Intercontinental of its day.

Situated only a few hundred yards north of the ruins of ancient Luxor, the stately hotel faced the Nile, about fifteen minutes by boat upriver from the entrance to the Valley of the Tombs on the opposite bank. The four-storied structure was a marvel in time and place. It had 200 rooms, beautiful gardens, and an enormous dining room, and was lavishly appointed throughout. Painted in the darkest shade of burnt sienna, the Winter Palace had purple shutters gracing each elongated window. The rooms had extraordinarily high ceilings, about twenty feet, and each room boasted its own small terrace overlooking the Nile, an area just large enough for a rattan table and two chairs. Everything about the Winter Palace was grandiose and elegant. The corridors were terribly long; and the main foyer, enormous.*

The mortally ill Lady Lucie Duff-Gordon did not live to fully enjoy her success. Her desire, expressed to her daughter Janet, was to lie among "her own people" at Thebes—the Egyptians, who, taking to her instantly, referred to her as the "great lady." But in the last minutes of her life in a Cairo hospital, when she felt she would never see her beloved Luxor again, she gave orders to be buried as quietly as possible in the Cairo cemetery. She died at the age of forty-eight, four years after the publication of *Letters*.

By then Luxor had achieved an international reputation as a health resort as, it should be noted parenthetically, it had in the days of Rome when Celsus sent his rich patients, dissipated by hedonistic Augustan living, to Thebes to recuperate in the invigoratingly dry climate. Thus, writing in 1873, only a few years after Lady Lucie's death, Dr. Dunbar Walker enthused: "Nice has got its advocates; Mentone is considered by others to be unrivalled in producing a salutary effect on . . . patients. San Remo has been upheld, and seems to be drawing away numbers from her sister towns in the Riviera. Other authorities point to Italy as possessing a climate unequalled by any other part of the world. Spain has been shown, especially the southern coast, to outstrip other winter sanitaria. Sicily, Algiers, Malta and Tangier have all their advocates, but weighing all things, Egypt has advantages that far outshine any other winter resort, and will give results never afforded by any other spot on the habitable globe during the winter months."

Another prominent physician, Dr. John Dalrymple, was more to the point: "Egypt . . . is to the languid invalid like a new lease of life."

Thus, as if the residue of design, the broken pieces of Carnarvon's life fell together into a new whole: his father's interest in antiquities and journey to the Valley of the Tombs of the Kings; the family's massive art collection at Highclere; his own love of the outdoors, of adventure, romance, self-reliance, and independence—all now seemingly barred to him because of his broken body; and the urgings of old family friends, such as Sir Wallis Budge and Sir Evelyn Baring, that he immerse himself in Egyptology. Sir Wallis was the keeper of Egyptian antiquities at the British Museum; Sir Evelyn, appointed British agent to Egypt in 1883, served as *de facto* ruler of the country for the next twenty-four years.

The excavation of lost worlds, a treasure hunt of sorts, also appealed to Carnarvon's gaming instincts and gambling nature. Schliemann had uncovered dazzling hoards of gold at Troy and Mycenae; Sir Austen Henry Layard, the ruins of Nimrud, Nineveh, and Babylon; Sir Arthur Evans, a fabulous Minoan civilization. He, Carnarvon, would join their august company.

As his enthusiasm for the new sport waxed, he read everything available on the subject—the works of Belzoni, Birch, Petrie, and Amelia Edwards. He studied maps and familiarized himself with all things Egyptian, *shorghl-el-Mizr*. The spirit of scholarship, dormant at Eton and Cambridge, emerged. His interest in shooting parties and stud racing waned. Percy Newberry, a close friend and collaborator, later recalled, laughingly, "He told me he would rather discover an unrifled tomb than win the Derby."

---

*In 1975, during my stay in Luxor, I put up at the old Winter Palace Hotel, which, except for the replacement of gas lamps with quaint electric fixtures, remains unchanged from the Victorian era. The terminology "old" Winter Palace is mandatory; adjoining it on the north side is the New Winter Palace Hotel, a white, nine-storied hostelry, which boasts 700 rooms and is air-conditioned.

Carnarvon left for Egypt four years later, in 1907, when he regained the physical strength to do so. For the next sixteen years he plumbed the mysteries of the Upper Nile. His health improved, but he was never again robust; frequently, he was confined to bed. He aged prematurely and looked ten years older than he was. His marital relationship with Almina was strained.

But all the while, his collection of art expanded. Sir Wallis Budge marveled at his acquisitions: "His taste is faultless," the great Egyptologist said in admiration. "He has a boyish enthusiasm for Egyptology." Carnarvon won further plaudits from the scholarly establishment. Together with Howard Carter, he wrote *Five Years at Thebes*. He also acquired a multitude of friends in Egypt, from the pashas at the apex of the social pyramid to the fellahin at the base. Apolitical as he was, he sympathized with the aspirations for independence felt by the peoples of Egypt, who had been successively ruled since pharaonic times by Persians, Greeks, Romans, Arabs, Turks, and Europeans (the country was now largely Arabic, the original Egyptians having been reduced to a minority's minority, the Christian Coptics). In the course of time, Egyptian delegations to London, dispatched from Cairo to plead the case for independence, put up at Highclere as house guests.

Carnarvon's mother had spoken to him, as a child, only in French—the family tree was traceable to Normandy—and his facile command of the language endeared him to the Egyptians, who preferred French to English as their lingua franca. "Lordy," as they fondly called him, was a familiar sight as he threaded his way about Cairo, Luxor, and Karnak with his white hat and walking stick.

But as summer blended into autumn, in 1922, Carnarvon knew he would have to tell Carter that it was time to abandon the treasure hunt.

A New Compact

Carter came to call, as usual, at Highclere Castle. Although he was slightly broader and heavier than Carnarvon and eight years his junior (it seemed much more), the collaborators bore a striking general resemblance to each other in mien, an air of English aplomb and civility, and in physical appearance—medium height, ample dark hair, trim moustaches. They even dressed similarly, in tweedy jackets, white shirts, and bow ties. Carter, however, preferred a homburg to Carnarvon's porkpie. An outsider observing the scene through the study's French windows would be pardoned if he thought he viewed brothers or first cousins or, perhaps, a double image. As an ancient Egyptian would have expressed it, Carter appeared to be Carnarvon's *ka*, his other self, his double, his soul, his spirit, his aura.

But beneath these similarities were completely different personalities.

Carter was an introvert: shy, diffident, retiring, more comfortable in the background than in the forefront. Uneasy in large groups, he lacked the ability to make small talk. Whereas Carnarvon made friends easily, Carter made enemies easily. Carter was a man of uncompromising, inflexible integrity and honesty. If he were in the right, as he saw it, he was obstinate to the point of sheer pertinacity. His character was explosive. It was perhaps an inferiority complex, springing from his low estate on the social ladder in a feudal-minded society, that he covered with a quick temper. High-strung and taut, constantly on the defensive, he was, among his countrymen and among Europeans generally, aggressive. With Egyptians, however, he felt at ease, among equals.

He was a lonely man whom one of his closest friends described as "a strange fellow in many ways." He lived alone in a small adobe house he had built near the Valley of the Tombs. "Castle Carter," the fellahin called it. He was unmarried, and there were no women in his life. He had received no formal education in his youth, and, like his father, a superior draftsman and unheralded water-colorist who painted the portraits of the aristocracy's favorite animals—a Derby winner, a pet retriever—Carter had a long record of employment by the leisure class. Carnarvon was not his first benefactor. He also worked for Theodore Davis, the Rhode Island millionaire who had left an Egyptological legacy.

Frustrated by his lack of "good breeding" and absence of wealth, Carter was contemptuous of the dilettante, the collector. After the deaths of Davis and Carnarvon, Carter wrote sulfurously that "too many people—unfortunately there are so-called archaeologists among them—are apparently under the impression that the object bought from a dealer's shop is just as valuable as one which has been found in actual excavation." With contempt, he added, "There was never a greater mistake." Davis? Carnarvon? Perhaps; but also perhaps not—because they had both labored in the field. We shall never know. If nothing else, just as Carnarvon was the ultimate sportsman, Carter was the perfect gentleman. Carter strove through his life to prove that gentlemen are not only born but also made. This was the mainspring of his character and accounted for his fanatical integrity, his probity.

The one thing the two men unquestionably shared was a genuine passion for Egyptology. This dedication was enough to bridge the social abyss between them. They genuinely liked and respected each other beyond the patron-client relationship. Nonetheless, there was an unavoidable master-servant relationship between them, however subterranean, and they both knew it. Not that Carter felt that by working for Carnarvon he had accepted a grant, a free ride. Carnarvon's wealth may have underwritten his employment, but the job was hardly a sinecure.

While Carnarvon thought of archaeology as a hunt in which the player tracked for high stakes, Carter also thought of archaeology as a game. On one occasion he confessed publicly that he had taken up archaeology because of his strong inclination towards the science of deduction. "If I hadn't gone for archaeology," he explained, "I might have entered Scotland Yard."

That afternoon at Highclere, over whiskeys probably, the two men reviewed the year's "barren labor." This was Carter's own descriptive phrase for the last campaign. He did not try to hide the fact. Yet barren though it had been, Carter's hopes were unquenchable, in large part because his very way of life depended upon an endless quest, an interminable search. Thus, Carter began to talk with customary excitement about the upcoming winter season.

Carnarvon interrupted him, albeit gently. Postwar economic conditions, he said with discomfort, precluded continuing the quest. In a word, the search for the lost tomb of a pharaoh must be abandoned.

Carter was stunned. Despite those barren years, he was unshakably convinced that "at least one more royal tomb," as he frequently expressed it, would be found. Not simply one, but "at least one." Of one he was sure. That was the tomb of the youthful pharaoh Tutankhamen of the Eighteenth Dynasty. He had ruled in Egypt's Golden Age, more than thirty centuries earlier. The existence of such a tomb, Carter never tired of pointing out, was confirmed by clues that the Davis expeditions had unearthed in the Valley before World War I. Indeed, Davis actually claimed to have found the tomb; rifled, of course. Carter was convinced that what Davis found was not a pharaoh's tomb, but a hint of things to come. The evidence was circumstantial, Carter conceded, but would Scotland Yard abandon a case because the evidence was inconclusive?

Carter fought to control his poise. Then, in a desperate effort to win back his patron, he spread on the table before them the now familiar, smudged and frayed map of the Valley they had used over the years.

Since the days of Belzoni, explorers in the Valley had employed the system of sondages in their excavations—that is, they made pits in places where rubbish was detected, in the hope of finding the entrance to a tomb. What Carter had suggested doing was to excavate the Valley down to bedrock, as Schliemann had done at Troy, paying no attention to scattered deposits of rubbish left at or near the surface by the gangs of laborers and craftsmen who had cut the mysterious tombs into the facing of the cliffs so many thousands of years before. Influenced by the sophisticated development of artillery on the eve of World War I, Carter had hit upon another point of departure from the excavators of the past. Instead of directing their archaeological fire haphazardly, he and Carnarvon crisscrossed their map of the Valley like a checkerboard, in the manner of artillery officers who thereby are able to bring down a barrage on any given square within radius of their cannon's range. They had excavated to bedrock, square by square.

As Carter spread out the map, he conceded that they had probed virtually every foot of the Valley. But he pointed to one square, the area just below the entrance to the empty hypogeum of Rameses VI, with its plundered passages, chambers, gaily painted walls, and hieroglyphics. This particular area, shaped more like a triangle than a square because of the cliff's configuration, had never been excavated. Twice Carter had opted to dig at that very spot, but had been interrupted. For one thing, the Rameses tomb was a highlight on guided tours through the Valley during the winter tourist season. Carter was reluctant to close down the area, disappoint tourists, and interfere with the business of the Egyptian guides whose meager livelihood depended on free access to the tomb. Moreover, the spot was strewn with the ruins of stone huts and the rubbish of laborers and artists who had worked on the Rameses tomb. It was, therefore, a most unlikely spot to probe because it was inconceivable that the workers erected their shelters across the opening of a pharaoh's tomb—unless, of course, the entrance was lost in *their* antiquity, possibly as the result of a rock slide, an earthquake (such as the one in 27 B.C.), or one of those rare torrential rains that flooded the gorge and raised havoc among the boulders and loose rocks. These violent downpours, accompanied by thunder and lightning, periodically converted the Valley into a cascading canyon of foaming water that lifted and transplanted great stones with ease.

During Carter's thirty-five years of wandering in the Egyptian desert, he could recall only four rainfalls in the Valley, one in 1898, another in 1900, and two in 1916, one of which he personally witnessed at 4:00 P.M., November 1, 1916, when the Great Northern Ravine, north and collateral with the Valley and confluent at the mouth, was transformed into a bursting dam as literally tons of wildly crashing water tumbled headlong through the canyon, redesigning the shape of the Valley.

Carter clung to the remote hope that the entrance to the tomb of Tutankhamen had been covered over in such a fashion. "We had now dug in the Valley for several seasons with extremely scanty results," he later wrote, "and it became a much debated question whether we should continue the work." This line, incidentally, is the only hint Carter ever dropped that he and Carnarvon "much debated" the question at Highclere in 1922. "After these barren years," Carter asked, "were we justified in going on with it?"

Carnarvon's answer was adamant. He refused.

Because Carnarvon's license to dig in the Valley did not expire until November 16, 1923, and was, therefore, good for another year—no dig could be undertaken in Egypt without a government-awarded concession—Carter drew himself upright and formally requested permission from Carnarvon to work the concession once more at his, Carter's, expense. Carnarvon must have suppressed a smile. It cost a bare minimum of £2,000 ($10,000)—easily the equivalent of $50,000 today—to organize a season's work, and he knew Carter simply did not have that kind of ready cash.

Carter said that if he found nothing, he would agree that the Valley was indeed exhausted. If, however, he found the lost tomb, the discovery was Carnarvon's, as they had agreed when they shook hands and began their collaboration in 1907.

Carnarvon thought Carter's offer was too unselfish, too generous. As a gentleman, as a sportsman, Carnarvon could not accept that offer. It was simply not cricket to dump, not so much the project, but Carter and their team of *reises* and diggers so abruptly after so many years of teamwork. Very well, then, he would give Carter notice; he would agree to one—"one," he repeated—more campaign in the Valley at his, Carnarvon's, expense.

The collaborators once again shook hands to seal the new compact. Shortly thereafter, Carter left for Cairo to organize the last campaign in the Valley of the Tombs of the Kings.

Carter in Egypt

As was his custom, Carter returned to Egypt circuitously via the Dover-Calais ferry, the Calais-Marseilles express, and thence by a Messageries Maritimes steamship to Alexandria, Egypt's principal port of entry. Even at sea, he was not far from Egyptology. The best-known Messageries steamships making the run were the 12,500-ton, 495-foot long, twin-screw, $17^1/_2$-knot *Champollion*, named for the man who first deciphered the Rosetta stone, and her sister ship, the *Mariette Pasha*, named for the French Egyptologist, except that she did not have a Maier bow and was, therefore, two knots slower. The journey, made in late October of that year, marked the last time he ever traveled in anonymity.

Carter had been making the journey regularly ever since 1891, when, quite by chance, at the age of seventeen, he was seduced by Egyptology. Professor Percy E. Newberry, who served on the staff of the Cairo Museum and taught ancient Egyptian history and Egyptology at the University of Egypt, tells the story.* "It was in the summer of 1891," he recalled in a memoir. "I was then in need of assistance in inking-in the mass of pencil tracings that had been made the previous winter at Beni Hasan [Middle Egypt], and Lady Amherst of Hackney, with whom I was staying at Didlington Hall, Norfolk, suggested that Howard Carter, who was at the time living in the neighboring village of Swaffham, would be most useful for this purpose."

Samuel John Carter, the boy's father, was frequently employed by Lady Amherst to paint portraits of her favorite animals. At the time, Howard, who was born at Swaffham on May 9, 1874, the youngest son of Carter and Martha Joyce Sandys, sketched and painted under his father's tutelage. His father taught him such watercolorist tricks as putting the sky into his paintings upside down so that the paint would run darkest at the top of the picture. At an early age, the youth earned pocket money by painting pictures of the pet cats, dogs, parrots, and canaries of his father's clients.

Sam Carter could not afford to educate the boy in public schools, and Howard was tutored at home. As a child, Howard brushed archaeology. Swaffham, a market town of about 2,500 people, famous as the site of cattle fairs, boasted the picturesque ruins of a Cluniac priory, which had been founded shortly after the Norman Conquest, and a remarkable series of earthworks erected by the Romans. The ruins of the church included the west front, arcaded with three Norman doors and a perpendicular window, with chapter house, cloisters, and conventual buildings. In Carter's childhood,

---

*The term "Cairo Museum" is often a source of confusion. This is the name used by foreigners. The official name of the museum and the name by which it is known among Egyptians is the Egyptian Museum (to distinguish it from the Islamic and Coptic museums in Cairo). The museum, built in 1900 and situated in the center of the city, fronting on Tahrir Square, contains more than 6,250 separate exhibits and is the world's principal storehouse of ancient Egyptian art and artifacts.

Roman coins and pottery were unearthed in Swaffham, the impetus given to the spade by Schliemann's excavation of Troy, Mycenae, and the Bronze Age civilization of pre-Periclean Greece at the time of Howard Carter's birth.

Given Lady Amherst's strong recommendation, Newberry promptly interviewed the lad and was impressed by both his portfolio of drawings and his infectious enthusiasm. Hired on the spot and provided with a modest retainer, Howard worked for the next three months at the British Museum. The Museum was equally impressed with his work; that autumn the Egyptian Exploration Fund, which had been set up nine years earlier to excavate in Egypt "to the further elucidation of the history and arts of ancient Egypt, and to the illustration of the Old Testament narrative," bundled him off to Cairo. There he was given a staff position as an assistant to Sir William Matthew Flinders Petrie, the man who, perhaps more than any other except Auguste Mariette, founded Egyptology as a science in the course of a career that spanned seventy-five years in the field. Long, lean, and flinty, with a billowing white beard, Petrie was the born archaeologist; at the age of eight he had suggested to his father that "the earth ought to be pared down inch by inch to see all that is in it and how it lies."

For the next six years, 1892–1898, Carter worked in Egypt under the guidance of Petrie, Newberry, and Swiss Professor Edouard Naville, copying scenes and inscriptions from the walls of Queen Hatshepsut's magnificent, terraced mortuary temple at Deir-el-Bahari, on the west bank of the Nile almost directly opposite the Winter Palace Hotel. Hatshepsut, donning a false beard and proclaiming herself pharaoh, ruled Egypt for twenty years while her husband and half-brother, Tuthmosis III, waited impatiently in the wings for her passing—just as Edward, the Prince of Wales, waited for Victoria to give up the throne in Carter's day. Immediately after Hatshepsut's death, Tuthmosis acquired the courage he did not have in her lifetime. He ordered her name to be stricken from the walls of the temple and he bricked up the stupendous obelisk she erected in her own name so that no trace of her works should be left for admiration. Her temple (a three-tiered structure built directly into the face of a burnt sienna cliff and approached by a pair of obelisks, a pylon gate, and an avenue of 200 sphinxes) is one of the architectural triumphs of the world.

As a taskmaster, Petrie bent the impressionable youth to fit his mold, admitting him into his inner circle of those "attracted by a real love of work, and not by publicity or the buttering and log-rolling of societies."

"Through archaeology, we begin to see a great past rising before us, dumb, but full of meaning," he counseled the youthful Howard Carter. "We are only yet on the threshold of understanding."

Then, as now, many people exhibited quaint notions about archaeology. A London matron once asked Petrie how she should excavate a ruined town—should she begin to dig at the top or at the side? A cake or raised pie was apparently in her mind, and the only question was where to best reach inside it. "Most people think of excavating as a pleasing sort of holiday amusement," Petrie said disgustedly. "Just walking about a place and finding things."

Among his camp followers, Petrie preached the principles of the new science. Carter quickly absorbed them. "The main requirements," Petrie restated in *Ten Years Digging in Egypt, 1881–1891*, "is plenty of imagination . . . Every ounce of earth [is to be] examined . . . Pottery is the very key to digging . . . Never dig anywhere without some definite aim . . . The most trivial things may be of value, giving a clue to something else . . . Keep a record of where everything is found . . . Soak all finds to prevent the corrosive effects of salt . . . Wrap finds in wax to preserve from air . . . One-fifth of the time of excavation is spent in packing a collection . . . Finding things is but sorry work if you cannot preserve them and transport them safely."

Today these homilies are considered pedestrian. In the last century, they were little short of revolutionary.

For an eager young man like Carter, Egyptology was more than hard work. It was also high adventure. To reach the enchanted hunting ground of the archaeologists in Upper Egypt, notably the holy trinity of Thebes, Karnak, and Luxor, slightly more than 400 miles south of Cairo, Carter traveled by boat upriver along the banks of the mysterious Nile. For the first time, he saw the verdure fields, the men attired in galla-biyas, the married women in the black, shroudlike gowns called *melayas*, the clusters of date palms, the villages of mud-brick huts, the camel caravans, the majestic mountains, and the seemingly limitless stretches of desert wasteland that made up the longest oasis in the world—Egypt.

At Deir-el-Bahari, Hatshepsut's mortuary temple, he camped out in a seven-foot-square tent; traveled from excavation site to excavation site by donkey; subsisted for days largely on rice, lentils, cooked tomatoes, and corn bread ("very good," he wrote home of the bread); dressed lightly by day and wore thick woolen sweaters in the evenings (he never went abroad in the noonday sun without a pith helmet—absolutely *de rigueur* among colonial Europeans in the tropics, as much a symbol of imperial authority as protection against the sun's rays). He also acquired his own batman or servant, a fellah lad, whom he paid four piasters (twenty American cents) a day.

Christmas came at the height of the digging season, in the trough of the Egyptian winter, the only truly bearable period in stifling Upper Egypt. On Christmas day, even Petrie put aside his shovel and pick and feasted with other campers on *samak*, a Nile fish; stewed pigeons; kebabs of lamb; braised mutton; a pilaf of rice; and turkey—yes, turkey. The following day, the team would reassemble at the excavation site of the moment and drive itself the harder, as if to make up for a lost day.

One evening at Thebes Carter climbed atop the pylon of the great mortuary temple of Rameses III by means of a stairway that ascended through the very center of the column itself. In a full moon, as if through the eye of Horus, the Egyptian god with the head of a falcon, Carter saw spread before him temple ruins that extended for miles. He recalled being momentarily paralyzed by their awesome beauty—the dazzling temple of Hatshepsut; the dark, brooding Libyan mountains shielding the Valley of the Tombs; the Colossi of Memnon, sandstone monoliths like sentinels in the green fields along the Nile's western bank. On another occasion, at Karnak, he pitched his tent along the Avenue of Sphinxes, not the familiar sphinx with a lion's body, but those with the heads of rams. He was moved to dip his hands in the sacred pool of the great red granite temple dedicated to Amen-Re, the sun god, where the dead bodies of the pharaohs were bathed before they were turned over to the embalmers. On still another occasion, he spent the night at the base of the pylon of the pharaoh Harmhab (Horemheb), a general of the army in the time of Tutankhamen, which stood within the shadow of the sixty-foot-high statue of Rameses the Great. Step by step, stage by stage, Carter became enraptured and ensnared by a world of the past.

In this formative period of his life, Petrie taught him not only basic archaeology and Egyptology, but also something of economics and sociology.

It was Petrie who introduced Carter to the roundabout, bargain route from London to Cairo. In the 1890s, when Upper Egypt was crowded with winter tourists and invalids, the typical well-to-do Englishman sailed on a Moss steamship from Liverpool to Alexandria. A first-class, roundtrip passage cost £60 ($300). Petrie demonstrated that the same trip, by ferry across the Channel and by a Messageries ship from Marseilles, traveling second class, of course, cost a mere £14 ($70) roundtrip.

As for dealing with the Arabs, Petrie taught Carter that "the cardinal principle to remember is that [the Egyptians] have no forbearance and know no middle course." They either love or hate, he said, and they do so with a passion. "They also have a positive dislike for making choices," Petrie advised. At the end of each season, they expected a five or ten percent *baksheesh* in a lump sum—an institutionalized form of bribery, not unlike tipping in the West.

The Islamic religion, Petrie impressed on Carter, is "everything to the fellahin." Robbery was the curse of Egyptology, he said; plundering was a national pastime because a man could always shut his eyes to the consequences of his own actions and claim it was kismet, or allotted fate. "The goose that lays the golden egg," Petrie laughingly told young Howard, "has a short and perilous life in Egypt."

With Petrie and Newberry as guides and mentors, Carter learned the Egyptologist's trade and taught himself colloquial Arabic and how to read hieroglyphics. He also came to appreciate why climate and religion fused in Egypt in perfect harmony. The country, he discovered, was literally an outdoor museum. As if by design, nature kept a finger on the thermostat, maintaining the air in an absolutely pure and dry condition that kept Egypt hermetically sealed off from the rest of the world, even its immediate neighbors.

In the Valley of the Tombs, as in Karnak, there was no humidity. Mildew was unheard of; dry rot, unknown. Almost nothing decayed. The art and artifacts of antiquity, the signboards of civilization's thrust, remained preserved in the dry air or under a coverlet of loosely poured, moisture-free sand, which acted as a sealant, like ship's caulking.

Thus, five thousand years and more of wall paintings, sculpture, and monuments—obelisks, pyramids, temples, sphinxes, and tombs—remained so pristine that they retained the wonderful freshness of having been fashioned yesterday. Inside tombs, fingerprints left by builders and grave robbers alike thousands upon thousands of years earlier, remained so clear that they seemed to have just been pressed onto surfaces.

The element of timelessness is overpowering. When Professor G. V. Schiaparelli, the Italian Egyptologist, brought to light the entrance to a tomb, he found the wooden door and its bronze handle were so wondrously preserved that they looked as if they had been installed the day before. He turned to his assistant and casually asked for the key. "I don't have it," the man replied solemnly.

Earlier, in 1905, Theodore Davis stumbled in the Valley onto the partially rifled tomb of two members of the nobility during the reign of Amenhotep III, around 1591 B.C. It was then the richest find yet made in Egypt. The tomb was "literally filled with gold," Davis recounted later; and his aide, Arthur Weigall, then supervisor of Davis's expeditions and later Egypt's inspector general of antiquities, recalled: "We stood really dumbfounded and stared round at the relics of life of over three thousand years ago, all of which were as new almost as when they graced the palace. There in the far corner stood an object gleaming with gold, undulled by a speck of dust, and one looked from one object to another with the feeling that the entire human conception of time was wrong. These were the things of yesterday, of a year or two ago."

Not only was there no speck of dust in the tomb, but over the large outer coffin they found a pall of fine linen, not rotting and falling to pieces like the cloth of medieval times, as seen in European museums, but as soft and strong as sheets on the beds of the nearby Winter Palace Hotel. Atop the linen was a small copper dish filled with ashes from incense. Those ashes glowed at a time when the Exodus had not yet taken place, when the glory of Greece and the grandeur of Rome were yet to unfold.

This quality of contemporaneity in Egypt confounded ancient travelers as well as modern archaeologists. In the age of Periclean Greece, Herodotus, the Baedeker of his day, attributed the character of the Egyptians themselves to their climate. "The Egyptians," he said, "far more than any other people in the world, devote themselves to the preservation of the memory of past actions." They were, in fact, the world's first historians; how could they have been otherwise when their past was preserved before their very eyes?

The Egyptian belief in life after death was the mainspring of their civilization. They believed, for example, that power grew out of the purity of the blood line. In an effort to avoid dilution of this power, they took to incestuous sheets: fathers married daughters, mothers married sons, and brothers married sisters. They did not distinguish between "good" and "evil" deities among their gods and gave their gods the forms of trees and animals as well as humans. (Think of the couchant lion with the human face —the sphinx.) In the pantheon of gods, Re, the divine disposer and organizer of the world, and Amen-Re, the sun god Re in human form, were the first among equals. Indeed, there was a strong monotheistic streak in the religion of the ancient Egyptians.

"Obscured as it is by a complex mythology, their religion has lent itself to many interpretations of a contradictory nature, none of which has been unanimously adopted," P. Pierret, the French Egyptologist, wrote in 1875. "But that which is beyond doubt, and which shines forth from the texts for the whole world's acceptance, is the belief in one god." However controversial this point of view among archaeologists even today, the seed of monotheism did flower at different times, notably during the theologically revolutionary reign of the pharaoh Akhenaten, one of whose daughters married Tutankhamen. Akhenaten was the king who preached that the lord his god, Aten, represented by a solar disk, was but one and that there were no other gods before him.*

Other ancient religious beliefs have persisted to the present among the Egyptians, notably circumcision and complicated laws about "clean" and "unclean" food. But at the core of Egyptian theology was an implicit belief in life after death, a hereafter of rewards and punishments, which all the great religions since then have also espoused. Yet no religion ever developed so complicated a death style as did that of the ancient Egyptians. And it was this death style that made Egyptology, in many ways, perhaps the most satisfying branch of archaeology.

Little wonder that Egypt seduced young Carter, like so many before him, and held him close for the rest of his life.

A Partnership is Formed

Carter's enthusiasm and industry won him the admiration of his superiors, and he rose rapidly to positions of responsibility and authority. He worked in Upper,

---

*As Arthur Weigall pointed out, the foremost law of Akhenaten's religion is identical with the first Mosaic commandment, namely, that no graven image either of the true God or of the older gods was to be either made or worshiped. In this connection, it is worth noting that Moses was a high priest in the Egyptian hierarchy and was privy to their secrets, "learned in all the wisdom of Egyptians." Six of the ten Mosaic commandments are found in Egyptian theology. The relationship between Akhenaten and Moses is a source of interminable controversy. See pp. 142–46.

Middle, and Lower Egypt; his superb drawings—collector's items today—were published by the Fund in six volumes over a twelve-year period, 1896–1908.

In 1899, Sir Gaston Maspero reorganized the department of antiquities at Cairo and appointed Carter, at the age of twenty-five, inspector-in-chief of monuments in Upper Egypt and Nubia, with headquarters at Thebes. Carter became, in effect, curator of open-air museums that embraced Thebes, Karnak, Luxor, the Valley of the Tombs, Deir-el-Bahari, and so on.

For the next three years he was Maspero's most efficient inspector. He restored temple ruins, built an electric power plant at Abu Simbel—the site of today's Aswan Dam—to provide lighting for the Valley's rock tombs (an inducement to the tourist trade), and policed the area against the continuing depredations of tomb robbers.

In 1902, Carter encountered the chain-smoking Theodore M. Davis, the eccentric American millionaire lawyer and financier, who had amassed a fortune in the brokerage houses of the world and for the past dozen years had devoted himself to archaeology.

Each year Davis summered at Newport, Rhode Island, the American Riviera of its day, and wintered in Upper Egypt, a style of living that Carnarvon, in part, later imitated. Davis's great desire was to be the first to find an intact, inviolate pharaoh's tomb. In the course of several expeditions, he had made a number of spectacular finds, enriching archaeology immeasurably.

Like Carnarvon after him, Davis assembled a priceless collection of Egyptian antiquities. He was infatuated by one piece, an alabaster bust of Queen Tiy that he had found in her plundered tomb in the Valley. The statue occupied a prominent place on his desk in Newport. "I always keep that portrait as a memento of a very beautiful and attractive woman," he explained to summer visitors. (His enchanting lady friend had lived three millennia before him.)

Davis had heard of young Carter and, on meeting him, was impressed with his dedication and drive. Carter encouraged the American to abandon his shotgun manner of digging and to focus his funds and forces on the Valley. He also persuaded Davis to "undertake a systematic exploration in the Valley," as Carter expressed it. Central to all of Carter's ideas about excavation was the imperative need for a "systematic" approach. Mobilizing a work force of 150 fellahin in January 1902, Davis and Carter established a base camp and started to scour the gorge for clues to a pharaoh's tomb. They began their search in the western half of the Valley and worked towards a sheer cliff. After a fruitless year, they reached the lower part of the cliff.

At this point, amid the debris, Carter detected the opening of a tomb. "In clearing down to the surface of the rock," he said, "I came upon two small holes which contained complete, undisturbed sets of foundation deposits bearing the name of the king, Tuthmosis IV." In great excitement, Carter cleared the entrance to the tomb—and his vision of finding a pharaoh's gold and jewels quickly dissolved. "We entered [the tomb], accompanied by the head *reis*, finding a passage partially filled with rubbish and strewn with broken antiquities," he recorded with disappointment. "This immediately indicated to us that the tomb had been anciently plundered." Sliding along the passage for one hundred feet, they found another opening, a stairwell, and a chamber sixty feet long. All that remained in the chamber was the lid of Tuthmosis' sarcophagus, fully inscribed with hieroglyphic texts and bearing the king's cartouche, or nameplate. But as their eyes grew accustomed to the dim light of their candles, they were chilled by a ghoulish scene.

"In the right-hand corner, resting in an erect position against the wall, was a denuded mummy," Carter later wrote, "whose stomach and cage had been ripped open by the ancient plunderers with a very sharp knife." In a second chamber they found "a mass of mummy linen-bindings, which had probably belonged to the mummy found in the first chamber, and this was, perhaps, the place where the plunderers had unrolled it." The grave robbers, of course, had sought the gold charms and amulets wrapped within the bandages to protect the pharaoh on his journey through Amenti, the netherworld of the ancient Egyptians.

Overjoyed by the find, Davis invited a number of officials from Cairo to the formal opening of the tomb in February of 1903. He fondly referred to Carter as "my admirable explorer." A year later, Davis, Carter, Newberry, Maspero, and G. Elliot Smith, the celebrated professor of anatomy at the Egyptian Government School of Medicine, coauthored an account of the adventure in *The Tomb of Thoutmosis IV*.

With great enthusiasm, Davis and Carter continued their excavations. Although Davis never found his unmolested tomb, he made a number of other important finds, including the discovery of the tomb and stripped mummy of what he believed was the last resting place of the radiant Queen Hatshepsut, who built the terraced mortuary temple at Thebes after usurping the throne around 1500 B.C.*

During his association with Davis, Carter once suggested that they dig around the mouth of the tomb of Rameses VI. Davis, citing a more promising location, dissuaded his young assistant. The area Carter had pinpointed was the very one he and Carnarvon agreed to excavate twenty years later in their last bid to find Tutankhamen's tomb.

Carter gradually acquired greater authority in Egypt, and then an incident at the end of 1903 wrecked his career as a government official—and almost terminated his career as an Egyptologist.

Petrie, his wife, and three young women students were excavating at Sakkara, copying hieroglyphics from the walls of mastabas, an early form of Egyptian tomb prevalent forty centuries ago. The tombs consisted of subterranean vaults for the coffin, or "house after death," and a network of rooms, protruding above ground, which were filled with food, weapons, and other articles for the mummy's use in the hereafter.

One Sunday evening, several intoxicated Frenchmen entered their camp, demanded a guided tour of the largest mastaba, and, as Petrie later put it, "tried to force their way into the women's huts." An ugly scene developed, and Petrie promptly summoned Carter. The chief inspector, accompanied by a squad of Egyptian guards, descended on the camp. Carter ordered his men to protect the women. A fracas ensued, and one of the guards knocked down a Frenchman.

Outnumbered, the French retired—but on returning to Cairo, they declared that the honor of France had been besmirched. They lodged a formal complaint against Carter and the "native" who had had the temerity to strike a European. The French consul general demanded an official apology. Carter told him to go to hell. Stiff-necked and uncompromising, Carter insisted that he had only carried out his duty. Carter's friends, including Maspero, pleaded with him to apologize. In a huff, Carter resigned

*Whether the mummy they found was that of Queen Hatshepsut or Queen Tiy, who lived 1397–1360 B.C., has been a matter of dispute ever since. In 1974, a team of archaeologists from the University of Michigan, headed by Professor James Harris, announced that they had found the mummy of one of the two queens, but, at this writing, still did not know which was which. The team discovered a sealed chamber in a tomb in the Valley that had been overlooked since Belzoni's time. It contained the mummies of three women. According to Egyptian funerary rites, queens were entombed with their arms straight down at the sides. But one of the three mummies had its right arm crossed over the chest, as if holding a flail and crook, the manner in which pharaohs were entombed. That mummy may have been that of Hatshepsut, who seized the throne and proclaimed herself a king.

from the government's antiquities service. The French Maspero, who, with his English wife, had tried to bridge the chasm between the French and English in Egypt, was dismayed. "I don't know what the department will do without him," he lamented.

The "incident," as it was called, mirrored the political undercurrents of the period. France and England had engaged in hot and cold wars for more than a century, shifting their competition from continent to continent and, in the process, covering the globe with their respective empires. In Egypt, their rivalry was unremitting.

Napoleon had arrived there in 1798 to challenge British power east of Suez. His fleet carried a team of scholars and draftsmen to study the monuments of ancient Egypt, a subject that fascinated him. As a consequence, the French acquired a headlock on Egyptology and, among many spectacular finds, recovered the stone near Rosetta that unlocked the mystery of hieroglyphics and demonstrated that the strange pictographic form of writing was in reality a highly developed alphabet. Following Nelson's defeat of the French fleet in Abukir Bay, near Alexandria, the so-called Battle of the Nile, the French surrendered. Under the terms of the surrender, the French were compelled to turn over to the British Museum their fabulous collection of Egyptian art and artifacts, including the precious Rosetta stone. The French never forgave the British for this indignity.

The hostility surfaced again at the beginning of the twentieth century, when, in the face of Germany's quest for a place in the sun, England and France were compelled to bury the hatchet and draw together. In 1904 they entered into the *entente cordiale*, the alliance that opposed German hegemony over Europe in World Wars I and II. To put an end to their fierce competition in the Mediterranean, the British acquired Egypt as a sphere of influence, and the French took Morocco. In that era, imperial powers traded subjugated lands like baseball cards. Archaeology should have been the farthest thing from their minds as they carved up North Africa. On the contrary, astonishingly, the *first* article of the alliance specifically held that Britain "is agreed that the post of director general of antiquities in Egypt shall continue, as in the past, to be entrusted to a French *savant*."

Thus, the *entente cordiale* notwithstanding, the cold war along the Nile between French and British archaeologists continued unabated. Maspero and his wife labored with indifferent success to make peace between the warring camps. They wrote Petrie, Newberry, and other friends and associates of Carter, including Davis, urging them to persuade the hotheaded young man to apologize and withdraw his letter of resignation. Egyptology, Maspero felt, was more important than this asinine squabble. "Carter, however," Newberry later reminisced, "was adamant in his refusal to apologize and preferred to return to private life." Reluctantly, Maspero was forced to accept Carter's resignation. Petrie was outraged. "This was perhaps the dirtiest act of the antiquities service's subservience to French arrogance," he declared.

On paper, Newberry's phrase, "preferred to return to private life," has a gentlemanly and misleading resonance. Carter was penniless.

Jobless at twenty-nine, he drifted back to his beloved Upper Egypt. There he was taken in by a former *reis*. It is an eloquent commentary on Carter's character, given the nature of the "white man's burden" in that haughty colonial era, that the "natives," as Egyptians and all other nonwhites were called, considered him as one of their own. For the next four years, he eked out a meager living painting watercolors for the tourist trade at Luxor's Winter Palace Hotel and spent his idle time scouting the region for clues to a lost pharaoh's tomb. Many of his old friends came to his assistance periodically—Petrie hired him for several weeks at a time, the Egyptian Exploration

Fund in London continued to publish his drawings, and, on one occasion, Davis hired him as a draftsman. But everyone moved warily, for a license was needed to dig in Egypt, and the concession could come only from the French-dominated department of antiquities. To befriend someone who was *persona non grata* with the French community in Cairo was hardly diplomatic.

The occurrence of these trials in Carter's life coincided with Carnarvon's motor accident in Germany and his subsequent decision to turn to Egyptology as a pastime. At the prompting of his physicians and friends, Carnarvon set off for Luxor in 1907 and obtained a permit from Maspero to dig at Thebes. He dug on his own. For six weeks, seven days a week, he tore into the sands with a vengeance. Anyone else might have found such work tiresome, but Carnarvon was exhilarated. For all his labor, however, he found only a mummified cat (the goddess Bast, symbolized by the cat, was revered as the defender of Egypt and worshiped by a cult known as the Bubastis).

Maspero watched Carnarvon from afar. When he realized the seriousness of the Englishman's amateurish endeavors, the director of antiquities insisted that he acquire the services of an expert excavator.

The abyss between dilettantes, collectors, and amateurs with bundles of money, and impecunious students and scholars—the relationship between rich patron and poor client—has persisted from time immemorial in many disciplines. The distance was especially wide in the early part of this century. "For many years European and American millionaires, bored with life's mild adventures, have obtained excavating concessions in Egypt, and have dallied with the relics of bygone ages in the hope of receiving some thrill to stimulate their sluggard imagination," an impoverished archaeologist of pre-World War I vintage wrote with a touch of bitterness. "They call it 'treasure hunting,' and their hope is to find a king lying in state with his jewelled crown upon his head. With this romantic desire for excitement one feels a kind of sympathy; but, nevertheless, it is a tendency which requires to be checked. The records of the past are not ours to play with: in the manner of big game in Uganda, they have to be carefully preserved; and the tombs, like elephants, should only be disturbed by those provided with a strictly-worded license."

These critics often sought the best of two worlds; that is, they were some of the same people who complained earlier that the leisure class wasted its money on breeding dogs and horses, financial resources that should be put to furthering the arts and sciences.

In any event, Carnarvon eagerly accepted Maspero's advice. He would get an expert excavator as an aide, but because he hardly knew anyone in the field, would Maspero recommend someone? Four years had passed since the "incident" at Sakkara, French passions had simmered down, the Germans provided a greater threat than ever to the Allies, and Carnarvon, with his fluent command of French and a lineage traceable to Aix-la-Chapelle, had charmed the French community in Cairo.

Maspero felt the moment propitious to summon Carter, and thus began the collaboration that was to make indelible archaeological history. Carnarvon and Carter met for the first time, not on the cricket field of Highclere or in the marketplace of Swaffham, but amid the incredible ruins of the oldest and richest civilization of the ancient world.

The Search Renewed

In notes made at Thebes during the first new seasons of their collaboration, from 1907 to 1911, Lord Carnarvon described the site of their endeavors: "Open and half-filled mummy pits, heaps of rubbish, great mounds of rock debris with, here and there, fragments of coffins and shreds of linen mummy wrappings protruding from the sand [are seen everywhere]," he wrote. "The necropolis itself extends for some five miles along the desert edge and evidence of the explorer and robber present themselves at every turn." (Like all archaeologists, he made a distinction between the "explorer and robber," an assessment which is sometimes as controversial now as then.) Few records of previous digs existed, and Carnarvon observed bleakly, "The work of the present-day explorer must be a heavy one."

With a view to systematic excavation, the imprint of Carter on Egyptology, the pair began to dig. Their work gangs of fellahin from neighboring villages fluctuated in force between 75 and 175 men. As Schliemann learned at Troy, the success of a dig depended in large measure on reliable foremen. Carter and Carnarvon employed three *reises* who remained at their side through the years: Ali Hassan, Mansur Mohammed-el-Hasbash and Mohammed Abdul-el-Ghaffar.

During these early years, the team dug in fifteen different locations in the Theban area (including Karnak, Luxor, and the west bank of the Nile). For both Carter and Carnarvon, the months passed with alternating phases of hope and despair. This was the nature of the gamble; the history of excavations in Egypt is marked with sharp contrasts. After seemingly interminable failure, de Morgan, the French archaeologist, turned up a vault filled with glistening gems in one of the Dachour pyramids. Petrie, on the other hand, working in the royal cemetery of Abydos, once uncovered a secret passageway in a tomb. In high excitement, after weeks of painstaking, teaspoon-paced excavation, the team arrived at the core of what turned out to be a "false" tomb designed to foil grave robbers. To their complete embarrassment, they found in the center of the so-called tomb a copy of a Parisian newspaper left behind by the last excavator.

As time passed in failure, Carter openly admitted that he and Carnarvon appeared engaged in "barren labor." Yet occasionally their patience was rewarded—once by the recovery of the Carnarvon Tablet and, much later, by the discovery of the long-sought-for tomb of the pharaoh Amenhotep I, who ruled in 1560 B.C. His tomb, like all others, had been plundered in antiquity; but to make sure that nothing should escape them, they sifted over the rubbish three times. As Carter later observed, "We removed many thousand cubic meters of sand [Carnarvon put the figure at 11,000] and days passed with hardly a single object coming to light." But Carter refused to be discouraged; he was determined to persevere. With the passage of time, the search for an inviolate tomb became an obsession with him.

To the ancient Egyptians, of all the components that went into the makeup of a human being—a corporeal being, an intelligence, a shadow, a name, a heart—the most important was the *ka*. Interminably and inconclusively, scholars have wrestled with the meaning of the word *ka* ever since it first turned up in the hieroglyphics translated in the first half of the nineteenth century. Amelia Edwards interpreted the *ka* as that "something," apart from the body, that is inseparable from the body during life, which survives the body after death and which is destined to be identified with the body through eternity. Soul? Spirit? Or, within a present-day context, personality? Or reputation? Or, as current experiments tentatively suggest, the Human Aura? The late German archaeologist Georg Steindorff concluded, "In my opinion the *ka* is not, as commonly supposed, a kind of ethereal facsimile or double of the man, but a guardian spirit or genius." Whatever the definition, the Egyptians were so deeply convinced that the *ka* was the irreducible essence of a human being that they even called the tomb "the house of the *ka*." In wall paintings and statuary, they glorified the *ka* as a bird in flight, flitting endlessly through the twilight zone between life and death.

At death, the palace gates of Osiris, the sovereign of the underworld, opened. The soul of the deceased passed into the hall of truth, where Osiris, surrounded by judges, held court. The judges listened attentively as the soul, in a confessional, recited the catalog of forty-two sins. Anubis, the jackal-faced god, held aloft a scale on which Horus, the son of Osiris, who possessed a hawk's face, weighed the heart of the deceased against a feather—the symbol of justice and truth. Crouched in the background was a terrifying creature with the head of a crocodile, the body of a lion, and the hindquarters of a hippopotamus. If the heart weighed more than the feather, the monster pounced on the heart and devoured it. If the heart were lighter, Thoth, the ibis-headed god of writing and computation, solemnly announced the verdict and inscribed it in the great book of judgment. The *ka* of the deceased was then led into the presence of Osiris, where it was pronounced fit to journey through the underworld in quest of immortality.

This story of judgment has a familiar ring in the literature and religion of other civilizations, including our own. Like most other peoples, the Egyptians established an ideal that was impossible to attain. Life after death was assured, and immortality was guaranteed as long as the lifeless body remained inviolate and undisturbed. "The immortality of the body was deemed as important as the passage of the soul," an official of the British Museum wrote at about the time Carter first arrived in Egypt.

"The Egyptians did not think of a corpse as 'life's worn-out shell,'" wrote Ann Terry White, who popularized archaeology on the eve of World War II. "To them it was a shell that would continue to be used as long as it was preserved." The Egyptians believed that death did not break the bond between spirit and flesh; the one was so dependent on the other that it could not exist alone—every step in the decay of the body robbed the soul of some part of itself, whereas complete destruction of the body meant total extinction of the soul.

But how is decay arrested interminably? How can the *ka* be eternally supplied with its needs? The Egyptians sought to resolve these twin questions through mummification and artistic representation. Not only was mummified food placed in the tombs, but representations of it as well. And there were statues of soldiers, servants, and slaves to render assistance to the deceased in the hereafter. These were called *ushabty*, or "answerers," because they "answered" the summons of the *ka* for assistance as the occasion arose.

Because the *ka* spent eternity in the tomb, ever faithful to the imperishable body of its infancy and maturity, it was also provided with such other articles as a chariot, furniture, weapons, and toiletries. The *ka* was even given game boards, for a form of backgammon, to while away the millennia.

The Egyptians embalmed their rulers, high priests, and nobles and secreted these objects in their tombs—many fashioned from gold or silver or from an alloy called electrum, others inlaid with jewels. "Consider then, what must be the number of those sepulchres, of those mummies, of these buried treasures!" wrote an enthusiastic explorer in the last century. "The graveyards of Thebes, Memphis and Abydos have enriched the museums of Europe and are not yet worked out. The unopened mounds of Middle and Lower Egypt, and the unexplored Valley of the Libyan range, undoubtedly conceal tens of thousands of tombs which yet await the scientific, or unscientific, plunderer!"

Mummification and religious beliefs, therefore, were inextricably interwoven, and the embalmer's process evolved into a sacerdotal function. A special order of high priests prepared the body and, in the process, gained an intimate knowledge of anatomy, chemistry, biology, and other sciences. They experimented with chemical compounds, invented surgical instruments, and even deified the most renowned physician of their day, Imhotep.

Carnarvon first learned of mummies in his childhood—who does not?—and, like many others, viewed his first museum mummy with the mixture of disbelief, fascination, horror, and humor that stirs most children. "To my mind," he once wrote as an impressionable youth, "mummies, at best, are unpleasant objects to look upon." But it was not until Carnarvon immersed himself in Upper Egypt with Carter that he came to understand that the life-style of the ancient Egyptians was, for all practical purposes, essentially a death style.

There is reason to believe that just as climate and religion complemented each other along the banks of the Nile, so did the embalmer's art. In a treeless land like Egypt, cremation was impractical on a mass scale. Fuel was in short supply. Burial was also discouraged very early in Egyptian history. The annual flooding of the Nile probably washed up the bodies of the dead, particularly if the first burials in Egypt occurred in the dry season or on the eve of the annual inundation that made the desert bloom. Strabo, the Greek geographer, observed in 25 B.C., when he journeyed up the river, "Herodotus was quite right in saying that the whole of Egypt is 'a gift of the river Nile.'" Indeed, without a Nile, there would be no Egypt, only sand.

Accordingly, the logical solution to the problem of disposing of the dead was to heap them up in the caves of the rocky spurs that line the river's banks. But piling them up like cordwood invited jackals and pestilence. By all accounts, Egypt was remarkably free of plague, and this led one observer to conclude quaintly, in 1851, that "this was owing, without doubt, mostly to the universal practice of embalming the dead, which cut off one main source of noxious vapors." Mummification may have evolved as a matter of public health, very much in the same manner that, ostensibly on religious grounds, the ancient Egyptians made a distinction between "clean" and "unclean" foods.

The implications of mummification are awesome. Samuel Birch, one of the early Egyptologists, amazed Victorian England in 1878 with the calculation that over a period of 2,700 years, the then estimated extent of Egyptian civilization, the Egyptians "embalmed no less than 420 million corpses." By the end of the century, on the basis of the new discoveries made by Petrie, Loret, and others, Egypt's funerary rites were ascribed to a span of 4,700 years. Accordingly, the number of mummies was put at 731 million, a figure that is still acceptable today.

Over the centuries, recurring invaders—Persians, Greeks, Romans, Arabs, Turks, and Europeans—ravaged the countryside for mummies. Some rifled them for treasure; others sought them as curiosity pieces; some, for scientific reasons. In time, no museum was worthy of the name without a genuine mummy on display. Mummies were also harvested for commercial reasons.

Up to the eighteenth century, for example, the brittle mummies were ground up for medicinal purposes. Mummy powder was as popular then as aspirin today. Genuine mummies, however, were so scarce and dear that the *Encyclopaedia Britannica* in 1771 indignantly warned its readers against buying substitutes at the local apothecary shop. "What our druggists are supplied with is the flesh of executed criminals or of any other bodies the Jews can get," the *Britannica* explained. "[The Jews] fill them with the common bitumen so plentiful in that part of the world; and, adding a little sloes and two or three other cheap ingredients, send them to be baked in an oven till the juices are exhaled and the embalming matter has penetrated so thoroughly that the flesh will keep and bear transportation into Europe." The result, the *Britannica* concluded, was that the medicinal value of these prefabricated mummies "depends more upon the ingredients used in preparing the flesh than in the flesh itself." The situation led Sir Thomas Brown to pen the following lines: "The Egyptian mummies, which Cambyses or time hath spared, avarice now consumeth. Mummy is become merchandise, Mizraim cures wounds, Pharaoh is sold for balsams."

In the enlightened nineteenth century, the market for the curative powers of mummies evaporated. But enterprising merchants discovered that mummies could be profitably ground up and sold for fertilizer as bone meal. The export of mummies as manure boomed. J. C. McCoan, writing in 1877, reported in his *Egypt as It Is* that up to 1872 the shipment of bones ranked high on the list of Egyptian exports with "mummy bones contributing nearly as much as those of modern cattle to the yearly total of 10,000 tons sent chiefly to England."

In New England, another purpose was found for mummies. A shortage of rags for making paper developed soon after the Revolution. In 1801, with proverbial Yankee ingenuity, Augustus Standwood, a Maine paper manufacturer, imported mummies by the shipload, stripped the bodies of their linen wrappings, and processed them as brown wrapping paper. The business was so profitable that Egyptian traders took to rendering the mummies in Egypt and exporting the wrappings alone in bales that resembled those of cotton or rubber. The stripped bodies, of course, were sold separately as fertilizer.

Standwood's business suffered a setback when cholera broke out in New England and, rightly or not, was traced to the wrapping paper. Even so, New York continued to import the wrappings for paper manufacture. The *Albany Journal* and the *Syracuse Daily Standard*, among others, waged a crusade against their import. In an editorial, on August 19, 1856, the *Daily Standard* chastized a local merchant who advertised "paper made from the wrappings of mummies": "Could anything better illustrate the practical character of this age, and the intense materialism of America?"

The subject of mummies has developed a rich literature. Herodotus was so fascinated by it that he recorded the embalming process in detail in his celebrated *History*:

[The embalmers] first take a crooked piece of iron, and with it draw out the brain through the nostrils, thus getting rid of a portion, while the skull is cleared of the rest by rinsing with drugs; next they make a cut along the flank with a sharp Ethiopian stone, and take out the whole contents of the abdomen, which they then cleansed, washing it thoroughly with palm wine, and again frequently with an infusion of pounded aromatics. After this, they fill the cavity with the purest bruised myrrh, with cassia, and every other sort of spicery except frankincense, and sew up the opening. Then the body is placed in natrum [soda] for seventy days, and covered entirely over. After the expiration of that space of time, which must not be exceeded, the body is washed, and wrapped round, from head to foot, with bandages of fine linen cloth, smeared over with gum which is used generally by the Egyptians in the place of glue, and in this state it is given back to the relations, who enclosed it in a wooden case which they have made for the purpose, shaped into the figure of a man.

Although Herodotus is revered today as the "father of history," he was a journalist at heart and spiked his copy with asides intended to raise Athenian eyebrows. He observed, for instance, that "the wives of men of rank are not given to be embalmed immediately after death, nor indeed are any of the more beautiful and valued women. It is not until they have been dead three or four days that they are carried to the embalmers," he explained. "This is done to prevent indignities from being offered them. It is said that once a case of this kind occurred."

Herodotus' report of seventy-day mummification is echoed in the Old Testament. Just as the Hebrews may have acquired monotheism, circumcision, the concept of kosher and nonkosher food, and six of the Ten Commandments from the Egyptians, they may also have learned the embalmer's trade in captivity. Thus, in Genesis:

> Joseph commanded his servants, the physicians, to embalm his father; the physicians embalmed Israel. And forty days were fulfilled for him; for so are fulfilled the days of those which are embalmed: and the Egyptians mourned him for three score ten days [seventy days].

In the early years of search with Carnarvon in the Theban countryside, Carter kept one eye on the ground, so to speak, and the other eye on the Valley of the Tombs of the Kings, where Davis, who held the coveted permit to dig exclusively in the gorge, pursued his quest. By 1912, the Valley had drained a weary Davis of his enthusiasm and vitality, but he was loath to give up a site where he had expended so much time and money. However impatient Carter and Carnarvon were to dig there, they had no recourse but to wait until Davis formally surrendered his right to the area. Among archaeologists there is a gentleman's agreement that the last previous excavator of a site has a prior claim to the right of digging at the site unless he either formally renounces that claim by not renewing his concession or by transferring his right to another party. Davis dallied. During the 1912–1913 and 1913–1914 seasons, he renewed his permit, but only went through the motions of digging. In truth, he never dug again in the Valley, but he could not tear himself away from it until the end of the 1913–1914 season, when he gave up his concession. Perhaps he felt the siren call of Osiris; a year later he died in Florida at the home of Secretary of State William Jennings Bryan. An exquisite figurine of the Egyptian lord of Amenti was near his deathbed.

While waiting for the Valley permit, Carnarvon and Carter switched their activities from Upper to Lower Egypt. It was Carnarvon's money; Carter had no say in the matter. They arrived at Sakha in the spring of 1914; the weather was abnormally hot, and the area turned into a snake pit. Newberry, who spent a couple of days with them, recalled, "After a fortnight, they were practically driven from their camp by the extraordinary number of cobras that infest the place." In a sense, the cobra, symbol of Lower Egypt, drove them back to their destiny along the upper banks of the Nile.

In June of that year, the Valley concession was awarded them, the permit renewable annually up to November 16, 1923. Although Carter and Carnarvon had already begun preliminary work, the original contract was not signed until April 18, 1915. Carter signed the lease on behalf of Carnarvon. Maspero was dead; George Daressy, then the acting director general of the antiquities service, signed on behalf of the Egyptian government.

The contract was routine. It contained thirteen clauses. Article 1 stipulated that "the work of excavation [in the Valley] shall be carried out at the expense, risk and peril of the Earl of Carnarvon by Mr. Howard Carter." The clause also stipulated that Carter, a professional excavator and Egyptologist, must always be present at the dig. The final article held that "any infraction on the part of the permittee or his agent . . . shall entail the cancellation of the present authorization." Other clauses stipulated that the permittee might open any tomb that was found and might be "the first to enter." In the event that mummies of kings, princes and/or high priests were discovered, they, together with their coffins and sarcophagi, would revert to the antiquities service. As a compensation, rights of publications with regard to the results of the expedition were accorded to the concessionaire. Articles 9 and 10 seemed harmless enough—yet they would cause international shock waves. "Tombs which are discovered intact," read Article 9, "shall be handed over to the [Egyptian] Museum whole and without division." In the case of "tombs which have already been searched," the department of antiquities reserved the right, in addition to mummies with their coffins and sarcophagi, "to all objects of major importance from the point of history and archaeology." The word "searched" was widely interpreted as a euphemism for "entered and robbed in antiquity"—plundered. And in a related clause, in Article 10, the department tacitly conceded that an "unsearched" tomb would probably never be brought to light.

"As it is probable that the majority of such tombs as may be discovered will fall within the category of the present article [that is, searched]," the clause read, "it is agreed that the permittee's share will sufficiently recompense him for the pains and labor of the undertaking." In sum, Carnarvon, at a minimum, was entitled to a return on his investment equal to the costs of his expeditions, a figure, as observed earlier, that crested at a quarter of a million dollars. As Carter remarked later, with customary understatement, "Although the concession gave rights to the concessionaire, they were not clearly defined."

Perhaps the principal reason for the permit's ambiguous phraseology was that nobody in Cairo seriously believed that the pair would find a rainbow, much less a pot of gold.

All the evidence indicated, however, that the tomb of the pharaoh Tutankhamen was buried in the Valley. Sir Charles Leonard Woolley, the renowned archaeologist, later observed that any success Carter and Carnarvon achieved was not owned "to a stroke of good luck but the patient following-out of a logical theory." The theory was deceptively simple. Inasmuch as the Valley contained the known graves of all the pharaohs of the Eighteenth Dynasty, clearly it was the burial ground of that dynasty, and therefore *all* the kings of that dynasty ought to have been found there, and because they had not, they were still to be discovered.

At the time of the contract signing, the legal ramifications of the arrangement were the furthest thing from the minds of the signatories. Daressy, like Maspero before him, had confidence in the integrity of Carter and Carnarvon. Carnarvon, who had worked in Egypt for seven years, was then fifty years old. Carter, with twenty-four years of experience in Egypt, was forty-two.

For the next eight years, intermittently during the Great War, Carter and Carnarvon worked in the unexplored areas of the desolate, somber Valley, shifting thousands of tons of glistening white limestone chips from the bottom of the gorge, scraping the cliff sides in search of possible doorways, clearing the rubble and debris left by other excavators, digging to bedrock wherever feasible, and combing every crevice of the mountain pass. Unlike others before them, they did not work haphazardly. Their field map was forever spread out before them.

First Clues

To this day there is no reliable chronology of the Egyptian age of pharaohs. Nobody knows how many sovereigns were buried in Lower and Upper Egypt during the royal past; nobody knows how long they reigned. The first "king list" was drawn up in 300 B.C., when the Ptolemies, remembered better for their Cleopatra than for anything else, ruled the Nile. The most recent edition of the guide to the Egyptian Museum in Cairo, published in 1968, confesses: "We do not possess a complete chronological list of all the kings; and there are 'Dark Periods' of which we cannot determine the length, even within a century or so."

In the 1930s, Petrie (who died in 1942 at the age of ninety-two) constructed the best list yet in existence, openly conceding that its foundations were shaky. Tracing Egyptian history from 9000 B.C. to the emergence of the First Dynasty in 4326 B.C. and through the millennia until 341 B.C., when the last native Egyptian sat on the throne, Petrie wryly acknowledged, "These dates are based on the annals of the early kings, the ancient lists of kings, the inscriptions dated in reigns, biographies and genealogies, epochs fixed by the calendar, the horoscopes, and new moons."

Two problems confronted Egyptologists in assigning events to their proper sequence. For one thing, although the Egyptians developed calendars, two in fact, they possessed no fixed system for measuring the passage of time. The reign of each pharaoh was recorded from his first year on the throne. Thus, a monument might be dated, "In the twenty-first year of the reign of Harmhab [also spelled Horemheb]." But how did this relate to the overall history of Egypt?

The second problem is political in character. On ascending the throne, some pharaohs sought to rewrite history, eliminating the names of predecessors and gilding their own lilies. Queen Hatshepsut not only erased predecessors' names from monuments, but altered her gender in the hieroglyphic documents of the period. Since then there have been many examples of men and women rewriting history to suit themselves or an ideology. Two thousand years ago, fifteen centuries *after* Hatshepsut, a Chinese emperor ordered the world's first massive book burning, and in Cromwell's time it was seriously proposed that all records should be burned and that the memory of the past should be erased so that history might start anew. The rewriting of history, of course, persists to this day, notably among the totalitarian powers of the right and left that have left their mark on the scarred twentieth century. In Egypt, the most significant attempt to rewrite pharaonic history was made by Harmhab, a general under

Tutankhamen, who seized the throne from Tutankhamen's successor, purged Tutankhamen's name from official king lists, hammered out his portraits and cartouches from temple walls, and expunged his name from hieratic steles. As Christiane Desroches-Noblecourt, an Egyptologist of the Louvre, observed, "Tutankhamen was the victim of a systematic attempt to erase him completely from history." But the revisionist general lost the day. A stone from a temple built by Tutankhamen, bearing his cartouche, was found among blocks sequestered by Harmhab for pylons erected to perpetuate his own name and to honor Amen-Re and the old gods. Reused Tutankhamen blocks were also uncovered at Luxor. Harmhab expected history to treat him as the immediate successor to the heretic king Akhenaten, who had espoused the revolutionary concept of monotheism, and to hail him, Harmhab, as the ruler who restored the old gods and goddesses to their proper niche in the drama of creation.

Carter's initial interest in Tutankhamen had begun in 1891 during his first year in Egypt, when he was dispatched to work in Petrie's camp. Petrie was then in the vicinity of Akhetaton (Tell el-Amarna today), the capital city that the heretic Akhenaten built to revere his discovery of the one, true, and only God, the Lord his God, the Lord who was one, beside whom there was no other God. This God, Aten, was represented not by an image (Akhenaten outlawed idol worship) but by a solar disk—the sun—without whose beneficial rays life on earth would perish. The rays, radiating like a comet from the orb's "tail," were depicted terminating in upturned hands, palms outward.

Petrie described himself in this period as working to "fill in the blanks" of the history of the Eighteenth Dynasty. At Gurob, Petrie had satisfied himself that Tutankhamen ("He who serves Amen") was originally named Tutankhaten ("He who serves Aten") and that he changed his name when he restored the seat of the Egyptian throne to its former capital at Thebes. Thus, Tutankhamen's reign marked the transition from the experimental belief in one Creator to a return to the tradition of worshiping the old sun god, Amen-Re, and a coterie of other gods.

At the time seventeen-year-old Howard Carter joined Petrie, only a few facts were known about Tutankhamen's personal history. From the number of small objects he found while digging at Akhetaton, the place of Tutankhamen's coronation, Petrie concluded that the young pharaoh had lived there only briefly, perhaps six years, before the capital was returned to Thebes. Petrie found neither a palace nor a tomb fit for a pharaoh at the new capital and therefore concluded—correctly, as it later developed—that Tutankhamen had reverted to tradition and was buried with the other pharaohs of his dynasty in the sacred Valley of the Tombs of the Kings.

Because pharaonic court records about plundered tombs made no mention of Tutankhamen's tomb being robbed, Petrie also drew the conclusion that tomb despoilers had overlooked his burial place or, more likely, that the location of the tomb had been lost in the antiquity of antiquities.

At the outset of the present century, the consensus among archaeologists was that all the major pharaohs of the Eighteenth Dynasty buried in the Valley were accounted for except three. Poetically, the three were the principal figures in the Akhenaten heresy. Among them were Akhenaten himself, the heretic, who had changed his name from Amenhotep IV when he discovered the true and only God, Aten; Tutankhamen, the great compromiser, whose reign sought to bridge the abyss between Thebes and Akhetaton; and Harmhab, the archrevisionist who fully restored the old gods to Egyptian religious belief. Many archaeologists doubted that the heretic's mummy would ever be found; as Sir Alan Gardiner, the English Egyptologist, observed,

"Conceivably Akhenaten's body had been torn to pieces and thrown to the dogs." As for Harmhab, the evidence at that time strongly suggested that the general was buried at Memphis or at some place in Lower Egypt. This left only the mummy and tomb of Tutankhamen unaccounted for. Because neither had been recovered, there was a persistent hope, albeit frail, that perhaps his tomb had eluded the "curse of Egypt," the tomb robbers.

Tutankhamen's name had been familiar to archaeologists since Napoleon's day. In the British Museum the pharaoh's cartouche adorned the lions found at Gebel Arkal: somehow they had escaped the hammers of Harmhab's stone masons. Early Egyptologists speculated a great deal about how this phantom pharaoh fitted into the historical matrix of ancient Egypt. Was he a commoner or a member of royalty, possibly related to Amenhotep III, Akhenaten's predecessor? In a slip, the commoner Howard Carter once wrote, "He may have been of blood royal—he may on the other hand have been a *mere* commoner." [Italics added.] The only point on which the scholars were in full agreement was that a king by that name once held the flail and crook and ruled Egypt at a crucial time in her development.

Fifteen years after Carter first landed in Egypt, a French Egyptologist provided the first tangible record of events attributed to Tutankhamen's reign. Digging at the base of a temple in Karnak on June 28, 1905, Georges Legrain recovered intact a red sandstone stele from under several feet of sand. The tablet had fallen from the pillar upon which it had been fixed and had been partly shattered by the fall. Apparently nobody noticed it at the time; perhaps a sudden sandstorm swirled through Luxor. Whatever the case, centuries of sand accumulated at the spot and preserved the pieces in excellent fashion. Harmhab's agents of destruction missed it completely.

The stele provided the initial insight into Tutankhamen's rule. Because in that age works were often written to flatter the ruler, it is sometimes difficult to distinguish between fact and fiction, but such records are evidence of the values and thoughts of 3,500 years ago.

When, in the aftermath of the Akhenaten heresy, Tutankhamen assumed the throne on the death of Akhenaten, the stele recorded "the land was overridden with ills." The shrines of the gods "ran to destruction." In turn, "the gods neglected the land." The farthest frontiers of the empire were reoccupied by barbarians. Tutankhamen appealed to the gods and goddesses for assistance, but they shunned him. Accordingly, the new pharaoh embarked on a vigorous program to win back the forsaken gods. "His majesty made rules for the land every day without cease," according to the stele. Tutankhamen restored the worship of Amen and "made his august image in pure gold"; he "raised monuments to the other gods"; he increased the number of sacred vases "in gold, silver, copper, and bronze without limit to their number"; he multiplied the riches of the temples "by two, by three, by four, in silver, gold, lapis-lazuli, malachite, precious stones of every kind, royal linen, white linen . . . no end of all precious things"; he built new ships to sail the waters and "covered them with gold . . . so that they lighted up the Nile." He surrounded himself, the high priests, and nobility with "slaves, male and female, singers, and tumbling girls." He was benevolent and dispensed justice evenhandedly. As a consequence, everyone everywhere "exulted, shouted, struck their chests, and danced for gladness."

Maspero, one of the earliest students of Tutankhamen's reign, held that the picture of the young pharaoh's life and times was probably accurate. "There is no doubt that the great mass of the Egyptian population must have experienced strong joy when the persecution [of former gods] ended, and the old order of religion was reinstated," he observed. And yet the archaeologists of Maspero's day were more mystified than ever because the stele showed, as had some of Petrie's earlier finds, that although Tutankhamen restored Amen, he also remained faithful to Akhenaten's vision of Aten, the one and only God, the sole Creator of the universe. A representation of the rays of the solar disk bathed the stele.

The Legrain discovery attracted the attention, of course, of Carter, who was then, as an outcast among Egyptologists, eking out a meager living through the sale of watercolors at Luxor's Winter Palace Hotel. Convincing proof of Tutankhamen's former existence came at a time when Carter's life had reached a low point.

Two years later, in 1907, when Carter's fortunes changed dramatically and he embarked upon his journey into history with Carnarvon, Legrain published a book containing a photograph of the rare stele. While the book was on the Parisian press, the authenticity of the stele was confirmed beyond doubt. The shattered fragment of a duplicate was recovered at Thebes.

At almost the same time, Theodore Davis turned up new evidence that Tutankhamen had indeed been buried in the Valley.

"While digging near the foot of a high hill in the Valley of the Tombs of the Kings," Davis reported, "my attention was attracted to a large rock tilted to one side, and for some mysterious reason, I felt interested in it." With the aid of an assistant, Edward Ayrton, Davis carefully extracted from beneath the rock an exquisite faience cup, pigeon blue in color. The Egyptians were (and are) masters of faience: a process in which clay is heated with glass. The glass melts and imparts a lovely color to the clay.

"The cup bore the cartouche of Touatankhamanou," the elated Davis reported. (*Touatankhamanou* was the accepted spelling at that time.)

The following season (1907–1908), Davis, assisted by E. Harold Jones, returned to the dig. In the course of a preliminary resurvey of the Valley, Davis and Jones came upon the unmistakable signs of a lost tomb. They put their fellahin to work immediately. "At the depth of 25 feet we found a room filled almost to the top with dried mud, showing that water had entered it," Davis recalled. They carefully sifted through the mud and, in great excitement, Davis said, "we found a broken box containing several pieces of gold leaf stamped with the names of Touatankhamanou and his wife Ankhousnamanou. . . . We also found under the mud, lying on the floor in one corner, a beautiful alabaster statue."

The discovery caused a sensation in Luxor and Cairo. Some of the gold pieces, very thin and flat, apparently had been stripped by plunderers from the furniture and funerary articles buried with the dead pharaoh; other pieces of gold leaf, slightly thicker, contained engraved scenes and had probably been nailed or stitched to other objects, such as a chariot. "After spreading [them] out," said George Daressy, then a Davis aide, "I succeeded in reconstructing some designs, more or less complete."

A number of pieces of leaf, some measuring eight by five inches, bore the cartouche of Tutankhamen and depicted his life-style. In one scene, the pharaoh stood erect in his chariot, bow poised, in the midst of a hunt. The scene was unique; for the first time a pharaoh was shown accompanied not by lions but by a greyhound. Another fragment of gold leaf bore the legend, "Lord of the two lands giving life forever like the sun." Still another scene depicted Tutankhamen with his youthful wife, her seductive figure discernible through a diaphanous negligee. She wore the headdress of Hathor, the cow-headed goddess of Amenti, a deity of the Egyptian Hades. Standing behind her husband, as he smote an enemy with a sword, she declaimed: "All protection of life is behind him, like the sun." Still other vignettes showed black Africans, with short frizzy hair, and western Asians, with curled beards, paying homage to the new pharaoh.

The alabaster funerary statue was a delight in itself, fifty-nine inches tall, carved from fine, translucent stone. The figure was that of a man in mufti, his arms crossed upon his chest. Unfortunately, the figurine bore no inscription.

Warming to the dig, Davis accelerated the pace of the excavation. Again he was rewarded with success.

"A few days after this we came upon a pit, some distance from the tomb, filled with large earthen pots containing what would seem to be the debris from a tomb, such as dried wreaths of leaves and flowers, and small bags containing a powdered substance," Davis reported. "The cover of one of these jars had been broken and wrapped about it was a cloth on which was inscribed the name of Touatankhamanou."

Davis did not recognize the monumental nature of his discovery. Instead, disappointed by the contents of the jars, he brushed them aside, storing them in the camp's warehouse.

Some months later, however, Herbert E. Winlock, who became curator of Egyptology at the Metropolitan Museum of Art and was then a member of the museum's Egyptian Expedition, examined the Davis find. His pulse quickened. Winlock considered the discovery incontrovertible proof that Tutankhamen was buried in the Valley. With the American millionaire's approval, Winlock repacked the jars and shipped them to the Metropolitan for a thorough examination. The New York word came back: "Extraordinary."

The articles packed into the jars included several clay seals of the royal necropolis; the dried leaves and flowers were of the style of floral collars worn at Egyptian funerals more than three thousand years earlier; and the piece of linen used to hold together the contents of the broken jar bore the inscription ". . . year of the reign of Tutankhamen." The conclusion was manifest: Davis's find was part of the funerary debris from Tutankhamen's burial service. In the dry climate of Upper Egypt, the objects were so well preserved that it seemed they were thrown aside only the day before—not, as in fact they were, literally, more than a million days earlier. Obviously, a mourner, perhaps a servant or a necropolis official, tidied up after the funeral, stuffed the odds and ends into the jars, and shoved them into a crevice in the rock—sweeping them under the rug, so to speak.

The excitement at the camp was transmitted to Carter and Carnarvon. "With all this evidence before us," Carter said, "we were thoroughly convinced in our own minds that the tomb of Tutankhamen [was] still to be found." Although he did not say so, he probably felt that Davis would beat him to it and turn up the lost tomb. Davis probably thought similarly.

Then, in 1908, Davis's decade of digging in the Valley was crowned with an irritating mix of triumph and failure.

On February 25 of that year, the Davis crew discovered signs of another tomb. After a day's feverish digging, they uncovered a stairway leading sharply down a few feet, where broken rock and sand filled the space almost to the top. "It was impossible to advance except by digging our way with our hands," Davis reminisced, "and, as we were most anxious to find whose tomb it was, my assistant, Mr. Ayrton, in spite of the heat, undertook the difficult task of crawling over sharp rocks and sand for some distance [to look for an inscription]."

Arthur Weigall, then working for Davis, recalled in his memoirs that they first thought they had discovered the tomb of Tutankhamen. "The size and shape of the entrance left no doubt that the work was to be dated to the end of the Eighteenth Dynasty," he said.

But their buoyancy was quickly deflated when Ayrton read the hieratic inscription* on a supporting beam of the tomb: it contained the name of Harmhab, the general who had sought to blot Tutankhamen's name from history.

Davis described the party as "astonished" by the discovery, as no doubt it was. But Weigall focused on another emotional reaction. "We were disappointed," he wrote.

Wriggling and crawling through the tunnel, accompanied by a small avalanche of stones, Davis, Weigall, and Jones joined Ayrton and continued to squirm deeper into the tomb's passageway.

"It was necessary to drag ourselves over the stones and sand which blocked the way, with our heads unpleasantly near the rough roof," Davis recounted. "There was little air, except that which came from the mouth of the tomb 130 feet above, and the heat was stifling."

The party dropped into a large room and in the center of it stood a red granite sarcophagus, 9 by 4 by 4 feet. Weigall provided this eyewitness account of the excitement: "Looking into the sarcophagus, the lid having been thrown off by plunderers, we found it empty except for a skull and a few bones." As usual, plunderers for profit had preceded the plunderers for art and science—by centuries, if not millennia.

Harmhab's stripped tomb was the last find Davis ever made in the Valley of the Kings, although he continued the search for Tutankhamen's tomb through 1912. Then, drained of his hopes and too tired to dream, Davis abandoned his quest.

The aging, eccentric millionaire consoled himself, however, with the conviction that the discovery of the blue faience cup and the gold leaves was proof positive that he had found Tutankhamen's tomb. "[These discoveries] lead me to conclude that Touatankhamanou was originally buried in the tomb," he wrote, "and that it was afterwards robbed, leaving the few things that I have mentioned."

Davis published his findings in *The Tombs of Harmhabi and Touatankhamanou*. It was a four-part collaboration. Davis wrote the section on the discovery of the tombs, Maspero provided the historical background on both pharaohs, Daressy prepared the catalog, and Lancelot Crane illustrated the folio. Daressy did not mirror the confidence Davis had reflected in the title of the book. He called his section of the work "Catalogue of the Objects Found in an Unknown Tomb, Supposed to be Touatankhamanou." This was the same Daressy who later, as acting director of the government's antiquities service, signed the Carnarvon-Carter concession in the Valley.

Carter scoffed at Davis's claim, which he termed "ludicrous." The Davis theory was "quite untenable," he said. No pharaoh, Carter argued, would be buried in a shallow pit grave. Inwardly, he must have been relieved that Davis had not found the tomb. History was still to be written.

Lost Years

Before receiving the cherished permit to dig in the Valley proper, but in the course of

---

*The eminent Egyptologist, Adolf Erman, is amused by the distinction made by most archaeologists between hieroglyphics and hieratic script. " 'Hieratic' . . . is just the cursive form of hieroglyphic writing," he points out, "and to distinguish the one from the other is as if we were to explain our own handwriting as something different from our printed type." He termed the distinction "somewhat absurd."

initial excavations, Carnarvon and Carter had, in the latter's words, "the good fortune" to locate the empty tomb of Amenhotep I, the second ruler of the illustrious Eighteenth Dynasty. The find, like so many others, was largely a matter of luck.

"The entrance was secreted under a huge boulder," Carter reported in his account of the discovery in the *Journal of Egyptian Archaeology* in 1915, "and a unique feature is that the debris coming from its excavation was removed in its entirety to a considerable distance away, and hidden in a depression in the ravine below.

"Thus," he wrote, "when the tomb was sealed up there could have been practically no visible indication of its existence."

They expected to find Amenhotep's tomb looted, and they did. Early in the Eighteenth Dynasty, after a series of frightful plunders in the Valley, the mummies of several sovereigns, including Amenhotep, were removed from their original resting place and deposited, family style, in a mausoleum. The location of the mausoleum remained hidden in the Valley until Loret's discovery in 1881, thirty-five centuries later.

Despite its being a plundered tomb, Carnarvon and Carter burrowed into it with zeal. There was always the off-chance that some of the treasure buried with the pharaoh might still be recovered intact, perhaps in a secret, walled-up chamber in the tomb.* But the Amenhotep tomb was shorn not only of its mummy and treasure—its galleries, passageways, and chambers were a shambles, evidence of extensive depredation. "All that was left of the king's funeral equipment was the debris of broken vessels and statuettes, fragments of alabaster, green feldspar, yellow limestone, red conglomerate, serpentine, and basalt," Carter reported. "They were broken with such method that hardly a fragment larger than six square inches was found among them, though apparently many of the vases had been of large dimensions." Among the fragments, fifty-four different vases were identified. Some of the broken fragments contained inscriptions, including the cartouche or elliptical frame bearing the name of Amenhotep I.

In July 1914, Carnarvon was officially informed that he would receive the permit to dig up the entire Valley. He and Carter set about drawing up their "elaborate campaign," as Carter called it. They crisscrossed their map of the Valley with plotting lines, like a mariner's chart; authorized their *reises* to raise a force of 275 men; ordered fresh supplies from Cairo to be shipped to Luxor and then onto the dig; and developed a scheme to dig up the Valley to bedrock. Their starting point: the area of Davis's discoveries.

In August, however, war broke out in Europe, and all was uproar and confusion in the Near East. The "elaborate campaign" was suspended.

Carnarvon hurried back to England and sought to enlist in the army, but he was turned down as physically incapable of service. The first battle of the Marne was fought that September, and trench warfare began as the British repulsed the Germans at Ypres. The number of casualties was unprecedented in military annals. Worse was yet to come.

Frustrated and restless at Highclere Castle, Carnarvon hit on a project to turn his palatial estate into a rest and rehabilitation center for the wounded, and he spent the remainder of the war in related work at Highclere or in London. For his part, Carter was caught up for a short time with wartime duties in Cairo.

At the outbreak of the war, the political situation in Egypt was roiled beyond belief. A weak khedive, or king, sat on the throne in Cairo as the nominal ruler of Egypt

*This is precisely what happened at another site in 1974. See fn. p. 32.

under the even more nominal suzerainty of the Turkish sultan in Constantinople, the seat of the Ottoman Empire. Real power in Egypt, of course, was exercised by the British (except in matters pertaining to the department of antiquities). The war, however, stripped away flimsy political camouflage. When Turkey declared war on the Allies and joined the Central Powers, the situation, from London's point of view, was impossible. Accordingly, on December 18, 1914, Britain announced that "in view of the state of war arising out of the action of Turkey, Egypt is placed under the protection of His Majesty and will henceforth constitute a British protectorate."

Realizing that the British were pinned down in various parts of their empire at the outset of the conflict, the Turks seized on the opportunity in 1915 to reassert their authority over Egypt and the Nile. The British turned them back. However, when the Turks in turn defeated the British at Gallipoli, they followed up their victory with a second invasion of Egypt in 1916. Once again, the British repulsed the Ottoman army and, in the process, overran the Sinai Peninsula and carried the war to the Turks by attacking Palestine. Thereafter, the war faded from the Egyptian theater.

During these attacks and counterattacks, the British became increasingly dependent on the recruitment of fellahin as labor levies to build fortifications and move supplies to the fighting fronts. With his working facility in Arabic and his knowledge of *shorghl-el-Mizr*, Carter was assigned to a department in charge of the mobilization of labor battalions. Their recruitment was one of the most sordid sideshows of World War I. Sir Davis Kelly, the former British minister in Egypt and an outstanding Foreign Office figure, denounced the whole operation in scathing terms as being carried out "with a maximum of waste, corruption and brutality."

Carter, as dedicated a public servant as Sir Davis, was also appalled by his countrymen's disregard for, and callous treatment of, the fellahin, whose stereotype in the West has been summarized by Professor Ayad al-Quazzaz as "dirty, dishonest, unscrupulous, inferior, backward, primitive, savage, sensual, oversexed, half-naked, fatalistic, lazy, unambitious, shifty, scheming."

The brutal treatment of the fellahin during World War I clearly ignited the flames of militant Egyptian nationalism that led to the rise of Zaghlul Pasha in the twenties and finally to Nasser's seizure of the Suez Canal in the fifties, which allowed Egypt to reemerge as an independent power.

In any event, with the failure of the Turkish invasions of 1915–1916, the war receded from Egypt, affording Carter an opportunity to carry out single-handedly the search for Tutankhamen's tomb. In point of fact, as early as 1915, the year he formally signed the Valley concession on behalf of Carnarvon, after the failure of the first Turkish offensive, Carter was dispatched to Upper Egypt to assist unofficially in policing the Valley. The absence of officials and the diversion of regular guards from Upper Egypt, owing to the war, spurred a revival of activity among what Carter called "local native tomb robbers." His choice of words implies that he made a distinction between "local native tomb robbers" and "foreign tomb robbers." The meaning was clear: theft and plunder are theft and plunder.

In 1916 a group of "local native tomb robbers" from a village near Luxor made a spectacular find in the Qurna hills adjacent to the Valley of the Tombs. In the prewar period, the area, which included peaks rising 1,800 feet above sea level, had been known to Egyptologists as the "lost cemetery of royal families"—the last resting place of the wives and children of the pharaohs. Why the archaeologists dubbed it "lost" is inexplicable.

At that time, the region was relatively unexplored except for one valley, Gabbanatel-Qirud, in which tombs abounded, hidden in clefts and crevices. Some tombs were cut high up into the rock faces of the perpendicular cliffs. All the known tombs had been ravaged in antiquity.

Through his contacts among the fellahin at Luxor, who respected his integrity, Carter learned of the fresh discovery. Acting on the intelligence, he gathered together a handful of former workers, including several, he later admitted, "who had escaped the Army Labour Levies." This was an extraordinary admission on the part of a British official during wartime: a clue perhaps to his intimate relations with the Egyptians in the colonial period. He and his men set off for the Qurna hills.

From the crest of a precipice, "Carter's irregulars" heard voices and noise below and saw the occasional flicker of a kerosene lamp. The robbers had found a hypogeum cut into the face of a cliff and were hard at work. The tomb's opening was cleverly concealed 130 feet from the top of the cliff and 220 feet from the floor of the Valley.

Studying the scene, Carter observed that the thieves had descended to the opening by a worn rope. He cut the rope, then secured his own stout line and shinnied down until he was parallel with the tomb's opening, dangling in space. "Shinnying down a rope at midnight into a nestful of industrious tomb-robbers," he recalled dryly, "is a pastime which at least does not lack excitement." Eight thieves were at work; at his sudden appearance, they dropped their tools in shock. "There was an awkward moment or two," Carter said.

He boldly offered them a choice: either ascend on his rope or remain where they were. They probably recognized him. After twenty years in Upper Egypt, the former chief inspector of antiquities was known in every village; more important, in this situation, he was also respected. The culprits departed peacefully—and Carter never reported them to the authorities.

To Carter's utter amazement, given the location of the tomb, he entered a lateral passageway that ran straight into the cliff for 55 feet and then opened onto a stairway. In a periodic report to Carnarvon to keep him abreast of developments in Egypt, Carter wrote, "I found that they had burrowed into it like rabbits as far as the sepulchral hall. The burrow made by them was some twenty-nine metres long and would allow but one man to pass at a time and then only by creeping upon his stomach. They had widened and deepened the burrow for further operations."

On his return to Luxor, Carter promptly notified the antiquities service in Cairo of the discovery and, with the approval of British headquarters, the department arranged for him to carry on at the spot.

For the next twenty days, relays of fellahin labored day and night to clear the tunnel and chamber. The job was arduous and dangerous. Because coming and going by a single rope was impractical for a large body of workers, Carter jury-rigged an "elevator" that operated on pulleys. "For anyone who suffers from vertigo," he remarked later, "it certainly was not pleasant." He himself always made the descent in a net!

As the work progressed, excitement at the camp rose. Surely so well-hidden a tomb, Carter reasoned, must be intact and must contain wonderful treasure. But the tomb contained only an empty, crystalline sandstone sarcophagus, which bore hieratic inscriptions and the cartouche of Hatshepsut, whose body had already been found in the Valley of the Tombs.*

In hieroglyphics he read the queen's moving, eloquent appeal: "Place me among the stars imperishable ... that I may not die."

*See fn. p. 32.

Clearly, this was the original tomb of the radiant queen of the terraced temple of Deir-el-Bahari, who usurped the throne at her husband's death and proclaimed herself pharaoh. "It is to be presumed," Carter wrote in a report that appeared in the *Journal of Egyptian Archaeology* in 1917, "that on her definite adoption of the dignity and predicates of the pharaohs, this great queen felt it beneath her dignity to be buried in the distant spot consecrated to the royal *harim*, and transferred her sepulchre to the same valley which was to become the regular burial place of the kings of the Eighteenth Dynasty."

If she had been buried in this secret place, her mummy would have remained undisturbed, at least into the early part of the twentieth century, three and one-half millennia later. Then it would have been plucked clean. A pharaoh she would be, Carter mused, and a pharaoh's fate she shared.

But how in the name of Aten (or Amen) did the ancient Egyptians cut the tunnel halfway up the face of the cliff? How did they move the sarcophagus, which weighed tons and whose lid alone measured $6^1/_2$ feet by $2^1/_2$ feet, into the burial chamber? The engineering feat was as puzzling as it was astounding.

"I have endeavoured to discover whether it was lowered into the tomb from the cliff above or whether it was hauled up from the valley below," Carter said, "but I have been unable to discover indications pointing either way. Far away on the lower foothills west of the Valley, I think I can trace a possible road by which it may have been brought, but the traces are too slight to be more than hypothetical."

The excitement surrounding the discovery incited Carter to transfer his search for an intact tomb from the Valley of the Tombs to the adjacent Qurna hills.

With his band of *reises* and unreported deserters from the labor battalions, he undertook extensive soundings in the area at Carnarvon's expense and with the approval of the wartime authorities in Cairo. (One wonders what the British Middle East command would have thought had they known that Carter sheltered deserters.) He uncovered potsherds of the Eighteenth Dynasty—Tutankhamen's dynasty—and fragments of granite, basalt, crystalline sandstone, and alabaster, the raw materials frequently found in and near Egyptian burial grounds. He also took rubbings of many inscriptions carved into the cliffs and chiseled "H. C. 1916" alongside them so that future explorers would know that they were already copied and cataloged. The initials, a lasting monument to his life and times in Upper Egypt, are still there. "On one of the ancient roads of the upper plateau," he wrote matter-of-factly, "I picked up a large copper coin of Ptolemy II Philadelphus."

But these finds were lowlights. As in the past, he wrote Carnarvon with an air of disappointment, "in this small valley I have been unable to find any traces of [intact] tombs." Nevertheless, he returned to the Qurna hills in early 1917 and pressed his dig. The end result was the same, and he ruefully concluded, "Though at present there are no visible traces, I believe there must be other tombs in this bay." His report was accompanied by a map, which illustrated the relationship of the Qurna hills to the Valley of the Kings and identified important finds in both places. There was a notable exception. Carter did not put an X to mark the spot where Davis contended he had found the tomb of Tutankhamen.

At this point, Carter realized, as sometimes happens to one in the midst of research, that he had backed off the main track and, out of curiosity, wound up on a siding. That summer, with the Americans now in the war and the Central Powers hard-pressed along the western front, Carter went back to the main line. "In the autumn of 1917 our real campaign in the Valley opened," he wrote in the 1923 edition of *The Tomb of Tut-*

ankh-amen, employing the modest first person plural. By describing the new expedition as "our real campaign," he implied that all their other campaigns constituted an idle effort, which was hardly the case. Most likely, Carter hoped to keep up Carnarvon's spirit—and keep up the flow of pounds from his treasury.

"The difficulty," Carter said later, "was to know where to begin, for mountains of rubbish thrown out by previous excavators encumbered the ground in all directions." Worse, no sort of record had ever been kept as to which areas had been properly excavated and which had not.

For a start, he tackled the square encompassing the known and plundered tombs of Rameses II and VI and Merneptah. He drew blanks. The following year, with the war over and the world made safe for democracy, Carnarvon joined him; and, in a renewed burst of ardor, the pair spent the next seven months digging in the Valley. They found nothing.

In 1919 they made their first important postwar find, a cache of thirteen alabaster jars bearing the names of Rameses II, the widely acknowledged pharaoh of the Captivity, and Merneptah, his successor and the ostensible pharaoh of Exodus. Both had lived centuries *after* Tutankhamen. "As this was the nearest approach to a real find that we had yet made in the Valley," Carter later wrote, "we were naturally somewhat excited."

Lady Carnarvon had joined them for this campaign, and Carter said, "I remember [she] insisted on digging out these jars—beautiful specimens they were—with her own hands."

The 1920 campaign was launched with fervor, given their minor success the year before. They spent eight months digging daily—in terrible heat and on inhospitable terrain. The following year, they dug for seven months. They found nothing, absolutely nothing. "We were again disappointed," Carnarvon told friends.

Was Davis right after all? Had he really found Tutankhamen's empty, plundered tomb? Was that the last tomb to be found in the Valley? Doubts even plagued the Pollyanna Carter from time to time. "We had now dug in the Valley for several seasons with extremely scanty results," he wrote, "and it became a much debated question whether we should continue the work, or try for a more profitable site elsewhere."

After these barren years, were they justified in going on with it? As Carter later observed, "We had worked for months at a stretch and found nothing, and only an excavator knows how desperately depressing that can be." And, he continued, "We had almost made up our minds that we were beaten...." The operative word is *almost*.

Stubbornly, Carter clung to the slender hope that his powers of deduction would win the day, that an inviolate pharaoh's tomb was yet to be found—Tutankhamen's—and that he would find it.

The year 1922 was eventually at hand, fifteen years and $250,000 after Carnarvon first took up Egyptology. He reached the decision at Highclere to abandon the whole business—only to be trapped by Carter into organizing one last dig in the vaunted Valley of the Tombs of the Kings.

As their close friend and colleague, the English Egyptologist Sir Alan Gardiner, put it, Carter's return to Upper Egypt in the autumn of 1922 was his "last chance."

As it turned out, all else was prologue.

1. View of the Valley of the Tombs of the Kings, ▷ with the tomb of Tutankhamen in the center foreground, in front of that of Rameses VI.

2. The staff visiting another royal tomb. From left to right: A. C. Mace, archaeologist; a guest; A. R. Callender, engineer and supervisor; Lady Evelyn Herbert, the patron's daughter and official hostess for visitors; Howard Carter; Lord Carnarvon; Alfred Lucas, chemist and conservator; Harry Burton, photographer.

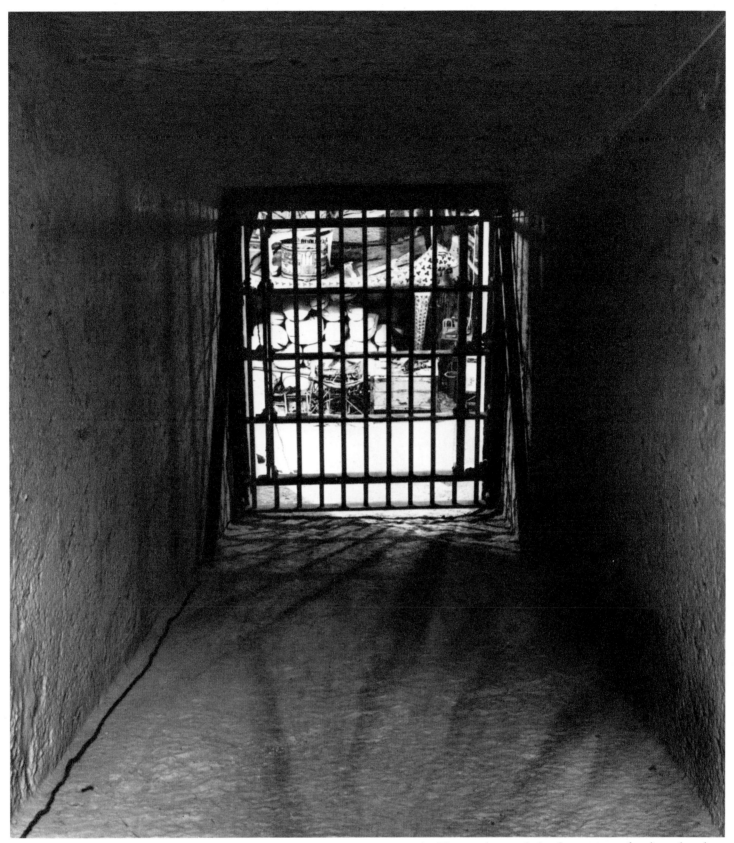

4. The passage and the doorway to the Antechamber.

◁ 3. The seal of the Royal Necropolis.

5. Funeral beds and other objects as they were found in the Antechamber.

6. The Antechamber as found by Carter.

7. The sealed door leading to the Burial Chamber between the *ka* statues of the King.

8. Lord Carnarvon (right) and Howard Carter opening the door to the Burial Chamber.

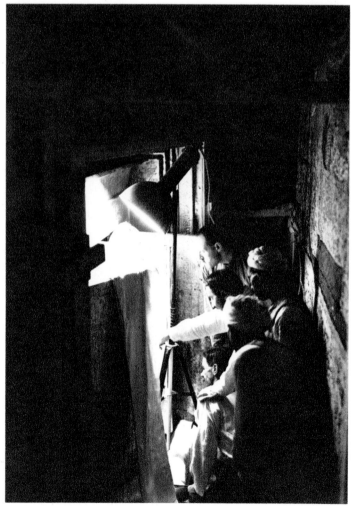

9. Howard Carter opening the doors of the third shrine.

10. The outside of the gilt shrine: the linen veil studded with gilded bronze daisies and the polychrome wall paintings in the Burial Chamber.

12. Anubis guarding the entrance to the so- ▷ called Treasury.

11. The oars placed between the outermost shrine and the wall of the Burial Chamber.

13. A detail of the stone sarcophagus showing the goddess Selkhet.

14. Howard Carter examining the third mummiform coffin.

15. The royal mummy within its coffin.

16. Objects found within the wrappings of the mummy.

17. Unguent jars and canes heaped up between the two outer golden shrines.

18. Ritual statuettes preserved in their coffers.

19. Ritual statuettes preserved in their coffers.

20. Objects stacked up in the Treasury, consisting of ▷ boats, coffers, statuettes, and a miniature granary.

21. The alabaster canopic chest with the lid removed.

22. Inside of the coffer in the shape of a royal cartouche containing precious objects, and earrings worn by the King as a child.

23. A small coffer in the shape of a royal cartouche.

24. The goddess Nephthys protecting the canopic shrine.

The Discovery

Before his departure from England, Carter casually mentioned to Carnarvon and others, including friends at the British Museum, that after living alone in Egypt for thirty years, he planned to return with a companion.

Cairo's foreign community was agog with speculation that October. Who was she? British, of course. Where had he met her? Nobody could recall a woman in his life until then. Well, as they said, life begins at forty. Most probably a sudden encounter.

At the Messageries Maritimes dock in Alexandria, Carter stepped off a French steamer with her in hand; that is, her cage. The "she" turned out to be a gold canary that chirped happily and sang almost incessantly.

On October 28 the odd couple arrived at Luxor, and the canary's cage was suspended from a stand on the second floor veranda of "Castle Carter." The house was situated between Carnarvon's and the Nile, within a thousand yards of the former. The internal layout of both bungalows (or mausoleums) was about the same, although Carter's cottage had one dome to Carnarvon's two and Carter's house was situated on a lower rise than Carnarvon's. When the two houses were viewed within one perspective, their size and location seemed to reflect the higher and lower social statuses of their owners at the time of their construction in the days of a still heavily stratified Edwardian England. In one respect, however, Carter's house was far superior: on the south side it boasted three trees, a thorny, small-leaved acacia and a couple of tamarisks, which required little moisture and provided excellent shade. Carnarvon usually tethered his donkeys, with Carter's, in the shade of those trees, the only touch of green—of life—between the riverine village of El Gournah and the barren, desolate Valley of the Tombs.*

Although Lower Egypt's ornithology is rich, birds are sparse in the country's upper regions. White herons are common in the morning along the Nile, and falcons soar over Luxor in late afternoon. But song birds, aside from a swallow-tailed bird

---

*Carnarvon's house today stands empty and unoccupied. But Carter's is livelier than ever, presently the home of Abdul Hamid el Daly, the inspector of antiquities at Karnak. He commutes daily to his job across the Nile, perhaps the most pleasant commutation route imaginable. Both houses overlook the road leading into the Valley. The programmed tourist hordes that periodically descend on the Valley are invariably oblivious to the colorful history contained within their tawny-colored walls. When I visited the el Daly home in early 1975, it seemed as if time had stood still. Donkeys were tethered outside, in the sparse shade, just as they had been when Carter inhabited the strangely shaped, domed bungalow.

THE GOLD OF TUTANKHAMEN

that closely resembles the chickadee, are uncommon. Thus, the canary was to the fellahin what the bird of paradise is to us—exotic. Little wonder that Carter's pet attracted widespread attention among the people on the west bank of the Nile.

In his memoirs, Charles Breasted, the son of James Henry Breasted, then doyen of American Egyptologists, recalled that, upon Carter's return to Luxor, word quickly passed among his workers that "the bird will bring good fortune."

After arriving home on the west bank of the Nile, Carter spent the next several days arranging for the movement of fresh supplies into the Valley, working out the payroll for his new labor force, conferring with his *reises*, and so forth. On November 3, with his frayed map of the Valley in hand, Carter outlined to his new assistant, A. R. "Pecky" Callender, who took up his residence at "Castle Carter," the final campaign. They were to excavate exclusively around the entrance to the tomb of Rameses VI, concentrating on the spot where some old artisans' huts of the Twentieth Dynasty (circa 1181 B.C.) protruded from the sand. Twice before Carter had been deterred from digging at this location—which was only one hundred yards from the spot where Theodore Davis, in 1907, found the funerary cache he mistakenly identified as Tutankhamen's tomb.

In an experiment that evening, the gallabiya-clad men removed enough sand from the location to indicate that they would have to clear the area to about three feet to reach bedrock. Carter ordered his labor force to dig a trench right through the spot. Arrangements were completed for the work to begin at daybreak the following day.

Most archaeological digs, including Carter's, follow a set pattern. The moment a pickman finds something of interest, he notifies the nearest *reis*. The foreman, taking pick or shovel in hand, satisfies himself as to what was found and either instructs the man to carry on or, in turn, summons the field archaeologist. As Sir Charles Leonard Woolley, the celebrated excavator of Ur of the Chaldees, once observed, "The Arab foreman is, next to the archaeologist himself, the most important person on the excavation, for on him depends the conduct of the whole gang of diggers."

On the morning of November 4, 1922, Carter rose shortly before dawn and took his customary tea on the veranda, feeding his cheerful yellow companion a small biscuit. Then he set off for the dig. But as he approached, he was greeted with complete silence. All work had stopped. The turbaned foreman, Ahmed Gurgar, who possessed a quaint but excellent command of English, was impatiently waiting for him, a group of fellahin clustered nearby. They had begun work about forty-five minutes earlier and had cleared the first hut for about two feet when they came upon a step cut directly into the limestone bedrock.

With Carter and Callender, who had now joined the group, supervising the operation, the workmen cleared the step completely. Creamy white, the first step led to another and then another, descending deeper and deeper into the floor of the Valley. Without the usual midday break, the work party labored on through the day, a fiery sun overhead, and into the cool twilight. "Think of it," Carter often said afterwards. "Twice before I had come within a yard or two of that first step."

Sifting the limestone chips that blocked their way, chip for chip, Carter and his men had cleared sixteen steps by the following day. Suddenly, astoundingly, their way was blocked by a sealed wooden door. The door bore the clay impressions of the high priests of the royal necropolis, a couchant jackal with nine prostrate prisoners. Anything, Carter realized, *anything* might lie behind that door. His first wild impulse was to smash the seals and tear down the door. But in the end, Carter, the archaeologist, the man of training, triumphed over the impulsive man of action.

To the utter astonishment of Callender, the *reises*, and the workmen, he ordered the staircase and entrance refilled with debris (mostly limestone chips), posted Callender at the spot with a loaded rifle, and ordered the *reises* to construct a wooden hut nearby for sentries. Then he rushed off for Luxor and arranged with the local authorities to have armed soldiers from the Sudanese Camel Coast Guard brought to the scene. These details completed, on November 6 he sent off to Highclere, from the Eastern Telegraph Company's office, the following twenty-word cable:

AT LAST HAVE MADE A WONDERFUL DISCOVERY IN VALLEY. MAGNIFICENT TOMB WITH SEALS INTACT. RE-COVERED SAME FOR YOUR ARRIVAL. CONGRATULATIONS.

Carnarvon was at dinner when the cable arrived. He promptly telephoned Gardiner, who later recounted the subsequent conversation to Leonard Cottrell, a writer on archaeology who is best known for his work with the B.B.C. "When Carnarvon had told me the news," Gardiner recalled, "his first question was, 'Do you think this could be the tomb of Tutankhamen?'" Gardiner was noncommittal.

In those days, it usually took a fortnight to make the journey by boat from Liverpool to Alexandria. Carnarvon spent the next day arranging passage on the first available steamer. On November 8 he dispatched the following cable to Luxor:

PROPOSE ARRIVE ALEXANDRIA TWENTIETH.

For Carter, the ecstasy of discovery turned into two weeks of almost unbearable torment. He was too excited to eat or sleep properly. After each restless night he revisted the scene of the discovery, but there was, of course, nothing to see, no tangible evidence of the find except the picturesque detachment of armed camel coastguardsmen with the stolid Callender in command. "The tomb had vanished," Carter later wrote, ". . . and I found it hard to persuade myself at times that the whole episode had not been a dream."

On November 18, Carter left for Cairo to greet Carnarvon, who was accompanied on this historic journey, not by his wife, the Countess Almina, but, as usual, by his daughter, Lady Evelyn.

Gentleman and loyalist that he was, as fitting tribute to his friend and benefactor, Carter erected on the site of the discovery a slab of rough stone, shaped like a stele, on which he drew in black paint a crude representation of the House of Herbert's coat of arms, a crest with three lions rampant, a panther with flames issuing from the mouth and ears, and a roaring lion standing upright on its hind legs. The crest bore the legend: *Ung je serviray* ("One I shall serve").

"A Wall of Gold!"

In anticipation of Carnarvon's impending arrival, Carter ordered the staircase reexcavated November 23.* The following afternoon, Carnarvon and his twenty-one-year-old daughter, in a broad-brimmed, black hat (she preferred that color, the repressive sun of Upper Egypt notwithstanding), reached the Valley. Both were in an understandably acute state of excitability, their British reserve jettisoned.

Closely reexamined, the sealed door had two different sets of seals. One bore the cartouches of Tutankhamen, both his nomen and prenomen; the other belonged to

*The creamy white steps are just as bright today as more than a half-century ago.

the officials who policed the royal necropolis. Hope was dashed when minute inspection of the door revealed that its bottom half had been rebuilt. Carter was mortified: the tomb had undoubtedly been broken into and then resealed in antiquity. Like Cinderella's golden coach at midnight, Carter's great discovery dissolved into a pumpkin.

With utmost care, Carter removed the seals and systematically dismantled the door, taking measurements and other notes and preserving as much of the door as possible for later reexamination. Behind the door, burrowed deeper into the earth, lay a passageway, dark and forbidding, blocked up with limestone chips. After a night's digging, Carter and Carnarvon cleared the passage. Among the rubble, they recovered fragments of broken boxes, vases, and jars—plunderers had beat them to it again. "Damn it," Carter cursed softly, convinced that they had found only the entrance to a funerary cache similar to Davis's discovery.

Then, on November 26, 1922, Carter went through what he later described as "the day of days, the most wonderful that I have ever lived through." In midafternoon, thirty feet from the outer door, the last stone chips were removed from the tunnel—revealing a second sealed door. It bore only the seals of Tutankhamen.

The moment of truth was at hand. Painstakingly, Carter made a small opening in the second door, and, his hand trembling slightly, he thrust in an iron testing-rod. The rod struck nothing. Whatever lay behind that door, was not filled with debris. As a test for noxious gases, Carter widened the breach and inserted a lighted candle. It flickered briefly as a rush of hot, entrapped air poured through the opening. But the candle remained lit. There was no poison gas behind the door; there was oxygen. Oxygen meant there was life. Just as death could not be avoided above the ground, apparently life could not be eluded below the ground.

His hands now trembling uncontrollably, Carter again widened the breach, reinserted the candle, and this time poked his head in. He was, as he remarked later, "dumbstruck with amazement." An eternity passed. He was paralyzed, speechless.

Carnarvon stood behind him, impatiently waiting for a firsthand report. "A long silence followed," Carnarvon recounted later, "until I said, I fear in somewhat trembling tones, 'Well, what is it?' "

Both men recalled different replies. Carter said, "It was all I could do to get out the words, 'Yes, wonderful things!' " Later that year he explained: "As my eyes grew accustomed to the light, details of the room within emerged slowly from the mist, strange animals, statues, and gold—everywhere the glint of gold."

Carnarvon remembered a slightly different response. He said Carter replied, "There are some marvellous objects here!"

Lord Carnarvon stepped chivalrously aside to permit his daughter to take the next peek into the kaleidoscope of the dawn of civilization. She did so and gasped. Then Carnarvon took his turn, while a dazed Carter and a dumbstruck Lady Evelyn stood transfixed. "At first sight, with the inadequate light," Carnarvon said, "all one could see was what appeared to be gold bars!"

Egyptologist Arthur Weigall, apparently drawing on Pecky Callender's recollection of the historic scene, offers a slightly different account of what transpired.

"Wonderful! Marvellous!" Carter is said to have exclaimed as Carnarvon pulled at his arm, shouting, "Hey! let me have a look." But Carter was immobilized by atonishment at all he saw.

"At last," Weigall wrote, "Mr. Carter was pulled from the hole, so the scene was jestingly represented to me, 'like a cork from a bottle,' and Lord Carnarvon took his place."

Whatever the case, the party's immediate impulse was to rip down the door and rush pell-mell into the Antechamber and touch the gold before the mirage disappeared, to fondle the gleaming bars as tangible proof that they were not living through a fantasy.

Some archaeologists refuse to admit it, but the spirit of the treasure hunt pervades the discipline. To his credit, Carter conceded the point forthrightly in *The Tomb of Tut-ankh-amen*, the classic account of the discovery he published the following year. The first sensation on entering a tomb, he wrote, is that time is annihilated and you are an intruder. Other sensations quickly follow—"the exhilaration of discovery, the fever of suspense, the almost overmastering impulse, born of curiosity, to break down seals and lift the lids of boxes, the thought—pure joy to the investigator—that you are about to add a page of history, or solve some problem of research, the strained expectancy—why not confess it?—of the treasure-seeker."

Carter, Carnarvon, and his daughter had seen something incredible: the Antechamber was packed, helter-skelter, with alabaster jars, strangely shaped boxes, gilt-covered furniture, including three colossal gilt couches with the heads of animals (which Carnarvon mistakenly took for "gold bars"), magnificent faience vases, statues and statuettes in gold and alabaster, golden chariots, and a gold throne with exquisite, inlaid semiprecious stones depicting Tutankhamen and his lovely queen, Ankhesenpa-aten, later called Ankhesenamen—a tableau that has since ranked as one of the world's greatest known works of art.

On the right-hand side of the room, along the north wall, the onlookers could see two life-sized statues of the king. These monarchial sentinels, facing each other, were attired in gold sandals and gold skirts. They brandished golden staves. Upon each of their foreheads was the sacred uraeus, the coiled cobra, whose magic powers had protected the tomb for more than thirty-three centuries.

Carnarvon, like Carter, fought to control his impatience. "It was a severe tax on one's curiosity not to demolish part of the door," he later admitted.

On a personal level, the discovery meant different things to each man. Archaeology aside, for Carnarvon it meant that he would recoup losses spread over almost twenty years. For Carter, it meant that he had at last come into his own; he, the commoner, was now rightfully Carnarvon's peer.

Howard Carter promptly exercised leadership. He redoubled the guard at the entrance; sent to Cairo for a steel door to be shipped to Luxor by train (then, as now, a journey of twelve or more hours); and hired his own platoon of ghaffirs, or watchmen, to watch over the guards who were guarding the tomb, in the hope of resolving the age-old problem: *Quis custodet custodes?*

He also issued an appeal for outside help, cabling A. M. Lythgoe, curator of Egyptology at the Metropolitan Museum of Art: "DISCOVERY COLOSSAL AND NEED EVERY ASSISTANCE . . ." The cable, partly garbled, is still in the possession of the Metropolitan in New York. In it, Carter specifically requested the services of Harry Burton, the Museum's staff photographer, who was then a member of the Metropolitan's expedition at an adjoining site in the Theban necropolis.

Lythgoe promptly cabled back: "ONLY TOO DELIGHTED TO ASSIST IN ANY POSSIBLE WAY." Thereupon, the Metropolitan's team descended on the Valley and put themselves selflessly at Carter's disposal. Among them was the aforementioned Winlock, then the leader of the expedition; Burton; and A. C. Mace, Petrie's nephew. It was a refreshing example of international cooperation in a field given to petty academic and national jealousies.

Among others who rushed to Biban-el-Moluk was the intrepid James Henry Breasted, accompanied by his son, Charles. "All my life I shall remember the picture," the son wrote in his memoirs, describing his descent with his father, Carter, and Winlock down the sixteen steps into that other world. "Through the steel bars we saw an incredible vision," he said, "an impossible scene from a fairy tale."

His father and Winlock, he recalled, turned and looked into Carter's face. Words failed the trio, and tears streamed from their eyes. They shook hands and, in a state of mild hysteria, broke into uncontrollable laughter.

Charles Breasted wrote that his first and lasting impression of the cache was the fantastically superb quality of the art and craftmanship of the ancient Egyptians, a craftmanship that made a mockery of Lorenzo Ghiberti and Benvenuto Cellini, artistic detail that surpassed Albrecht Dürer. "It made me fairly dizzy," he wrote.

An uneasiness that they could not articulate also overcame them, a mood that Carter had earlier described as the feeling of the "intruder." This sentiment persists in Egyptology to this very day. Working among the dead perhaps makes it unavoidable.

"There is something peculiarly sensational in the examining of a tomb which has not been entered for some thousands of years," wrote Weigall, Theodore Davis's former aide, in 1923, after a visit to Tutankhamen's tomb. "One cannot describe the silence, the echoing steps, the dark shadows, the hot breathless air; nor tell of the sense of lost time and the penetrating of it which moves one so deeply."

A generation after Weigall, the late Zakharia Gnomeim, chief inspector of antiquities in Upper Egypt, who discovered a lost pyramid in 1956, wrote: "Clearing the entrance corridor, I was strangely uneasy. It was certainly not fear of anything physical, such as the collapse of a roof or a fall of rock; it was something much less tangible, a mixture of awe, curiosity and uncertainty. No one who has not crawled along the galleries beneath a pyramid, and experienced the silence and darkness, can fully appreciate the sensation which at times overwhelms one. It may sound fantastic, but I felt that the pyramid had a personality and that this personality was that of the king for whom it was built and which still lingered within it [the *ka*?]."

The tomb of Tutankhamen, undisturbed for 3,500 years, exuded this forceful, intangible power more than any other ever found in Egypt. Plainly, to enter a tomb—the ultimate destiny of *all* mortals—is to cross the threshold into Amenti, into eternity and the underworld, and to do so when alive, to be conscious of it.

Breasted, in particular, entertained extraordinary experiences within the tomb. Left in the Antechamber to study, decipher, and copy the 150 almost illegible seal impressions on the walls, working alone and in silence, he suddenly heard strange rustling and murmuring sounds that rose and fell. For a moment, fear spread through him, and he had the impulse to flee. But the sounds were not those of ghosts, he reasoned; there had to be an explanation. Suddenly he hit upon it: the injection of fresh air into the hermetically sealed room had altered the Antechamber's temperature and humidity. Wooden articles like the spoked chariot wheels and the furniture groaned, creaked, and snapped as they adjusted themselves to the new atmosphere.

But for Breasted, the most terrifying experience was yet to unfold. In a scene out of the last act of Mozart's *Don Giovanni*, when the statue of the Commendatore comes to life to summon Giovanni into hell, Breasted reported a "curious incident."

As he labored over the seals in the half-dark, he happened to glance up at the face of one of the royal, life-sized sentinels. Unmistakably, he saw the eyes move. "For a moment," he later wrote his son, Charles, "this was strangely disturbing." That moment must have lasted an eternity. Once again he sought a rational explanation—and realized that as the humidity and temperature in the Antechamber altered, some of the pigment used in coloring the eyes of the twin statues dropped off in iridescent, shiny, mica-thin flakes. The flakes caught and reflected the light from his flashlight and gave the statues a frightening animation.

Eventually, a triumphant, albeit shaken, Breasted emerged with exciting news. The seals on the walls were indeed those of Tutankhamen. Thieves had broken into the Antechamber, as Carter feared, but they had been caught, and the tomb had been resealed. There was a reasonable chance, therefore, that the rest of the tomb was still intact.

At this point, Carter and the others realized that the most important object of all was missing from among the jumble of articles in the antechamber—the mummy of the king. Then they made another astounding find. Between the sentinels of the king was the bare outline of a plastered-over, hidden door. Behind that secret door, they surmised, lay the mummy of the pharaoh. "My God!" Carter exclaimed.

In their first joint public statement, issued on December 3, 1922, and written by Carter, the discoverers boldly declared, "We shall find Pharaoh Tutankhamen." They then gave a detailed description of what lay beyond the secret door. This foreknowledge confounded many observers and started rumors that the pair had been led to the spot by some secret papyrus rolls that had somehow fallen into their hands. In truth, they had reached their conclusions on the basis of having studied the Turin, Abbott, Meyer, and Amherst papyri. The Turin papyri, for example, specifically stated that the mummy of a pharaoh was housed not in one coffin but in a nest of three coffins, like a Chinese puzzle. Of course, nobody had ever found a mummy in such a state.

"We know that the custom was that the king would not only be buried in his sarcophagus enclosed in the three coffins, but that the sarcophagus itself was protected by a series of funeral canopies which, from the details in these papyri, seemed to have been constructed of wood," they said in their statement. Avoiding the use of the tantalizing word "gold," the pair forecast that within those canopies or shrines, within the sarcophagus, within the three coffins, "We shall be confronted with an unimaginably rich . . . result."

And Carter inserted a commonplace Moslem expletive into the statement. "*Inshallah* (May it please God), our expectations will be realized."

Invited by the London *Times* to write an article about their discovery, Carnarvon rushed into print with Carter's conclusion. In the article, which appeared a week later, Carnarvon wrote: "There is little doubt behind this wall there exists a chamber or chambers, and in one of those probably reposes, in his coffins and sarcophagus, the body of King Tutankhamen." Carnarvon used the plural, "coffins," as had Carter in the joint statement.

So meticulous were Carter and Carnarvon in their work that it took the party ten weeks to photograph, draw to scale, and remove, piece by piece, each object from the Antechamber. With the room cleared, the group was confronted by the mysterious seven-foot-high door that had been guarded by the life-sized sentinels.

Carter had a raised platform built at the base of the door and a series of wall supports erected on either side like the reinforcement of a coal mine facing. Then on February 16, 1923, he and Carnarvon and the rest of the team reassembled in the empty Antechamber. "Carnarvon was pale as he stepped slowly into the darkness and was lost in the shadows of ancient Egypt," a London *Daily Express* correspondent wrote from a vantage point outside the entrance to the tomb. "No matter how little superstitious a man may be, the act of breaking into a tomb must cause an emotion which time can never efface."

Within the Antechamber, Carter mounted the scaffold, sledgehammer in hand. As he struck the wall, the sound reverberated through the stillness of the underground vault. As the millennia dissolved with the last echo of that blow, as the party stood in the presence of a king who reigned more than three millennia earlier, did the mummy of Tutankhamen stir within its nest of coffins? Did the mummy anticipate its long-awaited resurrection as promised in the Book of the Dead? Was the moment of rebirth, for which it had waited patiently through the ages, as half the world's history was being written, at last at hand? Were those echoes the sounds of the last trumpet?

Carter worked for ten minutes, his white shirt drenched with perspiration. He had hammered out a small opening along the lintel of the doorway, a jagged hole large enough to take a flashlight. The beams of his Eveready played, in his own words, "on a solid wall of gold!"

It proved to be a gilded shrine of wood. The sepulchral chamber was 21 by 13 feet, the gleaming catafalque, or canopy, 17 by 11 feet. It all but filled the burial room, with a space of only 2 feet separating it from the walls on all four sides; above, it almost brushed the chamber's ceiling. "I am not ashamed to confess that [the scene] brought a lump to my throat," Carter said.

Then, along the right wall, beyond the Burial Chamber, he found the entranceway to another room, later dubbed the "Treasury." Within it, Carter discovered the canopic chest containing the king's viscera, guarded by four delicate little golden goddesses sculptured in transparent gowns; a great effigy of Anubis, the jackal god; strange-shaped, oviform boxes; golden chariots; and a heap of objects, looking like large white eggs, thrown under a gilded piece of furniture. As for the latter, Carter later explained to the press that they contained food for the dead—trussed ducks, haunches of mutton, all mummified. "The Egyptians," Carter said, "boxed food as Americans tin it today."

And Sir Alan Gardiner, who was a member of the party that memorable day, recalled to Cottrell his own impressions. "Beyond the Burial Chamber we found on the right the entrance to another room. . . . It was full of marvels . . . [including] a number of caskets. Carter opened one of these and on the top lay a beautiful ostrich-feather fan. The feathers were perfect, fluffing out just as if they had recently been plucked. Those feathers completely annihilated the centuries for me. It was as if the king had been buried a few days before. . . they made on me an impression such as I had never experienced before and never shall again."

It was a refrain echoed by each member of the party.

Said Weigall, who was present as the wall was breached: "There was something very solemn, and even tragic, in this awakening of the once great king, now when his empire was long fallen to pieces and his glory departed. And as I took my place at the mouth of the tomb I felt, if I may say without affectation, a sense of deep sadness weighing upon me."

A number of those on hand, overwrought by the excitement of the moment, became jocular under stress. When cane chairs were carried down into the empty Antechamber for the special observers, Carnarvon joked that it looked as if he and Carter were preparing to give a concert. "His words, though of little moment, distressed me, for I was absorbed, as it were, in my own thoughts, which were anything but jocular," Weigall recalled. "And I turned to the man next to me and said, 'If he goes down in that spirit, I give him six weeks to live.' I do not know why I said it . . ."

By now, of course, Carter and Carnarvon realized that they had arrived at the end of the rainbow and that there was indeed a pot of gold. Realizing that the discovery would draw the attention of every grave robber in Egypt, Carter moved to outwit them. In addition to the armed guard ensconced in the Valley, he arranged for the installation of a new, electrically charged steel door at the mouth of the tomb. A warning was issued: "Any tomb-robber who touches the door will be killed instantly."

Carter and Carnarvon also decided to end the season. Within a few days, the temperature in the Valley would rise above 100°F, and, until the following October, it would be humanly impossible to work in the suffocating, stifling rock tomb. Indeed, one newspaper correspondent reported that when Carnarvon emerged from the tomb on February 16, "he came up slowly into the air looking grey and old."

Accordingly, on February 26, the tomb was officially closed; scores of fellahin, acting as a fire-bucket brigade, discharged basket after basket of sand and limestone chips into the shaft. A cloud of dust hovered over the site, and from a distance, according to one eyewitness, a plume of "cloudlike smoke as from a great fire" rose over the Valley. Carter then busied himself for the next two months crating the objects for shipment to the Cairo Museum. In a neat hand, he wrote up a descriptive index card for each item.

Between the discovery of the tomb's first limestone step in November and the discovery of the shrines in February, the worlds of Carter and Carnarvon turned topsy-turvy. Just as Tutankhamen never rested in peace again, neither would they.

When news of the discovery of the tomb swept up and down the Nile, the fellahin attributed the find to Carter's pet canary. "The golden bird has done it," the villagers said. "The bird has led him to the tomb." Indeed, the Egyptians dubbed the sepulcher the "Tomb of the Bird."

Shortly after the discovery, however, a soft cry—"almost human," Breasted senior said—was heard from Carter's house. A cobra had slithered onto the veranda and entered the bird's cage. Among the Egyptians, the incident was widely viewed as an ill omen. "The serpent from the crown of the king has swallowed the golden bird," they lamented. The fellahin were convinced that the king's uraeus had struck to avenge itself against the bird for betraying the secret of the tomb.

Nor was it only the fellahin who drew this conclusion. The world's press splashed the story on the front page; The New York Times termed the canary-cobra affair "an interesting incident."

For the record, in Luxor and its environs today, there is another story still in circulation about the discovery of the tomb and the death of the canary. "Carter," an aged resident, who was thirteen at the time, told me emphatically in early 1975, "does not deserve the incredible fame he has achieved."

According to this version, a British soldier during World War I purchased a roll of papyrus from an Egyptian farmer who had found it accidentally. Later Carter acquired the roll. The soldier could not read it, but Carter could. The papyrus pinpointed the location of Tutankhamen's tomb and even listed its contents. Thereafter, keeping the knowledge of the papyrus a secret to himself, Carter concentrated his search around Rameses' tomb. It was not until 1922 that he succeeded in removing the thousands upon thousands of tons of lime chips that covered the area. It was then that the tomb was "discovered."

Moreover, my informant declared, shortly before, in the course of a trip to Cairo, Carter visited the Khan-el-Khalili, the fourteenth-century marketplace that still ranks as among the most spectacular oriental bazaars in the Near East. For a reason that even Carter could not fathom, he was attracted to a canary at a bird dealer's stall. The merchant realized that Carter found the canary irresistible and, accordingly, sold the ten-piaster bird for 100 piasters (one Egyptian pound). On the day Carter "discovered" the tomb of Tutankhamen, a six-and-a-half-foot-long cobra—so the story goes—emerged from the tomb and killed the canary. "The yellow bird shrieked so loudly that its cries reverberated through the hills of Biban-el-Moluk," the Luxor resident recalled. Tradition, he added, held that Tutankhamen's queen was the last to leave the tomb and that she carried the robes of mourning on which there was a scarab bearing the drawing of a golden bird. "Tutankhamen's soul did not die on the day Carter broke into the Burial Chamber," I was told with great sincerity. "It died on the same day as the canary, with the discovery of the golden shrines." My informant attributed these fantastic events to the powerful magic practiced by the high priests of ancient Egypt, especially Tutankhamen's successor, Ay, the grand vizier at the time, who held power briefly before General Harmhab usurped the throne.

Whatever the case, the consensus, then as now, was that the bird's death was a disquieting development. "There was almost universal concern," wrote Breasted more than a half-century ago, "that something terrible will happen."

The Aftermath

Carter and Carnarvon made their monumental discovery only four years after the end of World War I. The news of the day seemed serious, but was also somehow stale: Riots in India. Rebellion in Ireland. Tension Between Greece and Turkey. Power Struggle in the Kremlin. Moslem-Zionist Strife in Palestine. Civil War in China. Portuguese Cabinet in Crisis. The Franc Weak. Dictatorship in Spain. Unrest in Black Africa.

In America, a vice-president was sworn in as president. An Oklahoma governor was impeached because he "exceeded . . . his power." A newspaper publisher was convicted for advertising books on birth control, and "Darwinism" was outlawed in Florida. Former President Woodrow Wilson, with hardly anyone listening, warned the nation that America had "slipped into selfish isolation which is . . . manifestly cowardly and dishonorable."

Clearly, the world needed a breakfast table diversion. That search for escape earned the decade the sobriquet "Roaring Twenties," and the Tutankhamen discovery was part of the roar.

To the dismay of Carter and Carnarvon, the Valley of the Tombs was transformed into a circus ground as the world pitched a tent over Upper Egypt. One of the elements that made Tutankhamen so fascinating was what newspapermen call a "running story." It produced hotter and hotter copy for the remainder of the decade, through the Crash of 1929 and into the Great Depression which followed.

Among journalists there is the apocryphal story of the newsmen who descended on an English lord for an interview in connection with a political scandal. The butler retreated before the invasion and, rushing to the library, announced, "Milord, there is a group of newspapermen at the door, and also a gentleman of *The Times*." The lord of the manor replied, "Show in the gentleman from *The Times*."

The attitude is not altogether untypical of many members of the British peerage. There is more truth than meets the eye to this anecdote. Carnarvon, for instance, had been, from his youth, hostile to the press, although he maintained close and friendly relations with the *Newbury Weekly News*, his hometown newspaper.

News of the tomb's discovery traveled more than the length and breadth of the Nile. Wild rumors soon followed: three airplanes were said to have landed clandestinely in the Valley, loaded up with treasure, and taken off for a secret destination. Another rumor held that several mummies were found in the tomb, each covered with gold. Some said there were three mummies; others, eight.

With a view to "overtaking these rumors," as Carter termed it, he and Carnarvon decided to have a formal opening of the tomb on November 29, 1922. They invited a number of senior British and Egyptian officials and, from the press, the Cairo correspondent of the London *Times*, Arthur Merton.

In young Breasted's memoirs there is evidence that whereas Carnarvon favored admitting only the gentleman of *The Times* to the tomb, Carter leaned towards general invitation to Cairo's press, including both Egyptian and foreign correspondents. Whatever the case, the first story about the discovery, written from within the tomb, was a London *Times* exclusive. Merton, characterizing the find as "the most sensational discovery of the century," said, "The remarkable discovery announced today is the reward of patience, perseverance and perspicacity."

Reuters, the principal British news agency, and also the Egyptian and the world press, caught with their headlines down, recouped their loss the following day. In a Cairo dispatch, Reuters described the discovery as "astounding" and quoted Egyptologists terming the tomb's contents "beyond the dreams of avarice." The treasure found in the antechamber alone, the news agency reported, was worth "millions of pounds sterling." The American Associated Press described the find as "the most sensational in Egyptology" and reported "important papyri were also found" (as it later developed, to the dismay of Egyptologists, not a scrap of papyrus was ever found).

With these dispatches in print, the journalistic dam burst; and shortly thereafter, in the manner of the protagonists in Evelyn Waugh's brilliant *Scoop*, to mix a metaphor, the world's press descended on the Valley like owls hunting nocturnal rodents and their furry breed.

Placid, slumbering Luxor was thrown into bedlam. There were only two hotels worthy of the name: the huge Winter Palace and the Luxor—a five-minute walk from the Palace, set farther back from the banks of the Nile, but directly overlooking the town's ancient ruins. Neither hostelry was in a position to handle the influx, and they soon took to putting up army cots in their respective gardens to accommodate the journalistic horde. Fortunately, given the rainless climate, the scheme proved workable.

The Eastern Telegraph Company's Luxor office, designed to handle a modest amount of tourist traffic, was overwhelmed, and the government's Postal, Telephone and Telegraph Department was compelled to rush extra equipment to the scene. The PTT also opened a "press room" in a shopping arcade and wound up installing new telegraph lines to Cairo, some 500 miles to the north.

To reach the Valley, correspondents had to ferry across the Nile, and enterprising newsmen hired by the month the few feluccas available—riverboats with lateen sails, which had been working the Nile even before Tutankhamen's day. As news of the shoreside boom at Luxor spread up and down the river, a veritable flotilla of feluccas converged on the scene. To some, it looked like a new Battle of the Nile was underway.

Once across the river, on the west bank, the intrepid correspondents found that the principal mode of travel to the Valley was by donkey, a journey of six miles, which took a half-hour or more. At the site of the dig, chaos reigned. The London *Daily Telegraph* described the setting as reminiscent of Derby Day. "When the day's work was completed [at the tomb], involving the careful removal of treasure from the Antechamber," the paper reported, "correspondents began a spirited dash across the desert to the banks of the Nile upon donkeys, horses, camels and chariot-like sandcarts in a race to be the first to reach the telegraph office."

By the time the vanguard of the world's press descended on Luxor in mid-December, Carnarvon had left for England to report the discovery directly to the king. During an audience with George V at Buckingham Palace on December 22, a spokesman solemnly disclosed later, the king "listened with great interest to a description of the important discoveries made recently by him and Mr. Howard Carter as the culmination of the excavations which they have carried on for nearly sixteen years." Carnarvon, the spokesman said, assured the king that the mummy of the pharaoh would be found when each of the gilded shrines was dismantled, something yet to be done.

Carter, the commoner, was never invited to Buckingham Palace. Nor did he even make the New Year's Honours List, although such obscure personages made it in January 1923 as the head of the customs department in New Zealand.

For that matter, King Fuad of Egypt decorated neither Carnarvon nor Carter for their work, although, in a formal statement, he lavishly praised them. "The names of Lord Carnarvon and of Mr. Carter and of their zealous collaborators whom I am delighted to congratulate on their brilliant success," he said, "will remain ever linked with the archaeological splendor of our ancient country, and Egypt will always retain for them feelings of deepest gratitude."

Significantly, perhaps, on the very day that George V granted Carnarvon an audience, Carter flung open the tomb and invited all newsmen, including the "native" Egyptian press, to inspect the hypogeum firsthand. In reporting on Carter's bold action, *The Times*, in a surprisingly crude manner, reminded its readers twice within a three-paragraph story that *The Times* had scooped the world.

If Carnarvon was miffed by Carter's action, he did not say so publicly. He was perhaps too busy being lionized in London. On January 5, for example, he lectured before the Egyptian Exploration Society, whose president was General Sir John Maxwell, the former commander of British forces in Egypt. The crowd in attendance was so large that the meeting had to be shifted to Central Hall, Westminster. This was not surprising; at every London stop, Carnarvon, besieged by reporters, raised the thermostat of public interest in the discovery. "What lies in the third, yet unopened shrine?" he was quoted as asking. "Is it the mummy of the king?" In a burst of enthusiasm, the London *Daily Express* responded, "What subject matter for the conversation of a dinner party in Twentieth Century London!"

The London *Exchange Telegraph* reported that the treasure, not counting what might be found inside the sarcophagus, was already valued by art experts at £3,000,000 ($15,000,000). And a front-page story in *The New York Times* of February 18, 1923, datelined Luxor, began: "The gem-studded cavern of Ali Baba seems to have been a trinket shop in comparison, and Aladdin's lamp never realized such treasures as the flashlights from the torches illuminated to the lucky few who entered [Tutankhamen's] mortuary chambers yesterday."

Not only was there interest in the treasure for the sake of treasure, but also excitement in religious and art circles. "As Tutankhamen lived in the period of the Exodus," one British daily declared, "perhaps there is buried with him an account of Israel and Biblical times from the Egyptian standpoint. Possibly also a full account of Akhenaten . . . [who] preached Christian doctrines."

Pierre Lacau, the French director of the department of antiquities, told the Cairo press that the discovery was the "greatest find in the history of archaeology, and probably in the history of art." And the senior Breasted openly declared, "The craftsmen of Greece were mere hacks compared to the masters who designed and adorned [Tutankhamen's] throne."

Neither Carter nor Carnarvon anticipated the world's reaction to their discovery. Clearly, they inherited a monumental public relations problem. But the problem was hardly insurmountable.

As a former foreign correspondent myself, the obvious solution was to form a rotating pool at Luxor, picking the name of a correspondent out of the hat each day and having him or her cover the tomb and share the resultant report with the rest of the press. This is SOP in comparable situations. But Carnarvon, perhaps in part disposed to consider newsmen scavengers (except for the gentleman of *The Times*) and also in part to earn a justifiable return on his enormous investment, entered into an exclusive and controversial agreement with *The Times*. He gave the London daily a news monopoly in return for £5,000 ($25,000) in cash and three-fourths of the profits from the syndication of *The Times'* reports abroad. As Carnarvon's agent, *The Times* promptly sold its coverage around the world.

Carter was horrified by his colleague's decision. "Over Carter's emphatic protests," Charles Breasted wrote later, "he [Carnarvon] presently entered into an agreement with his friend, John Jacob Astor, chairman of the London Times Company, Ltd., where *The Times* was given a world copyright on all news, pictures, etc."

Conflicting versions of how Carnarvon came to give Astor exclusive rights to the story were recounted by Sir Alan Gardiner, Carnarvon's intimate friend, and by *The Times* itself.

Sir Alan told Cottrell, who reprinted this version in 1961 in *The Lost Pharaohs*, that over lunch, during his London visit, Carnarvon expressed concern about "press publicity."*

"I can't get a night's rest," he complained. "As soon as I am in bed, there are telephone calls. If I walk out of my house, I am stopped by some pressman." Gardiner sympathized, but observed that, given the enormous public interest in the discovery, such incidents were bound to occur. During lunch, Geoffrey Dawson, *The Times'* editor, stopped by and told Carnarvon *The Times* wanted exclusive rights to the story. "Carnarvon said he'd never been in such a position before," Gardiner recounted. "Dawson pointed out that by making *The Times* his sole agent for the distribution of news and pictures, he would be saved an enormous amount of trouble. Carnarvon said he'd think about it."

Later, Carnarvon and Gardiner conferred with the secretary of the Royal Geographical Society, who told them that the Society had made a similar arrangement in connection with the Mt. Everest Expedition and that it worked out very well. "As a result of this," Sir Alan continued, "Carnarvon decided to give *The Times* the agency."

The Times itself, however, in a formal announcement designed to still the clamor over the deal, provided a different version. "*The Times* was approached by . . . Lord Carnarvon . . . with the request that it should relieve them of the task [of news distribution]," the paper said.

"There was never any question," it continued, "of securing a special advantage for *The Times*, which accepted the work on the understanding that the news and photographs thus obtained should be available at a price estimated to cover the cost to any newspaper in the world which desired to print them . . . No profit has accrued to *The Times* from the transaction, which cannot by any stretch of the imagination be held to constitute a monopoly."

---

*The phraseology is revealing. Clearly, Carnarvon confused spontaneous news with manufactured news, that is, publicity.

Be that as it might, when the nature of the transaction was made public, the world's press did not feel it necessary to stretch its imagination. The arrangement was universally condemned.

"The tomb is not his [Carnarvon's] property," the London *Daily Express* howled. "He has not dug up the bones of his ancestors in the Welsh mountains. . . . By making an exclusive secret of the contents of the inner tomb he has ranged against him the majority of the world's most influential newspapers."

Six days later, on February 16, 1923, *The Times* went to Carnarvon's rescue. Critics, the paper said, had charged him "with creating a monopoly of news from Luxor, and even of commercialism [although] he supplied the news through *The Times* solely because he thought it would be the best way, in fact the only practical way, of supplying it fully and independently to all newspapers."

As the protest mounted, *The Times*, in a second defense, denounced "misleading statements" about the transaction and said "it seems desirable to place on record the fact that the financial proceeds of *The Times*' arrangement . . . are wholly devoted to the cost of the work at the tomb. The sole beneficiary is the cause of scientific research."

The Times also wheeled in a battery of "experts" to support its stand—among them, Jean Capart, secretary of the Royal Cinquantenaire Museum of Brussels and one of Belgium's outstanding Egyptologists.

"No obstacle whatever must be allowed to intervene between examination of the pharaonic treasures and the immediate distribution of the news to all papers," Capart wrote in a special article. "If Lord Carnarvon does not give way, if he does not cancel the agreement with the London *Times*, the Egyptian government must intervene and the concession must be declared forfeit!" he continued. "One would almost think one were dreaming when one reads such things. On the contrary, archaeologists feel Carnarvon has given the public daily information through the intermediary of the greatest newspaper in the world."

Events at the tomb sometimes belied these words. For example, when an American newsreel company arrived in the Valley, a gilded chariot was in the course of being removed from the tomb. The cameramen had no sooner set up their equipment than a sheet was thrown over the chariot. The Americans complained bitterly that they were standing in a public roadway, but Carnarvon and Carter were unmoved. A European camera company proved more resourceful. After arriving in the Valley, its team perched their camera equipment atop a nearby cliff and, according to a local report, "with the aid of a telescope [undoubtedly a telescopic lens] took some pictures." Even so, the report said, "A warm discussion ensued."

Finally, Ernest Shipman, the film maker, secured the motion picture rights for the United States and Canada of the official film portraying the exploration of the tomb. But his rights were limited to the footage shot by an English syndicate under contract to Carnarvon.

As a result of this infighting, the public soon found itself engrossed more in the mudslinging among the lords of the press than in the fate of Tutankhamen.

General Sir John Maxwell, the ex-field commander and friend of Carnarvon, soon joined the press fray. Writing from his suite in the Winter Palace Hotel at Luxor, he took umbrage with reports that Carnarvon was "prostituting science to commercialism."

"The arrangement appears to give entire satisfaction to everyone except the proprietors and representatives at Luxor of certain journals," wrote Sir John. His article, which appeared in *The Times* on March 21, 1923, contained a significant paragraph—on Carnarvon's intentions about the ultimate disposition of the mummy. "I happen to know that Lord Carnarvon himself does not wish its removal [from the tomb]."

The great press debate acted, of course, as a stimulant to the tourist trade. The Beautiful People flocked to Luxor like birds heading south for the winter. A typical news dispatch on February 21, 1923, reported from Luxor: "The Tutankhamen craze continues here and new arrivals who were thinking of nothing else drove and rode in column formation to the tomb this morning." From another dispatch: "Boatloads of rich Americans and Englishmen arrive every week, and numbers of curious Japanese." The descending herd of tourists prompted the *Philadelphia Ledger* to remark, "Tutankhamen is doing more for the prosperity of Modern Egypt than he appears to have done in his own time."

When the S.S. *Adriatic* sailed from New York in early 1923 for Europe, almost half of its 600 passengers were bound for Luxor (three thousand packages of fruit, candies, and flowers were sent to the ship on the night of its departure). Among the luminaries aboard were Senator Oscar W. Underwood (D., Ala.), Congressmen Allen T. Treadway (R., Mass.) and Wallace H. White (R., Me.), and their wives. "I hope Lord Carnarvon will permit me to visit the tomb he has discovered," the senator explained, "as it would be a great disappointment to find it sealed up after traveling 7,600 miles to be there." Compared to the very important persons arriving at Luxor, such as the rajah of Poona, senators were treated as little more than carpetbaggers.

When Elisabeth, queen of the Belgians, accompanied by Prince Leopold and Lord Allenby, the Allies' wartime commander in the Near East and then British high commander for Egypt, visited the Valley, the whole distance was guarded at fifty-yard intervals with ghaffirs in blue uniforms and black tarbooshes with red, green, and magenta stripes. The road was patrolled by Egyptian cavalry and members of the Sudanese camel corps. It must have been, in a word, a spectacle.

Indeed, so many "personalities" made the trek to Luxor that newspapers began to report their arrival in the manner of ships on the shipping page: "Arrivals this week include Sir Lloyd George [former prime minister] on his way home from India . . . Mme. Cecile Sorel, who has just concluded a successful season at the Royal Opera House, Cairo; and Baron and Baroness de Mayer." Sometimes Tutankhamen got his revenge, as in the case of the Belgian queen who no sooner arrived than she came down with a case of "indisposition," a code word for what was cockily known in the colonial era as Malta dog or Delhi belly.

By the end of the year, there was "an extraordinary invasion of visitors from the north, due, to a great extent, to the Christmas festivities"—Luxor was drawing trade from Bethlehem. An agent for the International Sleeping Car Company announced in New York that Carnarvon had guaranteed the company that American tourists would be permitted to view the tomb. (Carnarvon had promised no such thing.) But the Egyptian State Railway did open a new train service between Cairo and Luxor, officially christened the "Tutankhamen Special."

Few tourists, of course, ever negotiated the mysterious sixteen steps into the tomb. Carter made sure of that. At best, the curious clustered around the entrance to the tomb and, amid gasps of astonishment, clicked their inevitable cameras as objects were carefully removed from the tomb by the fellahin workers.

There was always a festive air around the pit entrance. Women in filmy, light summer dresses ensconced themselves on the walls of the tomb—holding green, red, blue, and yellow parasols to shade them from the burning sun overhead. European men wore pith helmets; the Japanese, despite the oppressive heat, were in black suits. A sprinkling of Egyptians in flowing white gallabiyas completed the picturesque scene.

By January 1923, on the eve of Carnarvon's return from England—again, in the company of his devoted daughter, Lady Evelyn, and not his wife—a besieged Carter showed signs of strain. Terribly irritable, he frequently snapped at colleagues and workers and simply refused to talk to the press. The constant flood of "celebrities" to the tomb, the glare of the press, and the circus atmosphere had interrupted his routine. For thirty years, largely in solitude, he had labored in Upper Egypt, immersed in what he was doing. Now he suddenly found himself at stage center, and quite unable to work. Worse, he was inwardly infuriated by the realization that most of the visitors to the Valley were not even mildly interested in archaeology. They had come to Luxor, he wrote later, "because it is the thing to do."

"Can you imagine anything more maddening, when you are completely absorbed in a difficult problem, than to give up half an hour of your precious time to a visitor who has pulled every conceivable kind of wire to gain admittance, and then to hear him say quite audibly as he goes away, 'Well there wasn't much to see, after all'?" Carter wrote a year later. "That actually happened last winter—and more than once."*

Carter was especially annoyed by newsmen who, barred from the tomb by the Carnarvon agreement, seized on every scrap of news and blew it out of proportion. On one occasion, as a case in point, the perennially cloudless, blue sky of Upper Egypt turned black. Fear spread in the Valley that a rarity of rarities—a rainstorm—might erupt and send tons of cascading water crashing through the chasm and into the open tomb. European and American newspapers, not privy to the London *Times'* reports, played up the angle. A New York headline read: "PANIC SPREADING/GRAVE POSSIBILITY/ PRICELESS ANTIQUITIES/MAY BE HOPELESSLY DESTROYED BY TOMORROW."

While this commotion was in progress, a correspondent from the London *Daily Mail* reported that an attempt to photograph the treasure in the tomb *in situ* had failed completely. There was fear, he wrote, that the flashlight powder would ignite the intensely dry, inflammable wooden objects in the sepulcher, turning the tomb into a bonfire. This, of course, was nonsense.

"From a tourist viewpoint," began a *New York Times* report on January 8, 1923, "it was a dull weekend outside of Tutankhamen's tomb, as nothing has been removed since the king's throne was taken [from] the tomb . . . on Friday." But, to justify his paper's expense in maintaining him as Luxor correspondent, the reporter found an enlivening angle:

"For the expert staff," he wrote, "it was exciting enough with the discovery that a huge rat had taken up his abode in the tomb . . . with the intention of making banquet of the most luscious and priceless objects stored there. A general rat hunt was organized without result, and now a trap has been set and all are hoping for the best. It would be most bitter tragedy if some of the objects after being most expensively and most carefully treated were knawed [*sic*] to pieces by rats."

When Carnarvon returned that January from his audience with the king at Buckingham Palace, he brought with him a new motorcar, a Ford. It was ferried across the

---

*And still does. In 1974 William E. Simon, then the newly appointed U.S. secretary of the treasury, led a stooping train of newsmen, secret service agents, aides, and members of his family through a low and narrow passage in the Great Cheops Pyramid at Giza—on the outskirts of Cairo—and up into the interior chamber to look inside an empty pharaoh's sarcophagus. When told there were more chambers higher up, Simon, sweating profusely, remarked, "When you've seen one sarcophagus, you've seen 'em all."

Nile, one of the first automobiles to appear along the west bank of the Theban necropolis. The London *Times* treated it as a major event, observing that the vehicle "created no little excitement among the people." Barred from publishing its own photographs, the *Illustrated London News* had a field day with imaginative woodcuts of Carter and Carnarvon at work within the tomb. And the rest of the press kept up its assault on Carnarvon.

"So far," said the *Daily Express* at one point, "Lord Carnarvon's treatment of King Tutankhamen [is] suggestive of a gentleman who has hit upon a patent corn cure."

Bedlam

A postwar upsurge of Egyptian nationalism coincided with the discovery of Tutankhamen's tomb. Its highlight was the return to Egypt in 1923 of Zaghlul Pasha, the nationalist leader who had been imprisoned by the British at Gibraltar and elsewhere. Only the year before, after riots in Cairo and the assassination of several British officials, London had sought to placate Egyptian ire by lifting the British protectorate and formally declaring the country independent—that is, except in matters of defense and foreign affairs. The Egyptians denounced this "independence" as a sham.

The country was divided politically into two camps: the popular Wafdist (nationalist) party of the returned Zaghlul was supported by a coalition of intellectuals, students, and the mass of politically credulous and unsophisticated fellahin; King Fuad was backed by the wealthy pashas and their middle-class effendi allies. In the intricate maneuvering for political advantage, each side accused the other of permitting itself to be used as a pawn by the British.

Indeed, on the very day that the London *Times* scored its November 30, 1922, beat on the tomb discovery, filling two columns of pages 13 and 14 with that news, page 12 of the same day reported the collapse of the Egyptian cabinet over "differences with King Fuad [as a result of] continued intrigues."

Carnarvon, as noted earlier, was largely apolitical. (Had he inherited a modicum of the brilliant political skill of his father, the fourth earl of Carnarvon, he probably would have thought twice about selling exclusive rights to a British newspaper, however prestigious a journal.) In any event, as a result of the arrangement, the Egyptian press was in the awkward position of relying on an English newspaper for stories about a marvelous discovery in its own country. The Egyptian government was as outraged as the Egyptian press. By the time Carnarvon realized his error, he felt compelled, as an English gentleman, to stand "loyally by his bargain," as one observer said. (It was this same strength of character that induced him to underwrite Carter's last expedition in the Valley of the Kings.)

Whatever the case, all hell broke loose.

"By handing over what may be called journalistic rights in the Valley of the Tombs to the sole control of *The Times*, they [Carnarvon and Carter] treated the find in advance as their own private property," the *Daily Express* charged on January 11, 1923. "The Egyptian government, with its newly awakened sense of nationality, has forwarded the contrary view that King Tutankhamen and his belongings are the national treasure of Egypt."

To compound matters, the Egyptians felt slighted in other ways. Most of the visitors invited inside the tomb were European VIPs. A random day, picked from the visitor's log, showed that on February 13, 1923, a Tuesday, when the fellahin laborers took their traditional day of rest, thirty-four "celebrities" and "personalities" visited the tomb. Six were Egyptians.

In defense of Carnarvon and Carter, it should be observed that at first the Egyptians did not realize the significance of the discovery. A check of the Egyptian press for the first week after the discovery reveals that the story of the find was downplayed in favor of politics. But as the world beat a path to Luxor, the Egyptians, especially those studying abroad, recognized its import and felt themselves reduced to the role of spear carriers.

"Egyptians in London who have read Lord Carnarvon's [latest] article," reported S. S. Ahram, London correspondent of the *Egyptian Gazette*, "feel indignant because Egyptians are thanked only for guarding and serving." Refreshingly, however, Ahram then laced into his compatriots: "But what else can they expect when there are hardly any Egyptians studying Egyptology?"

As they came to realize that there was nothing bogus about the treasure, Egyptian nationalists publicly advocated that the treasure be sold and the proceeds used to pay off the national debt. Indeed, in his formal statement on the discovery, in which he congratulated Carnarvon and Carter, King Fuad, in a poetic sense, had used the word *profit*. "As an Egyptian I also could not fail to reflect on the weighty inheritance which imposes on every Egyptian the duty to show himself worthy of such a great past. I am certain that this discovery is one of the greatest and most fruitful ever made, and Egypt's history will derive from it the greatest profit."

For many Egyptians, notably those connected with the tourist trade (since Caesar's day one of Egypt's most important industries), the discovery spelled profit for travel agencies, guides, hotels, antique dealers, and others. Thus, in the face of rising nationalist sentiment, the Cairo government announced that all tourist applications would be promptly serviced and that "excellent arrangements [had been] made by the authorities to insure the comforts of visitors."

Meanwhile, a struggle was incubating over the ownership and disposition of the treasure. Even the Copts—strictly speaking, the only native Egyptian race, true descendants of the ancient Egyptians—put in a claim to the treasure. In Cairo, a Coptic Christian, Athanasius Bokter, proclaimed, admittedly to almost everyone's amusement, that he was a direct descendant of Tutankhamen and that the contents of the tomb rightfully belonged to him.

Earlier, overcome by euphoria, Carnarvon unintentionally touched off the battle for possession of the treasure. During his London sojourn, he told newsmen that since the tomb had been rifled in antiquity, half the treasure was his by the terms of his contract with the Egyptian government. He also indicated that he would donate part of his share to the British Museum and the Metropolitan Museum of Art.

These remarks enraged Egyptians. *El Ahram*, an influential Egyptian journal (not to be confused with the name of the *Egyptian Gazette*'s London correspondent), expressed "doubt whether the government will take the same view." And the Ministry of Public Works, of which the department of antiquities was a branch, put out an official statement that claimed the treasure on behalf of the Egyptian government: "There is no question about this. . . . Egyptian public opinion should not be disturbed."

Although regulations provided that the discoverer should receive half of the objects found in a rifled tomb, except for articles that the Egyptian government reserved for itself, the Ministry claimed that Carnarvon's license expressly provided that he should have no right to any objects that he might find. In a subtle ploy, the government appealed to Carnarvon's sense of fair play. Carnarvon, the statement alleged, had "accepted with pleasure a condition in the license that he was entitled to nothing [thereby] giving a clear proof that he did not entertain any material ambitions in the matter and that he was devoted to the service of science and art."

This was news to Carnarvon and also to Carter.

On December 23, Carter announced that he and his assistants, including the outside archaeological help he had recruited, conclusively established that the tomb had not been entered into since about twenty-five years after Tutankhamen's death, circa 1377 B.C. "When the inner [sealed] chamber is opened," Carter said with relish, "we shall find the king [unmolested] in all the magnificence of his state religion."

Cairo promptly interpreted Carter's statement to mean that the tomb itself was undisturbed and that the contents were therefore outside of Carnarvon's contract and that he was not entitled to a single object. Like the *Daily Express* before it, on the other side of the Atlantic, *The New York Times* also concluded that Carnarvon was "partly to blame" for this state of affairs because he advanced the claim that because the tomb had been rifled in antiquity, half the contents belonged to him.

Then, in the realization that part of the treasure was slipping from their grasp, museum directors rallied to Carnarvon's side. The British Museum's Sir Frederic Kenyon declared that Carnarvon's share of the objects was his "own private property" and that he could keep the objects, sell them, or give them away, as he saw fit.

"If a country owning ancient sites adopts a policy of rigid exclusion or refuses to permit ancient objects to leave the country," Sir Frederic said with contempt, "it means that the hunting of old sites will be done largely by natives and art dealers." Under such circumstances, he said, "museums, private archaeologists and wealthy men would be deprived of fair incentive."

His views were strongly endorsed by Herbert Winlock of the Metropolitan. If Egyptian finds remained in Egypt, Winlock said, it would end excavations because all foreign digs were supplied by public subscription and philanthropy and their only reward was an "exhibition of at least a portion of the objects." Arrogantly, perhaps, but wholly in keeping with the colonial mentality of the period, Winlock pointed to the impact of archaeology on the Egyptian economy and labor market through the purchase of supplies, the hiring of donkey and camel drivers, and so on. "All this money goes to the miserable Nile villages which for a decade have been growing rich through trade with the excavating parties," he said.

As the abyss widened between Carnarvon and Cairo on the ultimate disposition of the treasure, there was a renewal of Anglo-French friction along the Nile. It was reactivated by the speech of Professor Percy E. Newberry at Burlington House, London, in the rooms of the Royal Society, one of the most prestigious bodies in the country, founded in 1660. Members of the group appended the letters F.R.S. (Fellow of the Royal Society) to their names. In the course of presiding over a meeting of the Egyptian Exploration Society in conjunction with the Society, Newberry said: "We may congratulate ourselves that Lord Carnarvon and Mr. Carter persisted and that it has fallen to the lot of two Englishmen to make what may be the last, but is certainly the most important, find ever made in this necropolis." The French and Egyptians smarted over the remark.

Rumors then spread in both Cairo and London that Pierre Lacau, a French Jesuit and the director of the antiquities service, was the *éminence grise* behind the Egyptian government's claim to the treasure of Tutankhamen. The English paper, *Westminster Gazette*, for example, claimed that "a certain French society" was trying to get a license to obtain some of the treasure, a charge that was patently absurd. Charles Breasted, returning to the United States in the spring of 1923, told the New York shipboard press that anti-British feeling was inflamed by "wealthy young Egyptian agitators . . . abetted by the French."

"Regardless of Lord Carnarvon's agreement, under which he was to have one half of what he found," Breasted said, "there is little possibility that Egypt will give up any material part of the spoils from the tomb of Tutankhamen, and the splendid things there will either fall into the hands of natives and be sold off piecemeal to dealers, or they will be placed in an Egyptian museum."

Then, in the light of his intimate contacts within the archaeological establishment, he made a revealing statement: archaeologists hoped that the treasures would be placed in an Egyptian museum. "This is generally felt to be the place where they belong," said the son of the dean of American Egyptologists, a close friend of Carter.

Lest he be misunderstood, given the political climate of the era—imagine handing the treasure over to a "native" museum!—young Breasted explained: "There is nothing in common, however, between this feeling on the part of scientists and that of the native Egyptians, who are inspired by spite against England and to some extent by the thought that they may sell off these things and put the money into the treasury."

Americans at first found Anglo-French rivalry in Egypt inexplicable. C. W. Barron, founder of *Barron's*, the financial weekly, and the owner of *The Wall Street Journal*, writing from Luxor, confirmed the claim that Lacau was advising the Egyptians to cancel Carnarvon's concession in the Valley and confessed his perplexity at French behavior. "Why this continued antagonism between the two great European allies of the late war?" he asked. "No American should presume to intermediate or decide on issues between the French and the English, but America must . . . understand the growing bitterness between the French and English."

Meanwhile, just as Carter had disagreed with Carnarvon over his arrangement with *The Times*, Carter now took issue with his benefactor over the disposition of the treasure. In view of the magnitude of the discovery, Carter felt that the tomb's contents should remain intact and should not be scattered indifferently around the world in public museums and private collections. The treasure should never leave Egypt, he argued; it should be housed in a special wing of the Cairo Museum. The sporting thing to do was for Carnarvon to renounce all rights and claim to the tomb with which ever thereafter the name of the House of Herbert would be associated. Compensation for Carnarvon's investment could be worked out with the Egyptian authorities, Carter contended. The Egyptians, Carter reasoned, would behave responsibly; it was in their interest to promote tourism, goodwill, and future digs.

Both men were so distraught at this point that they sometimes acted irrationally. By spring their friends thought each was on the threshold of a nervous breakdown. The rapture of discovery, the joy of accomplishment, had given way to heartache—and even agony. It seemed that Carter and Carnarvon could never again confide in each other without winding up in a row. The senior Breasted was so disturbed by this "painful situation," as he called it, that in a private letter dated March 12, 1923, he expressed concern that "a complete break seems inevitable" between the two longtime friends and associates.

The break was not long in coming.

A few days later, in the course of a visit at Carter's house, situated only a few hundred yards from Carnarvon's, they got into a shouting match. In a burst of fury, Carter ordered Carnarvon from his home. Carnarvon stormed out and never again went back.

The two houses were the only signs of life between the Valley of the Tombs and the Nile village of El Gournah—six miles of desolate, inhospitable wasteland. In the days that followed, the only two neighbors in that no-man's land ignored one another completely.

Their friends and associates—the James Henry Breasteds, the Sir Alan Gardiners—tried in vain to repair the breach. The disaster inherent in the magnitude of the discovery was complete.

Still smarting over mistreatment at their hands, real or perceived, the press now had a field day.

"Where the carcase [*sic*] is there are the eagles gathered together, even at the tomb of Pharaoh Tutankhamen," the London *Star* said. "And the eagles, after the manner of eagles where carcases are concerned, are merrily engaged in pecking out each other's eyes. 'My carcase,' says the London *Times*. 'Mine,' says the Egyptian government. 'Ours, surely,' say other eagles in a chorus, and feathers begin to fly."

"There was something inherently indecent in the original plan of rifling a tomb and unwinding the mummy of a dead pharaoh in the interest ostensibly of science," the *Star* went on, "but in reality of the first, second and third rights of publications, the book rights, photographic rights, cinema rights and all the rest of the elaborate commercial bargaining which precedes an attempt to reach the North Pole or in the marketing of an ex-Minister's literary indiscretions. But it becomes amusing when specialists in archaeology fall to quarreling among themselves over the spoils like pariah dogs over a scratched up corpse."

Then, suddenly, a new and wholly unexpected development restored the focus of attention to the tomb itself and provided the Tutankhamen story with a dimension that guaranteed its place in the annals of the Roaring Twenties.

To the credulous students of the occult sciences of the ancient Egyptians, the next development came as no surprise.

Carnarvon's Fate

As the various storms swirled overhead that March, like the khamsin, or sandstorms, that periodically sweep the Nile, Carnarvon was bitten on the right cheek by an insect. The bite turned septic.

Carnarvon himself believed he was bitten by a mosquito. Others thought he had been bitten by an insect and then, while shaving, he had accidentally removed the scab. Another belief was that he nicked himself one morning while shaving and that a mosquito or fly had alighted on the wound. Professor Newberry, for one, dismissed the mosquito thesis. In the Valley itself there were no mosquitoes, he pointed out, so that the poisonous bite must have occurred at Luxor, on the other side of the Nile.

The existence of deadly insects in Egypt was recognized as early as in the Book of the Dead, which was written in Tutankhamen's age. Isis, for example, recounted the death of her infant child, Horus: "he bedewed the ground with water from his eye and the foam from his lips, his body stiff, his heart still, and no muscle in his limbs able to move." Thoth, using magical powers, restored the child to life.

Sir Wallis Budge, in a footnote to his translation of this passage, recalled a strikingly similar episode while in Egypt. "This is an exact description of the state of an animal which has been stung by the small black scorpion in Egypt," he said. Sir Wallis wrote that he witnessed such a case in 1897 and that the bitten animal, a dog, was revived by immersion in hot water.

After penetrating the Antechamber in November 1922, Carter and Carnarvon had pursued a meticulously scientific program before going into the sealed Burial Chamber. The morning after they breached the secret door, five sterile swabs, obtained from Dr. A. C. Thaysen of the Bacteriological Laboratory of the Royal Navy, were carried into the farthest corners of the Burial Chamber, to a point where no human had trod for more than 3,000 years. The swabs were wiped on the walls and floor and then sent to the Royal Navy's Wareham laboratory for examination by H. J. Bunker, a senior chemist. Four swabs were sterile. The fifth, reported A. Lucas, a Fellow of the Institute of Chemistry, contained several organisms that had probably been wafted into the tomb with the circulation of outside air. Lucas concluded, "No life of any kind, even of the lowest form, existed in the tomb when it was first found." The fungus growths on several walls were dry and "apparently dead."

For the scientific record, specimens of dead insects in the burial chamber were sent to entomologists at the Egyptian Ministry of Agriculture and to members of the Royal Egyptian Agricultural Society. The insects proved to be small beetles of the kind that feed on dead organic matter. All were of a common variety still prevalent in Egypt; despite more than thirty centuries, there had been no evolutionary change or modification in their size or structure. The remains of small spiders and their webs were also found.

Whatever the case, Carnarvon's health had so worsened by late March that his daughter, Lady Evelyn, rushed him by train to the Cairo Hospital. Five physicians were consulted, and Lady Evelyn cabled her mother, the Countess Almina, at Highclere and also her brother, Lord Porchester, who was then in India on military duty, to come to Cairo. The first announcement of Carnarvon's illness had been officially made on March 19: it was an infection attributed to "an insect bite." The news hit the front pages worldwide.

Dramatically, Lady Carnarvon flew to her husband's side. This was news in itself, for flying was still a novelty. But after crossing the English Channel, Lady Carnarvon's plane put down at Paris's Le Bourget airfield—the scene of a wild celebration four years later when Lindbergh crossed the Atlantic. Apparently Almina had been taken ill on the flight, and she was forced to complete the dash to Cairo by boat from Marseilles.

With his family at his side, Carnarvon rallied magnificently, displaying the remarkable desire for life that had carried him through his automobile accident of almost twenty years earlier. His physicians were astonished by his progress and, with confidence, announced to the press that he would recover completely.

During this period, a remorseful Carter visited his stricken friend's bedside and made peace. Both men realized that their harsh exchange reflected not so much hostility and antagonism towards each other as the strains they had been put to by one of the world's great voyages of discovery.

But, suddenly, barely a week after Lady Carnarvon arrived at the Cairo Hospital, her husband suffered a relapse. Anxiety alternated with hope as his life ebbed. He remained conscious to the end, his wife, son, and daughter at his side. His last words were: "I am ready."

At 2:00 A.M., April 5, 1923, at the age of fifty-seven, less than twenty weeks after he first emerged from the mummy's resting-place, Carnarvon followed Tutankhamen into the netherworld of Amenti. Officially, his death was attributed to lobar pneumonia, complicated by pleurisy, both the result of blood poisoning from an insect bite.

"The excitement of his discovery and the lamentable worries it brought him," a London commentator said, "must have done much to sap the vitality which was needed so sorely this last week."

At the exact moment of death, something strange happened in Cairo. The city's electric lights flickered and went out. Briefly, the Egyptian capital was in total darkness; the only visible light was that overhead of the stars imperishable. "This curious occurrence was widely interpreted by those anxiously awaiting for news as an omen of evil," wrote H. V. Morton, a veteran foreign correspondent.

The incident caused a sensation in Cairo. Lord Allenby, the British high commissioner, ordered a British Army colonel, an engineer in charge of the Cairo Electricity Board's generating plants, to launch an official inquiry into the power failure. After a thorough investigation, he could not explain what had caused the outage.

Carnarvon's sudden passing stunned his family, friends, and associates. "I have learned with great regret of the death of your father," King George V cabled Lord Porchester, the new, sixth earl of Carnarvon, "especially after the splendid fight he made for his life." Reuters, in a dispatch from Newbury, the family seat, reported: "The news of the earl's death greatly shocked the tenantry of his estates in Derbyshire and Notts by whom he was revered as a genial and large-hearted landlord."

Deeply shaken by the loss of a companion of so many years, Carter swore, "This tomb has brought us bad luck." But the work of excavating the tomb, he announced, would go on.

The archaeological establishment was dazed. "In the history of archaeological research, no such tragic event has taken place as the death of Lord Carnarvon," said Professor Newberry, who had picked Howard Carter for the assignment in Egypt thirty years earlier. "The fatigue and heat which he experienced in the Valley of the Kings no doubt contributed to lower his vitality." And the aging Sir William Matthew Flinders Petrie described Carnarvon's death as a calamity. "He financed the whole of that expedition, and as far as one knows at present there is no one to carry it on," he said. Professor E. G. Elliot Smith, who undertook the first scientific study of royal mummies in the *salle des momies* of the Cairo Museum, said, "That his death should have followed so closely upon the dramatic culmination of his sixteen years' task in Egypt is indeed poignantly tragic. But that it should happen now, when the years of difficult work and delicate negotiation in connection with the discovery demand in a very special sense his personal presence, makes it nothing less than a calamity."

Ironically, Carnarvon died without knowing whether or not the shrines in the Burial Chamber contained the vaunted mummy of the king. For that matter, he died without ever gazing on the features of Tutankhamen, the pharaoh, who, in the end, exercised such a profound influence on Carnarvon and the House of Herbert.

Carnarvon's body was embalmed and made ready for shipment to England for interment at Beacon Hill, Highclere. In the midst of these preparations, Carter became ill. Appalled, the Countess Almina postponed her departure for England with the body of her late husband. Although Carter threw off his strange illness within a few days, this sudden development gave rise to a popular view that the tomb was cursed, that Tutankhamen and/or the high priests of ancient Egypt sought to punish those who violated the dead. What a Perry Mason would entitle "The Case of Carter's Yellow Canary" was now revived.

Rational men sought to dam the flood of speculation. Said Dr. Leonard Williams, an eminent London physician, "Mr. Carter has undoubtedly been working very hard and working, too, in underground passages which cannot be particularly healthy. On top of all this, the anxiety caused by Lord Carnarvon's long illness and its fatal termination must have tolled very heavily upon Mr. Carter. It is no wonder he should become ill. I think the same thing would probably have happened to any one of us."

When Carter recovered, the Countess Almina accompanied her husband's body to England. The voyage was made without incident, although several people who had booked passage on the same ship canceled their plans, fearing that some disaster might befall the steamer.

At Highclere, on April 30, 1923, in an unmarked grave on the estate that overlooked his beloved castle, the fifth earl of Carnarvon was buried. The body was buried there at his request rather than in the estate's stone chapel—built in 1855 "for the comfort of those that mourn." Carnarvon, a gravedigger himself, may have thought that not all men find eternal peace even after death, whether buried in a cemetery later dug up for the passage of a highway or in Westminster or in the Valley of the Tombs of the Kings. Or he might not have wanted to be buried within the family crypt because it contained the coffin of Charles Herbert, fourth earl of Pembroke and Montgomery, who died in Italy in 1635. According to legend, his bones were "rudely scattered by desecrators" before being shipped to England for burial. Apparently *contadini*, believing his heart was encased in gold, had torn his body apart in quest of treasure.

On April 7, two days after Carnarvon's death, the London *Times* published Carnarvon's last article on the Valley, which he had mailed at Luxor. "Almost at the moment of its arrival," a *Times* editor wrote, "came the first news of the illness which had so tragic an issue." The opening line of Carnarvon's piece was: "We have come to the end. . . ." He referred, of course, to the closing of the tomb for the season.

If, as the ancient Egyptians firmly believed, the heart of the dead must be weighed against a feather to determine whether it is light enough to journey into immortality, then Carnarvon, to his infinite credit, may have absolved himself in Osiris' eyes for desecrating, in the name of art and science, the tomb of Tutankhamen.

"I very much hope," he wrote in that final article, "I can say I almost feel sure [that the king's body] will be allowed to remain where it was placed so many, many centuries ago." Carnarvon's last hope from his own grave, as it were, was that Tutankhamen would be provided the opportunity to rest in peace through eternity.

With interment at Highclere, memorial services were held in London and Cairo. At St. Margaret's, Westminster, the service was attended by the nobility and the military, by archaeologists, and by the curious. In Cairo, the service was attended by Egyptian officials, including cabinet ministers; Pierre Lacau and members of the department of antiquities; British officials; and the diplomatic corps. Howard Carter was not present.

At Biban-el-Moluk, where the temperature had climbed to over 100°F, Carter was busily supervising the last-minute details of closing the tomb until the start of the next season.

Among the first questions raised after Carnarvon's death was the future of his concession in the Valley. This was speedily resolved. The permit was inherited by the dowager countess, who at forty-seven was a radiant, if mature, beauty. Before the year was out, Almina married Lt. Colonel Ian Orislow Dennistoun, a divorcé four years her junior, who had been in the Grenadier Guards. The only witnesses present at the marriage ceremony were her daughter, Lady Evelyn—who had married Brograve Campbell Beauchamp six months after her father's death—the family solicitor, and a friend.

Other questions were raised: What about the Carnarvon collection at Highclere? What about Carnarvon's share of the Tutankhamen treasure?

In England, the principal focus was on the disposal of the collection, the most complete collection of Egyptian antiquities in private hands. "Unless there is a will leaving them to the nation," a British journal suggested, "it is possible they will be sold abroad." This was an era in which *nouveau riche* Americans busied themselves around Europe outbidding one another for European castles and art collections.

But there was a last testament, and England sighed with relief. Carnarvon had left his collection to Almina, but he had added a codicil shortly after the Tutankhamen discovery. "I suggest," the postscript said, "that the nation—that is, the British Museum—be given the first refusal at £20,000 [$100,000], far below its value, such sum, however, to be free of all duties [inheritance taxes]." If the British Museum rejected the gracious offer, he left instructions that the collection should be offered to the Metropolitan and that Carter set a price and negotiate the sale.

Details remain sketchy to this day, but Carnarvon's instructions were apparently disregarded. Four years after his death, a shocked London learned that the collection had been sold to Edward S. Harkness, the American railroad tycoon and chairman of the board of trustees of the Metropolitan Museum, who bought it for the Metropolitan. The price he paid was not made public, but it was certainly far in excess of $100,000, and it was hardly unlikely that the family sought to recoup on the cost of Carnarvon's hobby over the years. Be that as it may, many pieces are still on display in New York at this writing.

London was appalled by the sale. British archaeologists publicly termed the collection's disposal "a severe blow" to the nation. A dumbfounded Sir Wallis Budge remarked, "It is a thousand pities that these art treasures have gone from England." Sir Frederic Kenyon charged that the British Museum had not been given the first opportunity to purchase the collection as provided for in the codicil.

Carnarvon's death also raised questions about his arrangement with *The Times*. After weeks of indecision, Carter—who had opposed the monopoly originally, but was now fed up with the rest of the press—consented to write a series of exclusive articles for the self-same *Times*. The first appeared May 31, with this prefatory note: "I desire to dedicate these articles to the memory of my generous friend, the Earl of Carnarvon, whose untimely loss the world now deplores. Without his lordship's unselfish cooperation and constant encouragement, our joint labours could not have been crowned with success. In the history of Egyptian archaeology, his honoured name will ever be remembered."

When Carter closed the tomb for the season, he estimated that only a fourth of the work of excavation had been accomplished. The mummy, of course (if there were one), was still to be found, and there were probably other hidden chambers to explore in the hypogeum.

Transcending other aspects of Carnarvon's tragic death was the persistent popular belief that he had been stricken by an ancient Egyptian spell. Indeed, ever since the death of Carter's canary, there had been talk of a curse. To the credulous, Carnarvon's death simply confirmed it, and the world's press pulled out all stops on this angle.

To appreciate the excitement that stories of the occult generated at the time, one must remember that, in the twenties, spiritualism and clairvoyance were at a popularity peak. Seers and mediums commanded attention and enjoyed prestige. Louis Hamon, who used the *nom de plume* Chiero, claimed that an Egyptian princess had appeared before him as an apparition and warned him that Carnarvon would die if he continued to dig in the Valley. According to Chiero, he informed Carnarvon, who rushed off to visit Velma the Great, among the most prominent mediums of the period. Gazing into a crystal ball—honestly, a crystal ball—Velma allegedly told his lordship, "I see great peril for you."

In the spirit of Reynolds Packard and his mythical Kansas City milkman, newspapermen love this kind of story, and many of them are apt to write tongue in cheek. Whatever the case, the suggestion that there might be an occult relationship between Carnarvon and Tutankhamen captivated the mass-circulation dailies and titillated the public.

Clare Sheridan, a columnist, wrote in *The World*: "Lord Carnarvon had to pay the price each one pays who dares to touch the Oriental dead. Other men have paid the penalty before. There is hardly a mummy in any museum in Europe that has not its sinister record for those who crossed its path. In my own family there is the same tale of disaster attached to the relic that a great uncle brought from Luxor."

In Paris, the world-famous Parisian seer, M. Lancellin, declared: "Tutankhamen has taken his revenge!" His rival, Madame Fraya, observed in turn that Egyptian occult science was highly developed and that Carnarvon had been the victim of the *ka* "or what is known in Egyptian and Oriental occult science as the 'doctrine of the double.' "

Sir Arthur Conan Doyle, a London literary giant of the era, held that an Egyptian mummy could radiate evil "elements." "It is impossible to say with absolute certainty if this is true but if we had proper occult powers we could delineate it," he contended. "In Lord Carnarvon's case, human illness was the primary cause of death. Yet the 'elementals' may have brought about the conditions which caused his illness." Accordingly, he said, "A malevolent spirit may have caused Lord Carnarvon's fatal illness."*

When Sir Arthur spoke, an enraptured public, perhaps naturally enough, did not hear *his* voice, but that of Sherlock Holmes. And one word from Holmes was enough to cause a panic. A front-page headline in the London *Daily Express* of April 7, 1923, read: "EGYPTIAN COLLECTORS IN A PANIC/SUDDEN RUSH TO HAND OVER THEIR TREASURES TO MUSEUM/GROUNDLESS FEARS."

However groundless the fears, parcels containing Egyptian relics poured into the British Museum; a number of owners acknowledged fear that Carnarvon had been killed by Tutankhamen's *ka* or double. "These fears are, it is hardly necessary to state, absolutely groundless," a museum spokesman said. Packages containing the shriveled hands and feet of mummies, faience, and wooden statues and other Egyptian antiquities arrived daily for the Egyptian rooms, the entrance to which, as one London guide then put it, was marked by a "gruesome . . . vitrified corpse, in crouching posture, of a man of the Neolithic period, probably 7000 B.C." The British Museum, said the *Express*, had become a "godsend to the superstitious."

All this astonished and annoyed the archaeological establishment. Sir Wallis Budge called the curse theory "bunkum!" and Dr. H. R. Hall, curator at the British Museum, commented wryly, "If there had been such a curse there would not be any archaeologists left today!"

Even G. E. Wright, secretary of the London Spiritual Alliance, of which Carnarvon had been a member, said: "There can be no possible connection between Lord Carnarvon's death and occult influence."

But Ralph Shirley, editor of *Occult Review*, injected a note of uncertainty: "I should not like to say one way or another, with regard to Lord Carnarvon, since there is no

---

*Before his death, Sir Arthur entrusted to Dunninger the Great, who billed himself as "Mastermind of Mental Mystery," a coded message. Dunninger, on tour or stage, at private soirées or banquets, on radio and television, until his death in 1975, repeatedly challenged mediums and other practitioners of the occult to disclose the message. He offered a $10,000 prize. He had no takers.

evidence. It may have been that some native Egyptian, indignant at the Luxor operation, put poison in the tomb."

Algernon Blackwood, a popular writer of the twenties whose bestsellers included *The Lost World* and *Pam's Garden*, both of which were set in the world of dreams and the supernatural, scoffed at the idea of a curse. "To credit any Egyptian magician of several thousand years ago with sufficient power to kill a man today is to lay a heavier burden upon a 'curse' than it can bear," he said.

As for Shirley's poison theory, Blackwood asked, "How could this poison be contained to a single individual only?"

This led to a new theory—that ancient high priests had impregnated some objects in the tomb with poison and that Carnarvon had accidentally nicked himself.

But a French professor provided a more titillating answer to the question of why Carter was not felled by the same curse. Carter himself, he implied, might have been responsible for Carnarvon's death. A pharaoh's tomb could not be explored with impunity by inexpert hands. Carter was a professional Egyptologist, an expert. Thus, under identical circumstances, Carter lived and Carnarvon died—because Carter knew what to touch and what not to!

Carter refused to dignify any of these tales with denials or libel suits. But in Volume II of *The Tomb of Tut-ankh-amen*, which was published in 1927, Carter felt compelled to abandon a position of reticence and refute the wild stories. "The sentiment of the Egyptologist . . . is not one of fear, but of respect and awe," he wrote. "It is entirely opposed to the foolish superstitions which are far too prevalent among emotional people in search of 'psychic' excitement."

He denounced the storymongers as "mischievous . . . unpardonable . . . mendacious . . . and . . . malicious." "If it be not actually libellous," he wrote, "it points in that spiteful direction, and all sane people should dismiss such inventions with contempt."

But Carter's bid to end the rumors failed; the stories were too good. The theme of the mummy's curse not only persisted, but developed an uncontrollable ground swell. The explanation for its durability was given by Morton, one of the serious journalists at Luxor. "The queer atmosphere which clings to all things Egyptian is responsible for the widespread story that in opening the tomb of Tutankhamen Carnarvon exposed himself to the fury of some malignant influence," he observed, "or that he was poisoned by materials left in the tomb thousands of years ago."

Indeed, the mummy's-curse theme was so captivating that *The New York Times*, on its front page, employed an *A* head of three decks of 30-point type with ten additional banks as follows: "CARNARVON'S DEATH/SPREADS THEORIES/ABOUT VENGEANCE." In an adjoining column, a comparatively modest two-deck *Y* head in 18-point type reported: "Lenin Critically Ill, May Die Any Minute/But Moscow Says He Still Keeps Control."

Suspended Animation

After a restful summer, Carter returned to Upper Egypt in October 1923, as he had done for thirty years, to mount the new season.

His hope for tranquillity was promptly crushed. Tourists flocked to Luxor in greater numbers than ever, literally by the thousands. A new hotel was under construction. The riverfront was crowded with an armada of feluccas and Toonerville ferries. Guides camped around the Winter Palace Hotel, and the world's press reassembled on both banks of the Nile, more determined than ever to crack *The Times'* monopoly

In truth, they already had, but they did not know it. Breasted's son Charles, in a secret arrangement with Carter's connivance, reported on developments from inside the tomb for the Chicago *Daily News* Syndicate under the pseudonym George Waller Mecham. Anonymously, he also covered events in the tomb for *The Christian Science Monitor*. His dispatches irritated *The Times* and puzzled the competition, but the source of the mysterious reports was not detected for months. The press viewed young Breasted's comings and goings in the tomb as that of a privileged person, the son of the renowned Breasted and a friend of Carter.

In January, as a result of a tripartite conference among Zaghlul Pasha (now the prime minister of Egypt), Lord Allenby, and Major Astor, Egyptian and foreign correspondents were admitted to the tomb once each week. By the time Breasted surfaced in March as Mecham, *The Times'* news monopoly was hardly that any longer.

At the start of the 1923–1924 season, there was new tension between Carter and the Egyptians as well as between him and the French. The latter were represented by M. Lacau; and the former, by the new minister of public works, a firebrand Wafdist, Morcos Bey Hanna, whom the British had once jailed for "treason." Both the bearded French Jesuit and the minister desired to put Carter, a former employee of the antiquities department, in his proper place.

For one thing, they showered instructions on the exasperated Carter, who later estimated that he lost fourteen working days out of the first fifty that season answering their stream of directives and rowing with them about how to carry on the work in the Valley. The Egyptian government—perhaps fearful that some of the treasure might be smuggled out of the country—put Carter under surveillance.

The tension was noticeable. "His [Carter's] face was lined and drawn with the heavy strain under which he has suffered during the past few days," the London *Daily Express* reported. "There is reason to believe that Mr. Carter's relations with the Egyptian government are becoming intolerable."

With the assistance of "Pecky" Callender and the Metropolitan staff, chiefly Mace and Burton, Carter reopened the tomb of Seti II, a pharaoh of the Nineteenth Dynasty, which Carter had converted the previous year into a laboratory and warehouse. At the tomb of Tutankhamen, under the direction of Carter's chief *reis*, Ahmed Gurgar, the limestone chips used to block it up were painstakingly removed, chip by chip; the job took about a month. In late November, additional power lines were installed in the tomb for the battery of klieg lights Burton imported from America—with the idea of making a frame-by-frame photographic record of the dismantling of the shrines and the opening of the sarcophagus of the king. (That there would be one was no longer doubted.)

In the Seti lab, Carter and his collaborators labored to preserve, in various chemical vats, the art objects that had been removed earlier and stored. They also crated objects for shipment to Cairo. Meanwhile, the dust from the Tutankhamen tomb was sifted for odds and ends. This effort produced spectacular archaeological results. In removing the gold and inlaid throne from the Antechamber, Carter had discovered that one of the four upreared uraei on the backrest was missing. In the tomb's dust, the missing piece was recovered.

With a view to dismantling the nest of shrines in the Burial Chamber, in order to get at the sarcophagus and the mummy, Carter planned to demolish the plaster wall that separated the Antechamber from the burial vault. Putting the project in motion in the limited space was an engineeering feat. Once the wall was torn down, Carter's team erected scaffolding in the tomb and an elaborate series of chain hoists, with differential gears, for lifting multiton loads.

Carter and his aides worked from 8:00 A.M. to 1:00 P.M., took a one-hour break for lunch, and then returned to work until 4:00 P.M. By late afternoon everyone was physically and emotionally drained.

Outside the laboratory, the Valley took on the appearance of a logging camp as teams of fellahin toiled in the burning sun, sawing freshly imported lumber and making shipping crates and scaffolding. Quiet descended during the lunch hour. Each day's luncheon, prepared at the Winter Palace Hotel and carried to the site, was like a working session between a field marshal and his staff. Promptly at 1:00 P.M., Carter, wearing a bow tie and a homburg, and his white-sleeved crew assembled in Tomb No. 10 at a long table covered with an immaculate white tablecloth. A year before, Carnarvon had been at the head of the table. Now Carter sat in that place.

It took Carter and his men eighty-four days to dismantle the four gold-sheathed shrines. The catafalques were composed of eighty separate pieces, each shrine of exquisite goldwork (the largest shrine, the outer one, was also inlaid with blue faience). The sides and ceilings of the shrines were dotted with religious texts and symbols and overlaid in gilt.

The largest shrine, known as the first shrine—although the eminent French Egyptologist, Alexandre Piankoff of the French Institute of Oriental Archaeology at Cairo, conclusively demonstrated that it was really the last and therefore the fourth shrine*— was 10.6 feet long, 10 feet wide, and 9 feet high. The smallest, fourth shrine within the nest (Piankoff's first), measured $9^1/_2$ by 4 by $6^1/_2$ feet. Each shrine fitted snugly into the other.

*Piankoff based his findings on the inscriptions found on the shrines; incidentally, the Tutankhamen shrines are still the only ones that have ever been found in Egypt.

Upon dismantling the outer shell, Carter was elated to find a rope around the second shrine, the intact knot bearing unbroken seals. The shrines had not been opened since the day they were sealed millennia earlier—these were genuine time capsules. "We had at last found what we had never dreamed of attaining—an absolute insight into the funerary customs followed in the burial of an ancient pharaoh," Carter wrote. "Years of toil had not been wasted."

In each succeeding shell, the gold was brighter. "The sight was dazzling, superb, almost blinding in its effect," Merton of *The Times* wrote on January 4, 1924, when the third shrine was opened to reveal still another.

Indeed, Merton, perched in the catbird seat (with "Mecham" at his elbow), ran out of superlatives as one shrine after another was dismantled. Here are samples of descriptive passages from his reports on the opening of the last three shrines:

> Carefully the cord was severed, the bolts drawn and the doors opened, and a third shrine was revealed, exactly similar in design, of gold throughout, like the other two, with similar ebony bolts across its doors, and its cord and sealing still in position. . . .

> Once more the bolts were drawn and the seal cord cut, and then the doors of this third shrine were opened, revealing yet a fourth shrine, also of gold, brighter and more dazzling than the last. . . .

> The decisive moment was at hand, and we all watched with tense excitement. The bolts of the last doors swung slowly open and there, filling the entire area within the fourth shrine, and effectively barring all further progress, stood an enormous sarcophagus of crystalline sandstone, intact, with the lid still firmly in its place.

Carter, the mummy-seeker, had found his mummy. The quest of a lifetime had ended in triumph.

On the door panel of the first shrine Carter and his band read: "Lord of Diadems, Tutankhamen . . . living forever . . . in the Region of Silence."

And on a panel in the second shrine, Isis, mother of Osiris, lord of the underworld, pledged: "I have come to be thy protection, thou art my son . . . May thou lift thy head to see Re, to stand on thy feet, to walk about in the forms thou likest, to move as before . . . To never decay!"

In the third shrine: "I have come to be thy protection, thy head is attached to thy body . . . I have given thee the day of eternity. . . . May thy house [tomb] prosper eternally as Re himself . . . Thy *ka* is stable, remaining forever in thy castle [tomb] . . . Thy heart is pleased . . . Thou livest forever and eternally . . . son of Re, Tutankhamen . . . Thou livest!"

The last shrine contained the most sorrowful lines found in Egyptian theology. "I have seen yesterday," the ancient Egyptian scripture concluded. "I know tomorrow."

With the shrines dismantled, a magnificent mural depicting Tutankhamen's passage into Osiris' world of the dead stood, totally unobstructed on the north wall for the first time in thirty-five centuries. The mural's color and vitality were such that it looked as if it had been painted only the day before.* Within the shrines, Carter discovered a treasure trove of smaller objects: silver walking sticks, models of Nile barges, gold statuettes—each designed to serve Tutankhamen in the afterworld.

Since the discovery of the sixteen steps fifteen months before, one supreme moment had dizzily succeeded another. Carter and the world now breathlessly awaited the most

*It still gives this impression. Egyptian art retains this freshness because the Egyptians used minerals in their pigments. Their paintings are as good as gold, therefore, in the sense that, like gold and other minerals, they never lose their inherent, natural brilliance.

supreme of all moments—lifting the lid of the sarcophagus. Compared with this prospect, the treasure that had already been found—and estimated to be worth $15 million—seemed relatively unimportant.

For the occasion, which fell on February 12, 1924, Carter invited nineteen guests: a mix of archaeologists, government officials, and VIPs. The group included two token Egyptians (the local governor and the undersecretary of state in the Ministry of Public Works), and three token Frenchmen (Lacau and the directors of the French Archaeological Institute and the French Expedition in Egypt). The other guests were Anglo-American—Gardiner, Newberry, Breasted, Mace, Callender, and others. Among the VIPs were two controversial figures, Major Astor and Edward S. Harkness, the American railroad mogul who would acquire Carnarvon's Egyptian collection right from under the noses of the British. Present, but not listed in the register of official guests, was Merton.

Carter spent the morning checking the makeshift contraption he had constructed in the Burial Chamber for lifting the one-and-a-half-ton lid, a series of blocks and tackles, ropes, and chain hoists. Iron clamps had been attached to the lid.

Promptly at 1:00 P.M., the guests assembled in Tomb No.10 for a bit of lunch. As usual, wine and tea were served, the tea in deference to the religious sensibilities of Moslem guests. The tension between Carter and Lacau almost crackled in the stifling tomb-turned-commissary. Carter seethed. The new minister of public works, Morcos Bey Hanna, the Wafdist firebrand, had sent him a telegram designating who might and might not in the future enter the tomb. Inexplicably, among those barred were the wives of Carter's collaborators. The directive, relayed by Lacau, forbade "until further notice access to this tomb by all ladies who have not received authorization." Lacau claimed the directive was "as annoying for me as for you," but that, as director of the antiquities service, which functioned under the ministry, he had no recourse but to enforce the order. Carter was sick of it all. "It makes me ill," he told Breasted.

At 3:00 P.M. the guests descended into the tomb. Klieg lights were turned on. As the temperature soared into the upper nineties, Burton's motion picture camera, poised on a tripod, began to whir. Carter signaled Callender, who was in charge of the blocks and pulleys. The chain hoists clanked, and the ropes grew taut. The lid trembled. Inch by inch, the rose granite cover, glistening under the klieg lights, was raised from the sarcophagus. When the lid was about two feet above the sarcophagus, Carter ordered a stop to the operation. Like a boat cradled aloft in a travel lift, the lid hung in midair.

Carter approached the sarcophagus, turned on his flashlight, and peered into its interior. For a fraction of a second, cold disappointment surged through his body. He saw nothing. Nothing, that is, except a discolored linen pall that covered the contents like a blanket. Gingerly, with Mace's assistance, Carter began to roll up the shroud. Sections of linen crumbled in their fingers. Their hearts pounded; their blood pressure rose; their mouths were parched. Perspiration streaked down their faces and stained their white shirts.

As they removed the linen, the gleam of burnished gold momentarily blinded them. Both men gasped aloud. A gold effigy of the youthful pharaoh filled the sarcophagus, rich goldwork on gesso. The face of the effigy was covered with a solid gold mask, brilliantly sculptured in Tutankhamen's image. On the forehead were the reared cobra and the vulture's head, symbols of Lower and Upper Egypt, poised to strike.

"Everywhere the glint of gold," Carter said in awe.

Upon the effigy was a graveside touch as common today as it was then: a wreath of withered flowers. Were they placed there by Tutankhamen's queen, Ankhesenamen? She had been the loveliest of the three daughters of Akhenaten, the heretic who destroyed the idols and preached the existence of one God, and his radiant queen, Nefertiti. Tutankhamen has given us license to dream.

In a memoir to his son, Breasted recalled the moment:

> As they [removed the pall], we suddenly saw the gleaming gold of the vulture's head and the up-reared cobra on the king's forehead. We saw his eyes, which seemed to look out upon us as in life; and soon the king's whole figure was revealed to us in all the splendor of shining gold. His gold-covered arms and hands were crossed upon his breast; in his right hand he grasped a crook or staff, wrought of gold and colored stones; in his left, he held the ceremonial flagellum or scourge [flail], also of gold. His figure was swathed in the gilded plumage of a protecting goddess.

What Breasted and the others saw was simply the outer coffin, cunningly wrought by the sculptor with the aid of lapidary and goldsmith into a portrait figure of a king lying, again in Breasted's words, "as if stretched out upon the lid like a crusader on his tomb slab in some European cathedral."

"I looked at my watch," Breasted remembered, "—scarcely an hour had passed since we had entered the tomb, yet we came away with a sense of having glimpsed the era and the last rites of Tutankhamen."

The party emerged from the tomb in a daze, unable to work further, the lid still suspended aloft some twenty-four inches directly above the sarcophagus. "Our one haunting regret," Carter remarked, "is that Lord Carnarvon was not spared to witness the fruits of his undertaking."

In Tomb No. 10, Carter and his guests toasted each other in champagne and tea.

The following morning, Carter led members of the press on a firsthand, two-hour inspection of the interior of the tomb and sarcophagus, partly a post-Carnarvon public relations campaign designed to assuage the press and partly in compliance with the newly negotiated contract between Almina, Countess of Carnarvon, now Mrs. Dennistoun, and the Egyptian government.

The press was also overcome. "I have never seen and never hope to see again such a magnificent sight," Merton cabled his paper. Reuters reported that "the view was dazzling . . . a more wonderful discovery has not yet been made." And the correspondent of the *Egyptian Gazette* wrote, "The great Tut stunt has reached and passed its climax. . . . . It was a thrilling moment."

With the departure of the correspondents scheduled for noon, Carter originally had planned to escort the wives of his collaborators into the tomb and then proceed to a luncheon in honor of his staff. But then came the ministry's directive, and that morning Lacau informed Carter that extra police had been dispatched to the site with instructions to bar the women if they sought to enter.

For Carter, the order evoked memories of his run-in, some twenty years earlier, with the French over the presence of women at Petrie's dig. Carter was visibly agitated, and on leaving the tomb that morning the correspondent of the *Egyptian Gazette* reported that he looked "strained and worried."

As noon approached, Carter told his aides what had transpired earlier. They, in turn, announced that they refused to work further in the tomb unless their wives were accorded the common courtesy of inspecting the object of their fifteen months' toil.

In character, Carter acted impulsively. He went directly to the tomb, cut the power lines, slammed shut the steel door, and padlocked it. He deposited the only set of keys in his tweed jacket, adjusted his bow tie, pulled his homburg down on his head, and, in a rage, headed for Luxor. At the Winter Palace Hotel Carter posted the following notice on the bulletin board:

NOTICE

Owing to the impossible restrictions and discourtesies on the part of the Public Works Department and its Antiquity Service, all my collaborators in protest have refused to work any further upon the scientific investigations of the discovery of the tomb of Tutankhamen. I am therefore obliged to make known to the public that immediately after the press view of the tomb this morning between 10:00 A.M. and noon the tomb [was] closed and no further work can be carried out.

[signed]   Howard Carter
February 13, 1924

If Carter was outraged by his treatment at the hands of the ministry, Morcos Bey Hanna and Lacau were livid. Lacau summarily ordered Carter to hand over the keys. He refused.

Meanwhile, the mummy of Tutankhamen lay stretched out in its nest of coffins. Overhead was more than a ton of granite sarcophagus lid, suspended by a series of multiple hoists designed to lift and lower the lid—not to hold it in suspension indefinitely.

In Boston, the staid *Christian Science Monitor* carried a headline that read: "LUXOR WRANGLES/AS SARCOPHAGUS/LID IS HELD IN AIR."

Fiction could not have created a more unbelievable plot line.

Carter in Exile

At Luxor, everyone from the world's most prestigious archaeologists down to the donkey boys and *gazooza* vendors was dumbfounded by the latest turn of events. So was the rest of the world. The Tutankhamen script had more climaxes, anticlimaxes, and anti-anticlimaxes than the *Perils of Pauline*, which was still captivating audiences in silent-film houses from Timbuktu to Zamboanga.

"To understand the dispute," said the *Egyptian Gazette*, "it is essential to disassociate it from Mr. Carter's personality, from his quick temper."

The *London Evening Standard* claimed that the dispute resulted from the Egyptian government's vision of gold. "Nearly every Egyptian," the *Standard* contended, "believes there is sufficient gold in the tomb to pay off the Egyptian national debt."

The specter of French intrigue was not far behind. Writing anonymously in *The Christian Science Monitor*, Charles Breasted confided: "The fact remains that the present astonishing attitude of the Egyptian government has the earmarks of being a put-up affair . . . fostered by the antiquity department's failure to offer Mr. Carter anything remotely approaching just and proper support since the resumption of work in the tomb last October 22."

Four Anglo-American Egyptologists, Gardiner, Newberry, James Breasted, and Lythgoe, went further. In an open manifesto issued on February 16, they pinned the crisis to the Egyptian government and its French advisers. "That unique discovery, with its wealth of historical and archaeological facts, belongs not to Egypt alone, but to the entire world," they proclaimed. ". . . you [Lacau], as director-general of antiquities, are failing completely to carry out the obligations of your high office to protect the scientific procedure of this all-important task."

In his book *Seventy Years in Archaeology*, the feisty Flinders Petrie also singled out Lacau as the puppeteer in the affair. "*Francia semper eadem*," Petrie wrote. And the London *Times* editorialized: "The friction which has led to the closing of the tomb and to the abrupt suspension of the work is, unfortunately . . . due largely . . . to the influence of unnecessary mischief-making from outside."

In Paris, *Journal des Debats* endorsed the Egyptian government's position and demanded that Carter hand over the keys to Lacau.

Whatever the truth about French intrigue, Carter portrayed a role of innocence. "It is a matter of surprise to me that, whereas every other department of the Egyptian government has shown only goodwill, kindness and eagerness to help," he wrote Lacau, "your department has, ever since the death of the late [*sic*] Lord Carnarvon, not only been endeavouring to frustrate the rights of the Carnarvon family but also to impede, hinder and delay this scientific work, without which the fruits of the discovery would be wasted."

"I am at a loss to find motives for this action," Carter said.

As for the vernacular Egyptian press, *Balagh* urged the government to cancel Lady Carnarvon's concession and declared, "Egypt has suffered enough from this foreigner [Carter] who, under the nose of the Egyptian public and of a high official of the government, violates the tomb of a pharaoh as though it were the tomb of his own father!" *Mahroussa* demanded that Cairo stand firm: "Let Mr. Carter know that we have a real government." *Akbar* said Carnarvon's concession in the Valley should have been canceled after Carnarvon's death: "We must put an end to the tyranny of Mr. Carter and those like him."

Only the influential *Siyasa* was embarrassed by the imbroglio. It accused the government of making "a great fuss about the wives" and held that it was "unworthy" of Cairo to behave in such an ungentlemanly manner. "Why did M. Lacau do it?" *Siyasa* asked. "It was only an act of courtesy to agree to the visit of the ladies. What patriotic interests and national dignity required the refusal of the request?"

The deadlock in the Valley was not so much an Anglo-French quarrel or a Carter-Lacau confrontation as an expression of the deep desire of articulate, politically conscious Egyptians to reassert their sovereignty in every field, especially against the British. Said Prime Minister Zaghlul Pasha: "Not at any moment has our action been influenced by Mr. Carter's nationality. I can assure all that if the concession holder had been an Egyptian we would not have treated him with as much consideration." Then he added: "I think that in England, as everywhere else, it is the duty of the government to defend the rights and dignity of the nation. That is what we have done. I do not consider that a Constitutional government can disregard the opinion of the country."

Carter had staunchly advocated from the outset—as, incidentally, had Lacau—that the treasure be kept intact, preferably in the Cairo Museum. But in a legal maneuver to win the right to sequester the tomb, Carter, meanwhile, modified his posture. "The tomb of Tutankhamen has been searched," he wrote Lacau. "It was not found intact. The conclusions to be drawn from [this] appear to me to be sufficiently obvious. . . . The articles found do not form a part of the public domain." In effect, Carter claimed the treasure for himself and Carnarvon's estate, certainly half of it under the terms of the 1915 concession awarded to Carnarvon.

But at the same time Carter sought peace. "The crisis," he said, "has compelled me to turn aside from the scientific work of recording the objects to consider what I still regard as a matter of altogether secondary importance, the question of the legal rights to which the discovery has given rise." The dignified, prudent course, he continued, would be "to postpone all dispute as to the ultimate destination of the treasure found until the continued existence of the treasures themselves should have been secured."

In New York, the Egyptian author Bishara Nahas, then on an American lecture tour, was outraged. "To say that the tomb was 'searched' is only a technicality which no sane person will ever admit," he argued. "The real difficulty lies in the division of what has been found, and not in the question of visitors." Recalling a conversation he had had with Carter the previous December aboard the Luxor-Cairo Tutankhamen Special, he disclosed, "Carter told me specifically that all that was in the tomb practically belonged to the Egyptian government except what the Egyptian government deemed as a proper compensation for the pains and undertakings of the excavators, which Carter estimated at about two per cent, adding that the Egyptian government would get ninety-eight per cent or practically the entire contents of the tomb."

In London, the *Daily Express* was acerbic: "The world does not really care very much whether Mr. Carter or M. Lacau unwraps the mummy, but it does care very much about Tutankhamen and the fate that awaits him at the hands of modern man." (The sarcophagus lid remained suspended.)

At this juncture, another crisis developed. Lord Allenby, British high commissioner and commander in chief of the British army in Egypt, was scheduled to make a formal visit to the tomb on March 6. The Egyptian government was thus confronted with three options: rescind the order against wives and have Carter reopen the tomb, which would have constituted an intolerable loss of face; inform Allenby that the tomb was closed and that the visit would have to be canceled, implying that Egypt lacked the authority to open it; or break into the tomb and sequester it in the name of the Egyptian government.

Zaghlul Pasha opted for the third alternative.

The cabinet authorized Lacau on February 20 to "reopen the tomb and resume work at the earliest possible moment." Lacking Egyptologists of its own, the government sought to make a deal with Lythgoe, Mace, and other members of the staff of the Metropolitan Museum of Art: the Museum was invited to take over work in the tomb. Acting as spokesman, Mace indignantly rejected the offer and termed it "an insult to all concerned."

In another maneuver, Lacau publicly announced that Carter might resume the work in the tomb at the expense—but under the control—of the Egyptian government. Still in a rage, Carter refused.

And so, in a formal statement, the government delivered Carter an ultimatum: return to work in forty-eight hours or face cancellation of the concession. ("Such a step is quite impossible," Lady Carnarvon said. "The license cannot be revoked after my signature is attached. No government would be so discourteous.")

Discourteous or not, on February 22, Lacau, accompanied by several Egyptian officials; the chief of police; a detachment of armed police; and a squad of workers armed with chisels, crowbars, axes, and hacksaws arrived at the tomb. They filed through the locks securing the outer door and then smashed the bolts of the steel inner gate and succeeded, finally, in opening the tomb.

"They descended into the tomb with lighted candles," a correspondent wrote, "like a band of conspirators."

In the Burial Chamber, the lid was still suspended in midair. Lacau and his men gently swung it aside and lowered it to the floor of the tomb. Their sigh of relief could be heard around the world.

On March 6, Zaghlul Pasha turned the incident to political advantage by deciding to visit the tomb himself. He and the Allenbys traveled to Luxor in separate trains. Along the route, tens of thousands of fellahin lined the tracks to shout their support of the prime minister and chant anti-British slogans. As the London *Times* dryly put it, the demonstration "removed from the minds of the government's guests any doubt in regard to the political sentiments of the populace."

Zaghlul Pasha had invited, in addition to Lord and Lady Allenby, a number of other luminaries to the official reopening of the tomb. There were several members of European royalty, including Prince Frederick Leopold of Prussia.

Like commoners before them, the celebrities descended the sixteen steps and gasped at the scene of golden grandeur before them. Tutankhamen still rested peacefully within his coffins, secure in the massive, open sarcophagus. The British guests applauded the excellent condition of the tomb and the superb theatrical lighting effects arranged by Lacau. Everything went smoothly. But all the Egyptologists in the country boycotted the ceremony, except M. Foucart, the director of the French Expedition and, of course, Lacau. That night the prime minister presided over a gala banquet at the Winter Palace Hotel. The Allenbys were conspicuous by their absence: they had gone directly from their special armored train to the tomb and then back to the train, leaving immediately for Cairo.

For ten days following the formal opening of the tomb, more than 2,000 visitors, including large numbers of fellahin, trooped down the limestone steps. Given the width of the passageway into the tomb, no wider than a subway car, the tomb must have taken on the appearance of a Times Square rush hour. If the din did not awaken Tutankhamen from his deep slumber, nothing would. As for his *ka*, it probably fled in terror.

In Cairo, Carter and Lady Carnarvon brought legal suit against the Egyptian government.

Gradually the principals hammered out an acceptable compromise: Carter was guaranteed freedom from harassment as he completed his work in the tomb, and in turn, he and Lady Carnarvon renounced all claims to the treasure. "I hereby voluntarily relinquish all claims on the part of Almina, Countess of Carnarvon, and the trustees and executors of the estate of the late Lord Carnarvon, to the antiquities in the tomb of Tutankhamen, and agree to withdraw all legal actions, as far as they relate to the enforcement of such claim," Carter and Lady Carnarvon declared in a joint letter sent to Morcos Bey. The settlement provided that the government would compensate the Carnarvon estate for its expenses in the Valley; a figure of £50,000 ($250,000) was bandied about. Finally, as a token repayment to the Egyptologists who worked on the tomb, Cairo also agreed to present "duplicate objects in the tomb" as gifts to the British Museum and the Metropolitan Museum of Art. Final details were put to paper March 11.

Egypt had yet to regain complete independence from foreign control, and the court system reflected the roiled state of affairs. Because the case involved foreigners, the suit came before a mixed tribunal presided over by a British judge. The judge appointed Breasted, Sr., as mediator. Even so, Carter and Lady Carnarvon engaged in overkill. In the selection of counsel, they retained General Sir John Maxwell, the former British commander in Egypt, executor of Carnarvon's estate, and an old friend of the family. Unfortunately, they also retained as counsel F. M. Maxwell, an able English solicitor in Cairo. An expert in Egyptian law, he had been, alas, the public prosecutor in the treason case that had put Morcos Bey Hanna, now Zaghlul Pasha's minister of public works, behind bars. During the treason trial, Maxwell had demanded the death penalty for Morcos Bey.

Carter's pact was about to be signed when Maxwell, talking aloud to himself, characterized the Egyptian government's behavior in the affair as "the action of bandits." Morcos Bey Hanna flew into a rage and broke off negotiations. Breasted and Carter hurried to repair the breach. Carter, at Breasted's urging, sent the minister a note of apology. "I wish to dissociate myself absolutely from the use of the word 'bandit' and to express my profound regret that such language should have furnished the just occasion for the termination of our negotiations," he said. But it was useless. The negotiations were never resumed.

An outraged Maxwell threatened to sue Breasted, the author of Carter's apology, for defamation of [Maxwell's] character. But nothing came of it.

"Heaven deliver me from ever again attempting to act as peacemaker in a lawsuit over the possession of a royal tomb of ancient Egypt!" Breasted, the court's mediator, wrote his son.

The consequences were profound. Neither the British Museum nor the Metropolitan received a single duplicate object from the tomb of Tutankhamen for their collections.

On March 12, the mixed court found in favor of Carter and Lady Carnarvon on all legal points in their applications for the tomb's sequestration. But it was a bootless award. The Egyptian government refused to discuss the matter further, and the court was unable to enforce its judgment without touching off a political crisis of incalculable dimensions.

The pendulum of political power was swinging in Egypt's favor, and, accordingly, later in the month the Egyptian government appealed the mixed court's ruling. A mixed court of appeal, sitting in Alexandria, reversed the lower court's decision. Egypt had won the day; indeed, the war had been won the day the government asserted its sovereignty and broke into the tomb.

Emboldened by its courtroom victory and probably prodded by Lacau, who sensed the opportunity for a kill, the Egyptian government barred Carter and members of the Carnarvon family from ever reentering the tomb of Tutankhamen.

The blow came that spring as Carter reached his fiftieth birthday. He was now at the crest of his fame and creative energy. He should have been in a position to savor his triumph. Instead, he was completely demoralized. Cairo's decision first stunned him and then plunged him into a state of deep depression.

Breasted's son, empathizing with Carter's plight, wrote in *Pioneer to the Past*:

> Since I had first met him in 1905 near this very spot, Carter has spent most of his career searching for this tomb. He had sacrificed health and large financial returns as a result of his insistence upon personally superintending almost every phase of the removal and preservation of the objects in the tomb. He had quarreled with his only friend, Carnarvon, because of his belief that the entire find should remain Egypt's. And now the same soldiers he had posted to insure the tomb's safety were marching up and down before me, under orders to prevent his access to it.

At a loss over his next course of action, Carter reluctantly accepted an avalanche of lucrative offers to hit the lecture trail in the United States. In a daze, during the last week of March, he sailed for England. At Southampton he booked passage for the United States aboard the Cunard White Star liner *Berengaria*.

This was the Golden Age of transatlantic service, when the queens of the oceans sought to outrival each other not only in speed but also in the galley. (In that era, a ship of the *Berengaria*'s tonnage would be stocked for one voyage with 25 calves, 75 oxen, 145 lambs, 20 pigs, 110 sheep, 10,000 oysters, 1,200 lobsters, 4 turtles, 3,000 chickens, 500 ducks, 280 turkeys, 450 brace of partridge, 450 brace of pheasant, 1,200 pigeons, 1,000 quails, and 1,800 tins of sardines.

But Carter's mind was not on any of life's pleasures—much of the time, avoiding the gaiety of the ship's companionways, he stayed in his cabin. On deck, he avoided fellow passengers and brooded in solitude about his fate. In the course of the voyage, he came to the sickening realization that his work in the tomb of Tutankhamen was finished—he would never return to his beloved Valley and would never gaze on the mummy of Tutankhamen.

By the time the black-hulled, red-booted liner tied up on April 20 in her slip on Manhattan's West Side, Carter had decided to embark on another fantastic voyage of discovery, an archaeological campaign he had once filed away in his mind for an unspecified future. This was to organize an expedition into eastern equatorial Africa in search of archaeology's missing link—a civilization originating in the heart of darkness that might have been the common mother of the civilizations that flourished in the valleys of the Nile, the Tigris, and the Euphrates. Carter's objective was the jungle-clad interior of Somaliland and Ethiopia, then called Abyssinia. He was moved in this direction, he later explained, by the results of archaeological research in northern African and western Asian valleys, each of which contained drawings and sculptures of animals found only in black Africa.*

In the United States, Carter was accorded honors of the sort his own country denied him. Never received at Buckingham Palace, he was invited to the White House, where he and Calvin Coolidge struck it off well. Both of them shared basic characteristics—frugality, modesty, and unpretentiousness. They were also plain in speech, appearance, and habit. Finally, both were self-made men. As he left the Oval Office, Carter told newsmen that he was "amazed and flattered" by Coolidge's familiarity with his work in Upper Egypt. Indeed, Coolidge was so impressed with his visitor that he invited Carter to return to the White House for dinner on May 9. That evening, in the warmth of the East Room, Carter enthralled the presidential circle with a talk about his search and discovery of the tomb of Tutankhamen. And although no university in England ever accorded him even an honorary degree, Carter was invited to Yale, which in the course of a ceremony that drew a large crowd to New Haven, bestowed upon him an honorary doctor of science degree. (He appended the title to his name with the publication three years later of the second volume of his trilogy, *The Tomb of Tut-ankh-amen.***)

Despite the accolades he received in the United States, Carter returned to England that summer a lonely, defeated, and embittered man. His depressive mood deepened when he found a letter waiting for him from Ahmed Gurgar, his chief *reis*. In English, in a shaky hand, Gurgar wrote: "Beg to write this letter hoping you are enjoying good health and ask the Almighty to keep you and bring you back to us in safety." All the *reises* and ghaffirs, he added, "beg to send their best regards." The letter ended: "My best remarks to your honorable self . . . longing to your early coming."

---

*Clearly, Carter was before his time. Meroitic archaeology, as it is now called, is a new discipline; and the question of which came first, ancient Egypt or ancient Meroë, the name of Ethiopia in antiquity, still baffles scholars. Sorbonne Professor J. Leclant, for example, has observed that the god Amen (as in Tutankhamen) appears in Meroë, and he asks whether Meroë absorbed the Amen cult from Egypt or whether the worship of Amen evolved in Meroë before civilization developed in the Nile Valley.
**Carter received one other academic citation: Madrid's Real Academia de la Historia honored him with the title "Correspondent."

Dispiritedly, Carter sought to work up enthusiasm for his new project, but Tutankhamen was uppermost in his thoughts—a light year beyond his reach.

In the House of Commons, questions were raised about the government's role in the Tutankhamen affair. Ramsay MacDonald, the Labour party's first prime minister, washed his hands of the matter. "Howard Carter," he told Parliament, "in his excavation work in Egypt [is] a private individual and subject to the provisions of the Egyptian law of antiquities." In the face of militant nationalist sentiment in Egypt, 10 Downing Street had enough trouble without getting involved in so sticky a wicket as Tutankhamen.

And so, by all rights, Carter's search and discovery of the tomb of Tutankhamen should end at this point.

Rescue from Oblivion

While Carter sulked in England, the political situation in Egypt deteriorated rapidly. Sir Lee Stack, the sirdar, or commander, of the Egyptian army and the governor-general of the Sudan—the most important British official in the area next to Lord Allenby—was assassinated on November 19 in the streets of Cairo. London seized on the incident to restore its pre-Wafdist authority in Egypt.

Britain leveled a series of demands at Zaghlul Pasha's government, including an apology, the prosecution of the murderers, a $2.5 million indemnity, an end to public meetings in Egypt, and, as *The Times* neatly characterized it, "a free hand for the protection of foreign interests" along the Nile.

Egypt's prime minister accepted some of the demands and rejected others.

In a no-nonsense mood, the British moved. British troops seized the Alexandria Customs, the principal source of Egypt's financial strength, and carried out maneuvers in downtown Cairo. To the music of fife and drum, units of the Duke of Wellington's Regiment marched down the avenues, fixed bayonets gleaming in the sun; then came the Highland Light Infantry, with kilted pipers and scarlet and white hackles tucked into their helmets; and the Hampshire Regiment, with machine guns packed on mules. While the columns paraded around Cairo, British forces along the Suez Canal were ordered to stand alert, and British gunboats took up positions in the roadsteads of Egypt's main ports, Alexandria and Port Said.

In the face of this show of force, Zaghlul Pasha resigned. He was immediately replaced by a British puppet who submitted readily to London's demands. Forthwith, political rallies were banned, the elected parliament prorogued, and scores of anti-British personalities detained in a series of sweeping razzias. British imperial power was restored over Egypt.

In a last attempt to retain a residue of respect and dignity, the Egyptian chamber of deputies addressed a note of protest to the secretariat-general of the League of Nations. But the deck was stacked. The secretariat met under the chairmanship of Britain's Sir Eric Drummond and, after an hour's deliberation, decided not to circulate the note among the organization's member states.

British behavior was hotly debated in London, both in and out of Parliament. George Bernard Shaw, the curmudgeon, issued a stern warning. "The British government has absolutely destroyed the League of Nations," he said. The League's effectiveness, Shaw argued, depended on its support by the Great Powers. Britain's failure to uphold the League in the Egyptian controversy, he said, was a "calamity." Calamity, indeed. A few years later, to all intents and purposes, the League collapsed when the Japanese refused to submit to the world organization on the Manchurian question, a slippery slide that led to World War II.

Whether Howard Carter pulled strings in the Foreign Office and/or Colonial Office and/or used the influence of the British Museum and the academic establishment in the bargain is still open to question. But the fact is that Britain had no sooner reasserted itself in Egypt than Carter turned up in Cairo. On January 13, 1925, a report from the Egyptian capital disclosed that the dispute over the tomb had been suddenly and "amicably" resolved. The settlement, it said, resulted from "the more reasonable attitude shown by the Egyptian authorities."

The accord was along the lines of the compromise agreement originally negotiated by Breasted. Carter and Lady Carnarvon renounced the treasure; the Egyptian government promised not to harass Carter in his work; Egypt pledged to compensate the Carnarvon estate to the amount of the expenses the late lord incurred in searching for the tomb; and, in recognition of the "admirable discovery," the government offered the Carnarvon estate a choice of duplicate objects from the tomb to either keep at Highclere or give to museums, as it saw fit.* Publicity arrangements concerning the tomb were placed in Cairo's hands.

With the settlement, an overjoyed Carter, oblivious to the political upheaval around him, rushed off to Luxor and his home on the west bank of the Nile. There he was warmly greeted by his *reises* and ghaffirs. It is a measure of the Egyptian character that in personal relationships the Egyptians are blind to politics, although politics is a strong suit in their nature.

In a simple ceremony on January 25, the tomb of Tutankhamen, which had been closed for eleven months, was reopened. To Carter's relief, only a few hardy tourists were on hand; the murder of Sir Lee Stack and the turmoil that followed had done in the tourist trade.

Within the laboratory and the tomb, Carter found everything in good order except the pall that had covered the coffin. It had been completely ruined as a result of exposure to the air.

*Five years later, in the depths of the Great Depression, the Egyptian chamber of deputies adopted the report of its financial commission and recommended the payment of £34,971 (around $180,000) to the Carnarvon estate as reimbursement for the moneys spent by him in search of the tomb. That same year, however, Wafdists returned to a reshuffled cabinet and canceled the clause that permitted duplicates to be turned over to the Carnarvon estate. In place of the objects, Egypt granted the estate a modest monetary recompense.

Work Resumed

"To begin a new season's work is a less simple task than is perhaps generally imagined," Carter once modestly observed. Nineteen-twenty-five was not an exception. He and his collaborators spent the first half of the year mapping a strategy for the realization of three terminal objectives: opening the coffins, removing the mummy, and unwrapping it.

New scaffolding was erected in the Burial Chamber for handling the coffins, new power lines were laid for X-raying the mummy, and a veritable laboratory was installed in the tomb for immersing the mummy's wrappings in vats of chemical preservatives.

In the light of Carnarvon's fate, Carter took one interesting, little publicized precaution. On several occasions, after detecting an invasion of "minute insect life," he sprayed the tomb with the primitive pesticides of the period.

It was the problem of preservation that especially worried the team. At the Cairo Museum, for example, where articles of gold from the previous season were on display, Carter found, to his dismay, that they already exhibited signs of discoloration. Worse, some of the wooden oviform boxes, chariot wheels, and statuettes developed cracks. "Everything may seem to be going well until suddenly, in the crisis of the process [of preservation], you hear a crack . . ." Carter wrote later. "Your nerves are at an almost painful tension. What is happening? . . . What action is needed to avert a catastrophe?"

He summoned a battery of experts to help: A. Lucas, the director of the Egyptian government's chemical department; Alexander Scott, the British Museum's director of scientific research; Douglas Derry, a professor of anatomy; and Dr. Saleh Bey Hamdi, the former director of the Egyptian University. In addition, Carter mustered one hundred experienced *reises*, ghaffirs, and fellahin.

On October 10, 1925, work inside the tomb had regained its old momentum. With two sets of three-sheaf pulley blocks, the heavy gilt wooden lid of the first anthropoid coffin, measuring 7 feet 4 inches in length, was slowly lifted by its original silver ornamental handles. With the lid raised, the curious band of archaeologists peered expectantly into the coffin. As their eyes adjusted to the shadows, they saw a linen pall covered with garlands of dried flowers.*

*Botanists later identified the floral garlands as fashioned from the cornflower, blue lotus, the olive, and the willow, among other plants. Because the cornflower to this day is harvested in Upper Egypt in late March and April, it was safely concluded that Tutankhamen was buried sometime between the Ides of March and the end of April.

When Carter drew back the shroud, he looked upon a magnificently gilded mummi-form coffin, 6 feet 8 inches in length, the head and shoulders of the effigy covered with a burnished, glistening funerary mask of solid gold.

At this moment of jubilation, Carter was confronted by one of the two great disappointments that clouded his discovery. The first and greatest disappointment was the failure to find a scrap of papyrus, even a hint of the life and times of the entombed pharaoh. The other disappointment was that, on closer inspection of the second coffin, Carter discovered evidence of dampness. "A rather ominous feature," he commented with typical understatement. ". . . Disconcerting." Moisture, of course, could destroy not only the linen bandages in which the king's august body was swathed, but the mummy itself as well.

On November 11, an odd work day because Armistice Day was then universally and reverently observed globally, the lid of the second coffin was raised. Although Carter and his associates expected to find a third coffin in the nest, the sight that they beheld left them numb. The third coffin, 6 feet $1^3/_4$ inches long, was solid gold.

Between $2^1/_2$ and $3^1/_2$ millimeters thick, it was an enormous mass of pure bullion, weighing 2,448 $^1/_8$ pounds. At the fluctuating price of gold today—around $150 per ounce—the third coffin was worth $6 million. (The weight of the three burnished gold masks found in the nest was, altogether, 581 $^7/_8$ pounds.)

Patently, these cost-price figures are absurd. The masks and third coffin represent, to this day, an unmatched pinnacle of art and craftmanship. Judging their value by weight is as ludicrous as judging the value of a Rembrandt by the cost of canvas and pigment.

Carter and his assistants were suddenly overwhelmed by the implications of their astonishing discovery. Tutankhamen, whose name would forever outshine and outlive the names of all the other kings of pharaonic Egypt combined—unless another intact tomb was discovered*—was, in historical terms, a lesser pharaoh who died, X rays later showed, at the age of eighteen. Tongue in cheek, Breasted, Sr., called him a "feeble pharaoh." Yet, if the treasure buried with him was so fantastic, how much more fantastic must have been the amount of treasure buried with such great pharaohs as Rameses VI, whose rock tomb, situated above Tutankhamen's, was a hundred times more cavernous?

"What riches that Valley must have once concealed!" Carter exclaimed.

Journalists had another heyday. One news agency dispatch from Luxor concluded ecstatically, "The astounding wealth of Egypt in that epoch outrivalled the wildest funeral extravaganzas of Rome and Byzantium." (The correspondent should have done his homework. The funeral pageants of Rome and Byzantium were bores and did not go much beyond marble and alabaster crypts.**)

Gold was, of course, not all there was to the third coffin. There was the mummy itself—literally covered in jewels.

"At such moments," Carter confessed, "the emotions evade verbal expression . . . Three thousand years and more had elapsed since men's eyes had gazed into that golden

---

*See p. 146.
**But the emperors of China were buried in pharaonic opulence as late as this century. In 1908, for example, the dowager empress of China, a Manchu, was interred outside of Peking, her body wrapped nine times by a single strand of matched pearls; her death robe embroidered with gold thread and studded with gems; her coffin lined with carved pieces of jade, green and rose quartz, amethyst, carnelian, and agate and exquisite porcelains, bronzes, silver ornaments, and ingots of gold; her coverlet shaped like a peony, fashioned from precious stones; her arms weighted down by heavy bracelets shaped like large chrysanthemums and plum blossoms set with diamonds; her fingers wrapped around a wand made of emeralds.

coffin. Time, measured by the brevity of human life, seemed to lose its common perspective before a spectacle so vividly recalling the solemn religious rites of a vanished civilization. But it is useless to dwell on such sentiments. . . ."

"The emotional side," he said, "is no part of archaeological research." (Nonsense. Because archaeology is a human endeavor, an emotional side to the discipline, however repressed, is unavoidable.)

Here is a partial count of what Carter recovered from the mummy after he removed the gold mask that covered the face, shoulders, and heart:

On the head, a royal diadem of gold with cobra and vulture, signifying Lower and Upper Egypt; *about the neck*, a pectoral of bejeweled gold and silver charms and amulets; *on the breast*, a series of small pectorals, arranged in sixteen layers, displaying extraordinary cloisonné work; *on the arms*, eleven magnificent bracelets, studded with semiprecious stones; *on the hands*, thirteen rings; *on each finger*, a gold sheath; *around the waist*, two girdles of gold and jewels; *at the hip*, a gold-handled dagger with an iron blade (of great archaeological worth, for it demonstrated that Egypt was already in the Iron Age); *around the legs*, a royal apron of inlaid gold; *on the feet*, gold sandals; *on each toe*, a gold sheath.

All told, Carter found 143 objects within the linen folds of the mummy. Each was worth a terrorist's ransom.

As for the mummy, Carter entertained great expectations that it would be found, as he put it, "in almost perfect condition." But "we found him [*sic*] in a terrible state," Carter said.*

The high priests had treated Tutankhamen in death as in life with reverence and respect. Swathed in yards of the finest cambric bandages, the mummy had been protected by a series of shells, seven in number, the four shrines and the three coffins.

When the last rites were performed, apparently, as sometimes happened in the case of other mummies, something had gone awry. Humidity—"a sore decayer of your whoreson dead body," as the gravedigger put it to Hamlet—was locked into the gold coffin. As a result, the unguents poured over the mummy before sealing the coffin had turned, with chemical action, into a pitchlike substance with the consistency of marine epoxy glue. This started a form of spontaneous combustion that destroyed the linen wrappings and caused the skin and underlying tissues of the mummy to become extremely brittle. Tutankhamen's mummy was stuck fast to the bottom of the coffin, and all of Carter's ingenuity could not move it.

Accordingly, the mummy had to be examined *in situ* as it lay in its gold coffin. The charred linen wrappings, which often crumpled to powder at the touch, had to be removed in bits and pieces, some no larger than a Band-Aid.

After seven consecutive days of work, with temperatures in the tomb in the high nineties, "the youthful pharaoh was before us at last: an obscure and ephemeral ruler, ceasing to be the mere shadow of a name, had re-entered . . . the world of reality and history!" Carter wrote. "Here was the climax of our long researches! The tomb had yielded its secret!"

Following the examination of the mummy, Carter directed his attention to a small opening along the west wall of the Burial Chamber. When he had first discovered it two years earlier, he had boarded it up so he would not be tempted to explore it until the shrines and coffins were dismantled and examined. This decision is a testimony to

---

*A slip; when referring to Tutankhamen's mummy, like most Egyptologists, Carter usually referred to the mummy in the neuter pronoun.

Carter's self-discipline and devotion to archaeology—a devotion to the past and the future at the expense of the present.

Dubbed the Treasury, this room, more than any other chamber in the rock tomb, a British Egyptologist recently pointed out, "was concerned with the mysteries of the world beyond the tomb." Roughly 15 by 12 by 7 feet, the room had a gilt-wood shrine as a centerpiece. On each side of the canopy, facing inward, were golden figures of slender, seductive goddesses in transparent gowns, their hands outspread, their countenances serene.

When Carter opened the shrine, he discovered an alabaster chest with a sculpted head divided into four compartments. Each compartment contained, in pure gold, a miniature coffin. This was the so-called canopic chest, containing the viscera of the mummy.* Carter gently opened the coffins: one contained Tutankhamen's liver, wrapped in linen; another, his lungs; the third, his stomach; and the fourth, his intestines.

Nearby were two small anthropoid coffins, each casket containing a second coffin. Within each of the second coffins was a stillborn child. One was the mummified body of what appeared to be a five-month-old female fetus, carefully wrapped in linen. But there was no abdominal incision and no indication of how the body had been preserved. The skin was gray; the body, shrunken and brittle. The second child, also believed to have been a girl, was also wrapped in bandages. The eyes were open; the eyebrows, distinct; a few eyelashes, still intact. The abdominal wall had been opened by an incision and closed with a sealing of resin. The abdominal cavity was stuffed with saline-impregnated lime. The baby had been about seven months old at the time of death.

"With little doubt," Carter wrote, "they were the offspring of Tutankhamen." If so, it is intriguing that the stillborn children were buried with the father and not with the mother (Ankhesenamen's tomb has never been found). Actually, to this day there is a dispute among Egyptologists over the parentage of the two babies: "Why should royal children, dying before their father, have been buried in his tomb?" asks Christiane Desroches-Noblecourt of the Louvre.

In this same chamber, Carter also found scores of clay and wooden *ushabty* figures. *Ushabty* were the answerers—the slaves, servants, and soldiers—destined to do Tutankhamen's bidding in the afterworld. The room also contained a fleet of model ships: solar barges in which the pharaoh might cruise in the wake of the sun-god Ra on his daily voyage through the heavens.

When he cleared the Treasury, Carter turned to the fourth and last chamber within the tomb. The Annex, he called it. Serving as the tomb's warehouse, this storeroom was filled with objects of every description in gold, silver, ivory, glass, and wood, from backgammon-style boards and toys to bedsteads, clothing, weapons, and literally hundreds of other items. They were thrown about helter-skelter.

Carter's meticulous work in the Treasury and the Annex occupied him for five seasons until 1932. One thousand seven hundred and three objects from the tomb are still on display in the Cairo Museum. To this day, their numbers follow the order in which Carter dutifully shipped them to the Museum between 1923 and 1932.

Carter's finds, after the reopening of the tomb in 1925, continued to make headlines and to draw ever larger crowds to Upper Egypt. In the first three months of 1926 alone,

*In ancient Egypt, at Canopus, the inhabitants worshiped Osiris in the form of a vessel with a human head. In the nineteenth century, Egyptologists mistakenly attributed these oddly shaped jars and chests to the influence of the inhabitants of Canopus. The heads, however, are representations of the deceased, not Osiris.

as the political situation momentarily stabilized, more than 12,000 persons visited Tutankhamen's crypt.

Next to the discovery of the tomb itself, the public was captivated most by Carter's discovery of the solid gold coffin and the mummy. Of the two, it is difficult to judge which created the greater sensation. As Dr. Derry, who examined the mummy with Dr. Hamdi, observed on November 17, 1925, in his press report, "The preservation of the dead body . . . has always excited the greatest interest."

In their report, the two anatomists placed Tutankhamen's age at about eighteen, certainly under twenty. They estimated that in life he stood five feet six inches tall. His skull bore a close resemblance to that of Akhenaten, the heretic who first conceived of his creator in monotheistic terms. Like Akhenaten, Tutankhamen had a platybasia skull, that is, flat-based: in profile, it resembled a lima bean. This abnormality is found in patients who have Paget's disease and in other conditions associated with a softening of the skull bones. However, such an odd-shaped skull is not conclusive evidence of a disease of the central nervous system. Platybasia *per se* is not necessarily associated with symptoms. In Tutankhamen's case, the deformity may be ascribed in part, perhaps, to taking to incestuous sheets.

The Derry-Hamdi report observed that all of Tutankhamen's limbs were wrapped separately; all his fingers and toes, bandaged individually. The eyes had been left partly opened; the eyelashes were very long and intact. The skull cavity was empty. The nose—a portion of it, flattened permanently by the pressure of the head bandages—was stuffed with resinous material in the manner employed by mummy makers after extracting the subject's brains through the nasal passage, as observed by Herodotus. Another note: Tutankhamen's penis had been drawn forward, wrapped independently of other parts of the body, and then kept in ithyphallic position by pelvic bandages.

In a final paragraph, the examiners noted: "On the left cheek, just in front of the lobe of the ear, is a rounded depression, the skin filling it, resembling a scab." A scab? "It is not possible to say what the nature of his lesion may have been," they said.

The insect that bit Carnarvon, it will be recalled, had struck him on the cheek and left a scab.

Thereafter, there was no stopping the legend of the curse of Tutankhamen.

Moral Outrage

Breaking into the tomb and stripping the mummy initiated an unprecedented debate over the relationship between archaeology and the rights of the dead. Moral outcry was heard from the pulpit, the press, and Parliament.

From the grave, Tutankhamen seemed to have wreaked his vengeance upon Carter: each successive controversy left him more drained, more embittered, more irritable, and more isolated.

Indignant letters in the press set the parameters of the debate. "It is hard enough, even in this twentieth century of the Christian era, to live according to the Golden Rule," went one of the milder letters to the London *Times*. "What must it have been for a pharaoh thirteen hundred years before Christ? . . . There are many who venture to hope that, after the legitimate claims of science and archaeology have been satisfied, it may be possible, in a spirit of pious regard for the religious convictions of the departed, to restore to their tombs the pathetic remains of those who, with many prayers and tears, were laid to their eternal rest."

Others were less charitable. Sir H. Rider Haggard, whose *She* was among the ten top bestsellers of the period, said Tutankhamen's fate appeared ultimately "to be destined to be laid half naked to rot in a glass case in the museum at Cairo, having first been photographed as he came from the embalmer's bath and meanwhile made the butt of the merry jests of tourists and the baser sort, as I have heard with my own ears."

"Is it doing as we would be done by others?" he asked. "Is it not an outrage and one of the most unholy?"

Across the Atlantic, similar letters arrived at the desks of editors. "Grave robbery is grave robbery," a Baltimore churchgoer protested. "Whether it be called archaeological exploration or otherwise, it does seem more or less shameful . . . that the Egyptian dead of 3000 B.C. are not allowed to remain undisturbed in their tombs, especially when it is so evident that they wished to do so."

The Villager, an avant-garde paper published in New York City, demanded to know what right Carter had to empty a tomb carefully prepared by a living person for his eternal well-being, especially in view of the obsessive fears of the ancient Egyptians about the afterlife.

A member of the House of Commons called upon the government to "use its influence" to see to it that "Tutankhamen's mummy remain in what the pharaoh desired to be its last resting place." But, as before, Whitehall, with an eye on what it considered more serious problems in the Anglo-Egyptian relationship, avoided public embroilment in the affair. Ronald MacNeill, undersecretary for foreign affairs, brushed aside the question with the rejoinder that the government would not intervene in a matter in which the decision rested with the Egyptian government. Given the extent of British influence in, if not outright control of, Egypt in this period, his reply was a cop-out.

MacNeill's posture did not still the critics. William Leech, an MP widely known for his wit, rose from his seat and matter-of-factly asked the prime minister "if he has received any request from Egyptian citizens for permission to ransack the tombs of British kings and queens in Westminster Abbey and elsewhere, if the British Museum has stipulated that relics, coffins, bodies, etc., shall be handed to them, and if requests have been received, what reply did he [the prime minister] propose to make them?" The question was disallowed.

But apparently Buckingham Palace was disturbed by the implications; and, according to the Cairo correspondent of Pulitzer's New York *World*, King George sent a message to the Egyptian authorities expressing his hope that the mummy of Tutankhamen would not be removed from the tomb and placed on exhibition in Cairo. The Egyptians were astonished by the message; they regarded George's intercession on behalf of Tutankhamen as another blatant example of British imperialist interference in Egypt's internal affairs.

"Topics of the Times," an unsigned commentary that formerly brightened the otherwise colorless editorial pages of *The New York Times*, observed that the Egyptians "seem to be unnecessarily disturbed, for King George merely did what anybody has a right to do—expressed an opinion as to what was proper or desirable—and he asserted no power and attempted no coercion." The writer doubted the propriety of drawing the line at the pharaoh's remains, however. "What he [Tutankhamen] would have called the desecration of his grave already has gone so far that it seems rather absurd not to carry it a little further and make the job complete."

Moral outrage at the treatment of Tutankhamen came from unexpected sources: the prospect of the body's removal from the tomb stirred the death merchandisers, the Associated Undertakers of Greater New York. Frank E. Campbell, whose New York mortuary facilities rivaled those of ancient Thebes, led the assault. "It is not pleasant to contemplate the prospect of having the bodies of Washington and Lincoln dug up after a couple of hundred or a thousand years and placed on exhibition in a public museum," Campbell asserted. "It is no less revolting to think of a similar indignity being inflicted upon the last earthly remains of King Tutankhamen."

At a meeting of the embalmers' organization, Campbell went a step further: "The mummies already in our museums have no business being there. They should be restored to the tombs from which they were removed."

In London, Sir John Maxwell, who had handled Carter's case before the mixed courts, scoffed at this line of reasoning. "If public opinion in this matter is germane, then, to be consistent, all bodies of rich and poor alike should be recommitted to the earth, and all national museums should take steps to return their mummies to Egypt for reinterment," he said. "But it might be as well to remind the good people at home," he added dryly, "that at all museums on a Bank Holiday the crowd dearly loves its mummy."

"The incident holds one moral," the London *Star* said editorially. "The superiority of incineration over embalming if a poor old king wishes his dust to rest in peace."

Arthur Weigall, the former inspector general of antiquities in Upper Egypt, acknowledged that he was besieged by people who asked: "How would we like it were foreigners to come to England and ransack our graveyards?"

He ascribed this widespread feeling against meddling to religious convictions. Some churchmen, he observed, held that the bodies of the dead should not be trifled with because they would rise again at the call of the last trumpet. To others, a corpse represented the total collapse of human expediency, the absolute paralysis of human systems and devices; and thus, in the mind's search for permanency, the bones of the deceased become consecrate. Indeed, Weigall, who was present when Carter broke down the wall and entered the Burial Chamber for the first time, recalled that he, Weigall, was "overwhelmingly conscious of the presence of God at that hour, and with all my heart I wanted the awaking king to know that he was safe in His hands, and that there was nothing to fear."

Nonetheless, as an Egyptologist, Weigall argued that the dead are the property of the living and that the archaeologist was the agent for the estate of the grave. The archaeologist is a gravedigger, if not of bygone individuals, then of bygone civilizations.

Even the critics were wont to admit that what was done cannot be undone. Once Carter discovered the tomb and unwrapped the mummy, the question of what to do with "it" became a matter not so much of ethics as of urgent practicality. Carnarvon before his death, as noted earlier, had expressed publicly the hope that the mummy would not be removed from the tomb. Carter, of course, entertained similar sentiments. During his American lecture tour, Carter told critics, "I believe myself that it is a wrong thing to disturb the dead." But, he added, "In no other way can we learn anything about unknown civilizations." In hedging, Carter implied that somewhere in time a line must be drawn beyond which the rights of the dead are terminated.

Carter's own moral dilemma runs as a submerged current throughout the trilogy he published in 1923, 1927, and 1933. In the first volume, he took issue with critics "who call us vandals for taking objects from the tombs." He argued that by removing antiquities to museums, Egyptologists really assured the safety of the objects, given the record of plunder in Egypt since antiquity. Four years later, in his second volume, he acknowledged that when he and his collaborators gazed on Tutankhamen's coffin, "many and disturbing were our emotions awakened by that Osiride form." Most of

117

these emotions were voiceless. "But, in that silence," he wrote, "you could almost hear the ghostly footsteps of the departing mourners."

The third and last volume, published a decade after he descended the sixteen creamy white steps, contained Derry's report on his examination of the mummy. "A word may fittingly be said here in deference of the unwrapping and examination of Tutankhamen," Derry wrote. "Many persons regard such an investigation as in the nature of sacrilege, and consider that the king should have been left undisturbed." He then pointed to the persistent record of tomb robberies in Egypt "from the most ancient times up to the present." Once the tomb of Tutankhamen had been discovered, he argued, Carter had no recourse other than to excavate it. Of course, Derry begged the question. The point was not whether or not to disturb the mummy of the youthful pharaoh, but whether or not Carter had the right to set out in quest of it.

Even so, the archaeological establishment missed the core defense for its behavior. Like climbing Mt. Everest or flying to the moon, Carter was driven to find Tutankhamen's mummy simply because it was there. He was moved to do so by man's irresistible and perhaps, given the emergence of nuclear weaponry—fatal—curiosity.

Yet what was to become of Tutankhamen's remains? One suggestion was that Tutankhamen's mummy should be mewed up in one of the empty chambers inside the Great Pyramid of Giza, on the outskirts of Cairo.

But Luxor was unhappy with the idea. Local merchants and others put pressure on Cairo to keep the mummy in its tomb. Luxor's interest was not so much ethical as commercial: as long as the mummy was within its tomb, the Valley would attract tourists.

Many archaeologists subscribed to Luxor's position, but for different reasons. Professor Newberry, sounding more like a man of the cloth than one of the spade, observed, "The exhibition of mummies in our museums serves no useful purpose, and personally I should like to see all the bodies of the pharaohs of Egypt, which now fill a large gallery in the Cairo Museum, taken back to their tombs and reinterred." Sir Martin Conway, former vice-president of the London Society of Antiquarians, agreed: "I think that after Tutankhamen's body has been examined and all desirable information obtained as to his age, racial type and religion, it should be decently buried out of sight and with such precautions as will prevent disturbances in the future."

Other Egyptologists were against leaving the mummy in its tomb. "The problem . . . is a very serious one," Flinders Petrie warned, "much more so than the average layman [and academic] imagines." Unless an armed guard were maintained around the clock, he said, "I believe an attempt will be made by robbers to despoil the tomb. Even electric wires and the sealing of the door with heavy rocks would be of no avail alone." Petrie pointed out that every Egyptologist had experience with grave robbers, and cited the case, from a generation earlier, of Amenhotep II. That pharaoh's bones, of no intrinsic value, were returned, because of public pressure, to their tomb, and an iron gate was placed across the entrance. "What happened?" Petrie asked, providing the reply: "One night an Egyptian ghoul smashed the tomb open and tore the whole mummy to pieces. It is astonishing how the idea of gold or treasure will tempt a ghoul in any country."*

Elliot Smith, the renowned anatomist-Egyptologist, concurred with Petrie. "There has been a good deal of not altogether relevant discussion about the ethics of desecra-

---

*Petrie had a point. In 1974, following reports in London newspapers that European art dealers planned to sell ten slabs from the Temple Hathor, Cairo dispatched 1,000 demobilized soldiers to the site to police it—a little like closing the barn door after theft of the cow. Colonel Ouda Ahmed Ouda, the tion, which is none the less unfortunate because it is inspired by ignorance of the real facts of the case."

"If archaeologists did not open and examine these tombs," Smith said further, "there is no doubt that in time the native [*sic*] tomb-robbers of Luxor, the most experienced members of their craft to be found anywhere, would in time discover the hidden tombs, plundering them and destroying historical evidence. There can be no question that the work of the archaeologist, when conscientiously done, saves the ancient tombs from willful destruction and gives the mummies and the furniture a new lease of assured existence."

These arguments aside, for scientific reasons, Petrie and Smith, among others, favored keeping Tutankhamen in Upper Egypt. For one thing, the mummy was in poor shape, and a long journey might do further damage. For another, the climate and humidity of Upper Egypt were better suited for the mummy's continued preservation. Carter agreed. So did Lacau.

They won the day. On October 31, 1926, after four years of debate, Carter rewrapped the mummy and placed it in the first, or outermost, wooden coffin. Then he lowered it into the great quartz sarcophagus, which had remained, unmoved, exactly where it had been placed in the Burial Chamber at the time of Tutankhamen's interment.*

It is still there.

The sarcophagus is open, and the lifelike, mummiform coffin peers up at visitors, bathed by a cluster of floodlights. In a sense, Tutankhamen lies eternally in state.

Never before, nor since, had the archaeological community been so buffeted by public opinion. This raised a question: Why should the fate of some obscure personage from the past matter so greatly? The answer is that the discovery had humanized Tutankhamen. Here was a flesh and blood creature, not a museum object. Here was an individual from the dawn of recorded history with whom people could identify, not some bloodless, abstract "ancient Egyptian." Tutankhamen did not belong to Egypt alone. He belonged to the world. As Samuel Mercer, the Biblical scholar and Egyptologist, wrote in 1923, "Today Egypt has become a household word." His explanation for the incredible interest in Carter's discovery transcended Tutankhamen.

"Now, why does all this interest the general modern public?" he said. "It is easy to create an interest in things Egyptian by invoking the aid of Christian and Jewish interests and tradition. Interest in Tutankhamen is natural and inevitable."

Perhaps. But Mercer's view should be modified slightly. It was not Egypt that became a household word. It was Tutankhamen—indeed, to such an extraordinary extent, that the world was caught up in—to mint a word—Tutmania.

Tutmania

Egypt and things Egyptian, the *shorghl-el-Mizr* of Carter's youth, were an uproarious

police commander in charge of protecting sites, described the theft as an "inside job" and said guards took part in the eighteen-month operation. Ahmed Sawy, head of the excavation section of the antiquities department described the slabs as "priceless and magnificent." With 40,000 sites to guard, Dr. Gamal Eddine Moukhtar, who presides over the antiquities department as secretary of state, said Egypt simply could not protect all the sites and that "99 per cent of lootings go undiscovered." The prison sentence for tomb robbery in Egypt is relatively light—three years. Following the Hathor scandal, the Egyptian parliament considered legislation to toughen the penalty and debated an ordinance that would bar local "antica" dealers from trading in antiquities.
*Interestingly, to date, the ground under the sarcophagus has not yet been explored.

theme in the twenties, especially among the young, carefree, and careless Americans who had emerged from World War I with, for the first time in their country's brief history, a world view.

The United States Patent Office was swamped by thousands of applications for trademarks using the name *Tutankhamen*. In New York, the Hotel Pennsylvania billed Vincent Lopez, a popular bandleader of the Prohibition era, as the man who played "Tutankhamen music," while at the Palace Theatre—the Mecca of the buck-and-wing brigade as vaudeville attained the height of its popularity—statuesque mannequins lined the runway in flimsy Ankhesenamen costumes. A corps of chorus girls in Tutankhamen bathing suits paraded around Miami Beach, and belly dancing was in all over the land. Tutankhamen umbrellas and walking sticks were the rage; one enterprising manufacturer sent a special Tutankhamen cane to President Harding. Every state fair in the land boasted a "Little Egypt." The Meade Hat Company—like vaudeville, hats were in vogue for both men and women—created, manufactured, and marketed "the Tutankhamen hat." In New Orleans, which boasted unique cemeteries, with the dead buried atop each other to save valuable delta land, "Tutankhamen-style" tombs became the vogue. At an international flower show, the W. Atlee Burpee firm, which marketed seeds through the mails, won a certificate of merit for its "King Tut" sweet pea, a deep, rich, rose pink variety that formed part of Burpee's "gold medal" collection. The sweet pea seed was sold at $50 a pound or 15 cents for a packet of fifteen seeds.

There were those who felt that commercialism had gone beyond the limits of decency and good taste.

"The other day," wrote one reader to a New York newspaper, "in a window of a Thirty-eighth Street shop, I saw a beaded handbag made to represent the face of the image that had guarded the tomb of the Egyptian pharaoh for more than thirty centuries. . . . In a department store [Macy's? Gimbels?], on the same day, I saw a number of leather dolls made to represent the pharaoh himself, and other objects, which the advertiser called 'King Tut's pups,' which represented the animals forming the sides of the king's couch."

"What would we think of Egyptian shopkeepers who would expose for sale as toys facsimiles of American coffins, funeral urns or hearses?" the reader continued. "What can be thought of women who would carry such trifles, of mothers who would give such objects to their children as playthings?"

The quickest—if not the zaniest—huckster was one Frederick Martin Burns. On November 19, 1922, three weeks after the Carter/Carnarvon announcement of the discovery, he composed, in a single night, a potboiler called *Tut-ankh-amen, or the Valley of the Kings*. Burns promptly copyrighted the title and sold the name *Tutankhamen* to Sanders and Carlo, coauthors of the Broadway musical *Tangerine*. Then, through a firm of patent lawyers, he copyrighted the use of the name on dozens of articles, ranging from tiny dolls, inspired by the *ushabty* figures found in the tomb, to bracelets and cigars. (A North Carolina cigarette manufacturer bought the name for a Tutankhamen cigarette.)

But Burns ran into a flood of other applications that gave rise to conflicting claims over the name and led to lengthy and costly litigation. Other promoters had sought to copyright such names as *Tut*, *Tut-Tut*, and *Two-Tank*. Obviously, Burns could not cover all the bases.

Shortly before Carnarvon's death, he was inundated with cables and letters from merchants as far apart as Japan and Switzerland, each proposing an arrangement whereby they would have exclusive use of the designs found in the tomb. One American businessman offered Carnarvon $100,000 outright plus a royalty for the use of such decorations. Clearly, Carnarvon was in a position to sell these rights country by country; it is to his honor that he rejected the overtures. On March 25, 1923, shortly before his death, Carnarvon's private secretary, H. Percy Robinson, announced that from his sickbed Carnarvon "asked me . . . to say that in due course photographs of everything discovered in the tomb will be available." This was widely interpreted to mean that Carnarvon would make no attempt to reserve the use of any designs found in the tomb, even if he could. By this gesture, Carnarvon gave the lie to attacks, notably in the British press, that accused him of crass commercialism.

Although the trademark division of the U.S. Patent Office declined to disclose the nature of the articles for which applicants sought to apply the Tutankhamen nomen, it was known that they were chiefly sought by fashion designers and textile manufacturers. The Patent Office never lost its cool, however. As the number of applications crested, the Department of the Interior, under which the agency operated, declared in an official statement that the Office refused to panic as "we know from long experience that every important historical event or discovery brought in its wake a rush of trademark applications."

While the Harding administration retained its aplomb, state legislators were alarmed by the sale of "relics" from the tomb at high prices to a gullible public. In New York, for example, sharpies no longer sold immigrants the Brooklyn Bridge; instead, they sold scarabs from Tutankhamen's hypogeum. In short order, the curio market was so glutted with fake antiquities that the State Assembly in Albany passed a measure known as the Tut Relic Bill. The bill made it a misdemeanor to reproduce or forge archaeological relics with intent to deceive. The original law, backed strongly by the New York State Archaeological Society, is still on the books.

In London, a similar situation developed. The British Empire Exhibition of 1924, opened by King George and Queen Mary, featured a facsimile, "an authentic reproduction," of the tomb. Two hundred thousand people crowded the Exhibition opening day, and the tomb was the hit of the fair. The directors of the exhibit charged an admission price of one shilling and three pence (25 cents) a head. Carter was furious and, to the exhibitors' chagrin, slapped a writ on the exhibit and sued the fair directors on grounds that the reproduction violated his copyright.

Carter was roundly criticized for his action, but, in truth, he never pressed the matter and never had any intention of doing so. His sole purpose was to alert a credulous public to the artificiality of the tomb. "I sued," he later explained, "to make it clear to the public that I accepted no responsibility for the exhibit."

In retrospect, Tutankhamen's broadest impact was on women's fashions in the twenties.* The American market in particular was captivated by the "Egyptian look," which helped prolong the postwar vogue for bobbed hair and short skirts. Dresses, hats, bathing suits—all were influenced from the grave. Russeks, a fashionable Fifth Avenue furrier, took top honors with a bisque, squirrel-collared coat featuring "Egyptian" embroidery. "The decorative splendors of the Tutankhamen period are repeated in the rich embroidery motif," the store proclaimed in its advertising.

---

*The Tutankhamen theme itself is alive and well at this writing. In March 1975, a Connecticut chapter of the Embroiderers' Guild of America exhibited its work at Simsbury. One of the most prominent pieces of work was a mixed-media creation by Rosemary Cornelius, called "King Tutankhamen." The face of the pharaoh was petit point; his headdress, appliqué.

121

Indeed, the Egyptian impact was so strong that Alexandre M. Grean, honorary president of the United Cloak and Suit Designers' Association of America, warned his fellow designers that Tutankhamen was "a dangerous theme. Do not exaggerate it," he cautioned. "Modify it, and choose the beautiful parts only."

Until then, Paris alone had set the pace for American designers. But, as a result of the Tutmania that swept the United States—while the French dragged their feet—American designers got an edge for the first time. "I am afraid the buyers who went to Paris this season for new models are coming home rather disappointed, as styles have suddenly changed," Grean said in mid-1923. "Paris has not taken up the Egyptian trend as vigorously as the designers of this country, and this new vogue will overshadow anything else."

But in 1925, Paris caught up with Tutankhamen and reestablished its leadership. Leon Bakst, for example, a Parisian pacesetter, labeled his line "The Isis Collection."

While New York and Paris were going at it, London entered the fray. The Tutankhamen look captured Brighton's fancy in the summer of 1923 with a Tut bathing costume that featured a cap modeled on the lines of an Egyptian headdress. By the end of the year, the *Daily Express* reported: "The inevitable has occurred: the Cleopatra Creation." This collection dominated Britain's annual fashion show at the Palladium. One enthusiastic fashion writer described a model who looked as if she "might have stepped from the walls of Tutankhamen's tomb." The model was swathed, like a mummy, in a dazzling creation of silver tissue, with a glittering cabochon in front accompanied by a regal headdress of pearls.

In Paris, New York, and London, the pipestem outline was elegant and in. To achieve the style, young women swathed their bodies in mummylike rigidity. "The straight silhouette may be aesthetically beautiful but it is full of peril for future generations," a Harley Street physician somberly warned British women, explaining that the mummy-wrap made breathing difficult and put undue pressure on the breasts and hips.

Zionists were dismayed by the growing enthusiasm for Egypt and things Egyptian. Speaking over the new medium of radio, Rabbi Solomon Foster, in a New York broadcast, sounded a warning to his coreligionists.

"As a human family, we are all deeply interested in the excavation into the soil of ancient Egypt. The vivid descriptions of the work of the patient and courageous scholars who are bringing to light memorials of an ancient civilization thrill us." But, Foster said, the real treasures of the Eighteenth Dynasty in Egypt were not the objects Carter recovered from the tomb. "We must look to a poor, obscure, weak and persecuted man by the name of Moses, a contemporary of Tutankhamen, whose work and deeds and precepts and commandments have come down through the ages as the most impregnable, most inspiring and most precious memorials of the ancient day."

The thought that Tutankhamen and Moses were contemporaries was news to many. However, the rabbi might have done well to consult the *Jewish Encyclopaedia*, which made the point that the Old Testament "seems to fix upon Rameses II as the pharaoh of the oppression during Moses' sojourn in Egypt." Rameses belonged to the Nineteenth Dynasty, of course, and lived more than a century after Tutankhamen. But the rabbi's peroration reflected one of the less publicized but more profound consequences of Carter's discovery: a review of the interrelationship between the monotheism of Tutankhamen's predecessor, Akhenaten, and Moses. Rabbi Foster would have been more upset some sixteen years later when, in 1939, the iconoclastic Sigmund Freud concluded that Moses was an Egyptian and that the religion he bestowed on the Israelites was nothing more than the monotheism preached centuries earlier by Akhenaten.

Museums also profited handsomely by the public's lively interest in Tutankhamen. Museum directors ransacked their storage bins to locate objects identified with the youthful pharaoh. The New York Historical Society enjoyed a windfall: in 1860, the Society had obtained the Abbott Collection of Egyptian antiquities, more than 3,000 objects. Reviewing the collection in 1923, a curator discovered a blue faience seal with ring that bore Tutankhamen's cartouche. Following the announcement of the discovery, long lines of people formed around the Society's building to view the find.

Not to be overshadowed, the Metropolitan dug up from its basement Theodore Davis's finds of the 1906–1907 season, the objects bearing the seals of Tutankhamen that misled Davis into thinking he had found the pharaoh's lost tomb. Literally thousands of people flocked to view the articles. One afternoon, attendants at the Metropolitan clocked the entry of 8,000 visitors, 6,800 of whom turned right as they entered the building. The Metropolitan's superb Egyptian collection is on the right, just as the Tutankhamen collection is in the Cairo Museum. To the amusement of museum officials, many of the visitors thought the exhibit had been shipped straight from the Valley of the Tombs of the Kings, once again attesting to the gullibility of "sophisticated" New Yorkers. Other museums reported similar excitement, notably those then active in Egypt, the Brooklyn Museum, Pittsburgh's Carnegie Museum, the Cincinnati Museum, Toledo's Museum of Art, and the San Diego Museum.

As Tutmania swept the world, Sir Rider Haggard's warning came to fruition. Tutankhamen soon became the butt of jesters. Perhaps the merriest prank of all took place at staid Cambridge. The students proclaimed a holiday and opened the tomb of "Toot-an-Kum-in."

Mysterious Egypt . . . tombs . . . ghouls . . . mummies . . . British explorers in pith helmets . . . above all, ancient curses—these were the ingredients to appeal to the writers of fiction and that new breed, the film makers. They lost little time.

Sir Arthur Conan Doyle, in a futile attempt to elude Sherlock Holmes, wrote a short tale of terror, "The Ring of Thoth," whose protagonists included an English Egyptologist and a mummy of the Louvre. There were no Holmeses or Watsons. Charlotte Eaton penned a poem to Tutankhamen; and the *Atlantic Monthly*, then in its salad days, published a poem by Preston Beazell, "Ravisher of Tombs."

Even before Carter's third volume appeared, the science fiction writers of the early thirties seized on Tutankhamen for plot lines. Charles R. Tanner, appearing in *Amazing Stories* in 1931, lightly disguised his chief character as "Tumithak of Loor." And a year later, in *Wonder Stories*, another pulp magazine writer, Jack Williamson, in the "The Moon Era," wrote about reaching the moon (surely nonsense). "What an adventure!" Williamson exclaimed. "To be the first human to tread this silver planet. To be the first to solve its age-old riddles. Why think . . . of Luxor and Karnak, when I might win the secrets of the moon!" Mary Gaunt, a popular Gothic writer of the twenties, was among the first to capitalize on the subject matter in a full-length book called *The Mummy Moves*.

Tutankhamen still stirs the minds of writers. In 1974–1975 two new books were high on the list of unpublicized bestsellers. One, *Carnarvon's Castle* by Jean Francis Webb, has an isolated castle, a sarcophagus, and a terrified heroine. The other, *The Curse of the Kings* by Victoria Holt, revolves around a bride's honeymooning in Egypt when the curse of the pharaohs strikes. This book sold 1.3 million copies, glowing testimony to the story line's indestructibility (*Inshallah*, May such a curse befall me!).

*For a fuller discussion of the Akhenaten-Tutankhamen-Moses relationship, see p. 142.

Carter's effort lent itself magnificently to the burgeoning film industry of the twenties. Within a week of Carnarvon's death in 1923, a Berlin producer announced plans for a film called *The Pharaoh's Revenge*. But it was not until 1932 that Hollywood produced its first classic in that mold. *The Mummy* had sand, tombs, pith helmets, mummies, Egyptologists, the Cairo Museum, and, inevitably, a comely heroine. Universal Studios boasted on billboards: "It couldn't be done—so Universal did it." Critics were impressed. "*The Mummy* beggars description," a *Los Angeles Times* film critic raved. "It's one of the most unusual talkies ever produced."

The film marked the emergence of a star named Boris Karloff. "Surely the mantle of the late Lon Chaney will inevitably fall upon the actor Karloff, whose portrayal of an unholy thing in this film, aided by magnificent makeup, establishes him as not just a good character actor, but a finished character star," said the Los Angeles daily.*

In 1940, stock footage from the flashbacks in *The Mummy* was shrewdly and effectively employed in a new version entitled *The Mummy's Hand*. And five years later, the same 1932 footage appeared in *The Mummy's Curse*.

The first horror picture ever filmed in England focused on the Tutankhamen theme. Gaumont-British produced *The Ghoul* in 1933 with Karloff in the feature role. Nearly thirty years later, *The Ghoul* was remade as a comedy.

To Carter's dismay, Tutmania revived and popularized in the English language the ejaculatory word "tut." Whenever Carter turned up, in hotels, on trains and ships, someone inevitably called out, "Tut, tut!" in jocular greeting. But in tracing the etymology of the word, the *Oxford English Dictionary*, in its 1933 edition, the year Carter's third and last volume was published, observed that the interjection was first employed in 1529 and that such "Gothic" writers as Goldsmith in *She Stoops to Conquer* and Thackeray in *The Virginians* made good use of it.

Perplexed by the world's reaction to his monumental discovery and wondering about the morality of it all, Carter might have profited by rereading Lewis Carroll's *Alice's Adventures in Wonderland*.

"Tut, tut, child!" said the Duchess. "Everything's got a moral, if only you can find it."

*Worldly, contemporary critics and late-late TV movie buffs still view *The Mummy* with awe. In 1975 one television critic commented, "First of the mummy films and the best." And another recently wrote, "Still about the best of these wrappings—sticks together nicely."

The Mummy's Curse

Of all the controversies in which Carter found himself embroiled—quarrels with the press, the dispute with Carnarvon, conflict with the Egyptian authorities, the row with the French, the moral disfavor generated by his work, and the excesses of Tutmania— none troubled or irritated him as much as the legend of the mummy's curse.

It all started, of course, with the death of Carter's pet canary. Carnarvon's death shortly thereafter strengthened the case. But what sustained it? With the passage of time, the curse not only came to haunt the story of Carter's search and discovery, but to overwhelm it.

It was in 1924, a year after Carnarvon's death, that Professor J. S. Mardrus, a French Egyptologist, gave credence to the curse business.

Citing the outburst of a severe case of plague in Upper Egypt and the deaths of four prominent persons directly or indirectly linked to Tutankhamen's tomb, Mardrus attributed these events to incomprehensible occult powers. At the core of his thesis was the established fact that the tomb, for the larger part, was the *first* intact, inviolate tomb of an Egyptian pharaoh discovered and opened in modern times.

"The twentieth century," he told a Paris news conference, "has treated as nonsensical superstitions those beliefs which existed during thousands of years of Egyptian civilization which were the most intellectual that ever flourished on this globe." Recalling the admonition of Louis Pasteur at the French Academy—"he who only possesses clear ideas is assuredly a fool"—Mardrus argued that Tutankhamen's tomb "contained, inviolate, all the things which the priests and masters of the funeral ceremony were able to place in the way of protection against profaners." Similar curses, he suggested, had overtaken the plunderers of the tombs in antiquity.

Mardrus cited other deaths connected with the Valley of the Kings since the opening of the tomb. George Jay Gould, the American multimillionaire, visited Luxor, was suddenly stricken by a strange malady, and died. Woolf Joel, a socially prominent, close friend of Carnarvon, while sailing up the Nile en route to Luxor aboard his yacht, was mysteriously swept overboard and drowned. (As Mardrus poetically described the incident, "An invisible watchman suddenly seized him and took him aboard the funeral skiff of Osiris, the blue god with the immobile heart.")

Then there was the case of Sir Archibald Douglas Reid, the noted British radiologist, who died of an unknown illness shortly after he signed an agreement with Cairo's department of antiquities to X-ray Tutankhamen's body.

Mardrus contended that, given the importance of magic, spells, amulets, and the like to the ancient Egyptians, Carter and Carnarvon should have realized that it was "an elementary necessity to be suspicious of the unknown and to take certain precautions, both against the visible and invisible." But, he charged, either through presumption or negligence, neither was done.

Then, in the autumn of the same year, H. G. Evelyn White, a professor at Leeds University who was well known for his work in Egyptology, committed suicide under bizarre circumstances.

White had recently returned from Egypt, where a monk had revealed to him a secret room in a Coptic monastery. There he found and removed a rich lode of apocryphal books, some previously unknown to have existed. In his subsequent suicide note, White confessed to deep-seated fears. "I knew there was a curse on me, though I had leave to take those manuscripts to Cairo," he wrote. "The monks told me the curse would work all the same. Now it has done so."

Two years later, Georges Benedite, director of the Louvre's department of Egyptian antiquities, and M. Cassanova of the Collège de France, both of whom had excavated in the Valley of the Tombs, died unexpectedly. Before the year was out, Leon Bakst, the fashion designer who had created the "Isis Collection," joined them on the eve of his Parisian show. Of course, there was no connection between Bakst's death and Tutankhamen other than the bond of Egyptian design; for that matter, there was even less connection between Gould, Joel, and Tutankhamen—but, as observed earlier, why ruin a good story with facts?

Besieged for comment on these deaths, Mardrus, who had been mocked for his earlier statement, rubbed it in. "I am, unfortunately, not at all surprised," he said.

"This is no childish superstition which can be dismissed with a shrug of the shoulder," he reexplained. "We must remember that the Egyptians during a period of 7,000 years, in order to assure the calm of subterranean existence which was supposed to delight their mummies, and to prevent all attempts to disturb their rest, practiced magical rites the power of which held no doubts for them. I am absolutely convinced that they knew how to concentrate upon and around a mummy certain dynamic powers of which we possess very incomplete notions."

Mardrus's observations now received more serious attention. Said *The New York Times*: "It is a deep mystery, which it is all too easy to dismiss by skepticism."

Mardrus now quickly attracted a number of supporters, among them Marie Corelli, the Victoria Holt of her day, whose tales of the supernatural captivated millions of readers (one of her novels went into forty editions). Miss Corelli* announced that she possessed a book, translated from the Arabic by a tutor of Louis VI, that claimed the Egyptian tombs contained caches of secret potions strategically placed to foil tomb robbers. The literary set of the twenties, who usually scorned her novels, applauded heartily when Ernest Wallis Budge, from his redoubt in the British Museum, denounced her claim. A copy of the book Miss Corelli referred to, he said, was in the British Museum. The translator had died in 1667 and, therefore, could not have been Louis VI's tutor because Louis the Fat died in 1137.

But in *Egyptian Magic*, published in 1901, Sir Wallis, the keeper of Egyptian antiquities, wrote, "The cemeteries were regarded with awe by the ancient Egyptians

---

*Given the chance, as she might today, of being called "Ms.," Marie Corelli would have insisted on "Miss." A staunch antifeminist, she described suffragettes as "the ladies who scream." She never married. "My three pets serve the same purpose," she once said. "A dog, who growls in the morning; a parrot, who swears in the afternoon; and a cat, who comes home late at night."

because of the spirits of the dead who dwelt in them." And he pointed out that Hebrew, Greek, and Roman writers invariably referred to the Egyptians as "experts in the occult sciences" and to Egypt as "a nation of magicians and sorcerers."

By 1929, the legend of the curse was firmly entrenched, and little wonder. Eleven persons associated with the Valley and Tutankhamen were dead. Among the new names on the list were Colonel Aubrey Herbert, Lord Carnarvon's half brother, who was present at the opening of the sarcophagus and died during a bout of "temporary insanity"; Lady Elizabeth Carnarvon, who, truly if unbelievably, died of an "insect bite"; Evelyn Greely, an American who killed herself on returning to Chicago after visiting the tomb; McGill University Professor M. Laffleur, a Canadian house guest of Carter who died the day after he inspected the tomb; Arthur C. Mace of the Metropolitan Museum of Art, who coauthored with Carter the first volume of *The Tomb of Tut-ankhamen*; and Dr. Jonathan W. Carver, another of Carter's assistants.

The curse, if there were one, was not limited to Western intruders. Several Egyptians associated with the tomb also died rather suddenly or mysteriously, including Prince Ali Fahmy Bey, who was shot and killed shortly after inspecting the tomb. Reports of the period are rather confused over the nature of his death. Some newspapers alleged that he was shot by his French-born wife; others thought that the murderer was never apprehended and that the police were unable to develop a motive for the killing.

The twelfth "victim" of the curse was the most spectacular. The seventy-eight-year-old Lord Westbury leapt to his death from a seven-story building near Buckingham Palace. He had been grieving over the strange death of his son, Richard Bethell, who had been Carter's personal secretary in the Valley. In 1929, young Bethell's body had been found slumped over in a chair at the fashionable Mayfair Club. The cause of his death was never determined. Like Evelyn White, Lord Westbury left behind a letter that served to promote belief in the "mummy's curse." "I really cannot stand any more horrors and I hardly see what good I am going to do here," he wrote. "So I am going to make my exit."

As a hearse bore the body of Lord Westbury to a crematorium (he had insisted on cremation to avoid being embalmed), the vehicle knocked down and killed an eight-year-old boy. And at this same time, Edgar Steele, a fifty-seven-year-old worker at the British Museum, a custodian in Budge's own department of Egyptological antiquities, died on the operating table in a London hospital.

By 1935, the number of "victims" attributed to Carter's discovery had risen to twenty-one. And just as Carnarvon had once received cables and letters from hucksters proposing various business arrangements for the commercial exploitation of his find, Carter received letters from cranks and others on how to deal with the curse. On dull days at Luxor, Arthur Merton, the London *Times* correspondent, dipped into Carter's mailbag and rarely failed to come up with a story. "The latest of these is a letter from a remote part of Ireland," Merton reported on one occasion, "recommending Mr. Carter, if there is any trouble, to shut the tomb and pour on it oil, wine and milk, when all will be well."

Some of the other recipes sounded as if they came from the witch's cauldron in *Macbeth*.

At first, Carter was reluctant to discuss the subject, apparently feeling that if he said nothing, the legend would fade away. But he finally broke silence by saying, "Rumours of a Tutankhamen curse are a libelous [*sic*] invention." At the British Museum, an official spokesman hurried to Carter's defense and observed that although thousands of persons had been indirectly associated with the Tutankhamen relics, there was no record of any overwhelming outbreak of mortality. "I've handled Egyptian relics myself many times, for years," the official told the press, "and I'm still as well as ever."

The museum of the University of Pennsylvania tried to put an end to the legend in a scientific way. A 1930 museum bulletin, prepared by Alan Rowe, a staff archaeologist, cited the excavation five years earlier of an Egyptian tomb plundered in 2800 B.C. The expedition had found a deep passageway choked with rubbish that led to the innermost chamber. The air in the passage was so bad that laborers could work in the tomb only about an hour each day. Even a short stay in the tomb produced a violent headache. In an experiment, lighted candles in the tomb were observed to expire after sixty or seventy minutes. Rowe attributed these phenomena to the lack of oxygen in the hypogeum and to the presence of carbon monoxide produced by the burning candles and by the crevices of the long-sealed chamber.

An individual who breathed such an atmosphere for too long a period, Rowe said, would not receive advance warning of its ill effects—carbon monoxide, of course, is odorless—but would simply collapse and die.

When a person is found dead in a garage, Rowe continued, the cause is attributed to carbon monoxide poisoning. When a similar fate befell a tomb worker in the modern era or a tomb robber in antiquity, "a guilty conscience and a lively imagination combined to attribute the deaths to a curse."

Three years later, the German Egyptologist Professor Georg Steindorff, director of the Egyptian Institute of the University of Leipzig, prepared a detailed monograph with a view to putting the curse to rest.* Steindorff had traced the deaths of the alleged victims of the curse and discovered that most of them had nothing to do with the tomb. He concluded that a "curse of the pharaohs" did not exist. He also demolished the tale, repeated in many versions of the curse, that Carter and Carnarvon had found an inscription in the tomb that warned, "Death shall come on swift wings to him that toucheth the tomb of the pharaoh." No such inscription was ever found.

Professor Jean Capart of the Royal Museum at Brussels, who also served as adjunct curator of Egyptology at the Brooklyn Museum, the same Capart who had defended Carnarvon's news arrangement with the London *Times*, supported Steindorff's analysis. The Belgian Egyptologist challenged those who wrote about the existence of the inscription "to give us a few particulars about the exact location of the text or to quote the book where a reproduction of it might be found." Nobody came forward with the information, and Capart dismissed the claim as "the product of the fancy of a storyteller in search of thrilling sensations."** He characterized the curse as "ridiculous."

Unfortunately for Carter, Rowe, Steindorff, Capart and others, Dr. Albert M. Lythgoe, friend of both Carnarvon and Carter, who was then curator emeritus of the Metropolitan Museum of Art's Egyptian collection, was hospitalized in 1934. According to newspaper reports, a team of specialists failed to agree on the nature of his malady. Lythgoe was described by the press as one of the few living survivors of the group that had attended the opening of the tomb. The switchboard of Boston's Massachusetts General Hospital was so flooded by telephone calls from a curious public

*See p. 138
**The inscription has become a hardy perennial. For example, in August 1975, a new book appeared, *The Curse of the Pharaohs*, which claimed that in Tutankhamen's tomb, along with the mummy and priceless treasures, Carter and his colleagues found "an ordinary clay tablet with this inscription: 'Death will slay with his wings whoever disturbs the peace of the pharaoh.'" Nonsense. Philipp Vandenberg, the author, gave no source for this claim.

that the operators were unable to conduct the hospital's regular business. Lythgoe died, and the "curse" had claimed another "victim." (Egyptologist Arthur Weigall also died that same year.)

Herbert E. Winlock, the director of the Metropolitan and Lythgoe's successor as curator of Egyptology, had for years declined to discuss the curse business in public for fear of lending credibility to the legend. But in light of the publicity accompanying Lythgoe's death, Winlock felt compelled to speak out against the curse as a "fiction."

In an interview in 1934, Winlock did more than any other archaeologist to debunk the myth by letting the hard figures speak for themselves:

On February 17, 1922, twenty-two persons were present at the official opening of the tomb. Of these, six had died by 1934. On February 12, 1924, twenty-two persons were present when the sarcophagus was opened. Of these, two had died during the next decade. On November 11, 1925, ten persons were present when the mummy was unwrapped. Of these, all were still alive.

As for Lythgoe, Winlock said, "There is nothing mysterious about his illness. He is suffering from cerebral arterio-sclerosis and has had a stroke. He is 66 years old, and in a precarious condition."

"The 'curse' is a superstition so wholly devoid of foundation," Winlock concluded, "that only the most credulous and ill-informed persons can give a moment's credence to it."

But what about persistent newspaper reports, including those in prominent newspapers, that twenty-odd persons associated with the discovery and opening of the tomb and sarcophagus had died? Bunk, Winlock said. Careful research showed only eight had died.*

Finally, he observed that "to the best of my knowledge, there is no inscription in the tomb or on any object inside it on which any curse was inscribed." Such inscriptions were simply not part of the Egyptian funerary tradition, he said, conceding that there was at least one such "curse" on record, an inscription found in the tomb of Amenhotep.

Roger Garis, an Egyptology buff, contended that Winlock had glossed over the curse found on the mummy case of Khapah Amen, a high priest whose mummy was discovered in 1879. "May the cobra on my head spit flames of fire into thy face, and may thy head be in the place of my feet" read a curse inscribed on his coffin. "Such a curse is the vengeance which is hidden in my body throughout all eternity, and which shall overtake whomsoever disturbs my body in its tomb. He or she shall have no grave, and after an arduous journey shall be attacked by wild beasts, and his or her bones shall be left to be washed by the falling rain."

According to Garis, Lord Harrington, a "collector" like the late Lord Carnarvon, acquired possession of Khapah Amen's mummy. Shortly thereafter, while on a hunting trip in the Sudan, Harrington was killed by an elephant. The safari party buried his body on the trail. Later, when an attempt was made to find the body so that it might be shipped to England, it was discovered that heavy rains had washed away the trail—and all trace of Harrington's remains.

While Carnarvon, Colonel Aubrey Herbert, and Lady Elizabeth Carnarvon may have fared poorly because of the curse, others of the House of Herbert enjoyed the

---

*Winlock weakened his case a bit in 1941. In a Metropolitan Museum of Art paper published that year, "Materials Used at the Embalming of King Tut-Ankh-Amun," he discussed Davis's 1907 find in the Valley, which Davis thought was the tomb of Tutankhamen. "Some old notes of mine," Winlock wrote, "tell of all the finders being dead within nine years of the excavations."

best of health. In a racy book called *Behind the Mask of Tutankhamen*, published in England four years ago, author Barry Wynne pointed out that Lady Evelyn Beauchamp, who was at her father's side when he entered the tomb for the first time, was still alive, a "sprightly and charming septuagenarian." Her brother, the present sixth earl of Carnarvon, who was at his father's side when he died, was just as sprightly and charming an octogenarian. Although they have had to put up with hearing about the curse most of their lives, they do not believe in it, Wynne wrote. (When asked if he would ever revisit the tomb, the sixth earl confessed, "Not for a million pounds!")

Inconceivably, perhaps, the legend of the curse recently acquired new stature and notoriety.

In 1966, at the urging of the French and with the approval of then President Gamal Abdel Nasser, Cairo shipped a collection of treasures from the Tutankhamen collection to Paris, where for the first time the objects were exhibited in the West. Mohammed Ibrahim, the director of the antiquities department, had strongly objected, but in the end he consented; he had no choice. He no sooner abandoned his opposition to the project, however, than his daughter was involved in a serious automobile accident and, in a state of despondency, he dreamed that he himself would meet a similar fate unless he blocked the removal of the treasures from the country. Ibrahim appealed to the government to reconsider its decision. In a final maneuver, he met with French officials in Cairo in the hope of getting them to withdraw President Charles de Gaulle's acceptance of Nasser's friendly gesture. They met on December 19, 1966, in Cairo. The French persuaded Ibrahim that, as a man of science, he should not treat superstitions and dreams so seriously, that there was nothing to the legend of the mummy's curse. Moreover, playing a political trump, they noted that only the previous year Nasser had cracked down on mystics and spiritualists in Egypt, branding them "antisocialist"—whatever that meant—and had at the same time officially denounced the curse of the pharaohs as myth. Apparently assuaged, Ibrahim left the conference with the French—he was struck by an automobile and died two days later from his injuries.

Two years later, a team of British radiologists, headed by Professor R. G. Harrison of Liverpool University, arrived in Egypt to X-ray the mummy of Tutankhamen in the hope of learning what had caused the young pharaoh's death. During their stay in Egypt, according to Harrison, the team was beset by "strange happenings." While the eight-man team worked in the Valley, the lights went out in Cairo, just as they had the night Carnarvon died. "And," Harrison said, "somebody connected with the research team died."

Something has been overlooked, perhaps, in the question of whether or not there is a curse on the tomb. Inside the third gold coffin, under the head-mask of the mummy, Carter and his assistants found a headrest made of iron. To the present, Egyptologists have regarded this object with special reverence. Like the blade of Tutankhamen's dagger, the headrest conclusively demonstrated that the Egypt of the Eighteenth Dynasty had crossed the threshold of the Bronze Age into the Iron Age, and all that that implies. But Egyptologists have been so engrossed with this spectacular discovery that they have failed to distinguish the forest from the trees.

In Carter's *The Tomb of Tut-ankh-amen*, Volume II, tucked away in Appendix II, which was written by his chemist friend Lucas and is appropriately entitled "The Chemistry of the Tomb," there is an innocent, short paragraph about the discovery of iron implements in the hypogeum. "*The iron* [Lucas's italics] are only three in number," he wrote, "namely a dagger-blade, part of an amuletic bracelet and a miniature head-rest, all of wrought iron."

In all my research on Tutankhamen's tomb, in Egypt and the West, only Penelope Fox, the assistant secretary of Oxford's Griffith Institute, where Carter's meticulous, handwritten card catalog of finds is stored, pointed out that in ancient Egyptian lore a coffin's headrest bore special significance. But she left the matter there and failed to draw further notice to a possible relationship between the headrest and the "legend of the mummy's curse."

The Book of the Dead, composed during the Eighteenth Dynasty, described the symbolic meaning of the mummy's headrest as follows: "Rise from non-existence, O prostrate one! . . . overthrow your enemies, triumph over what they do against you."

Epilogue

The discovery and excavation of the Tutankhamen tomb was, of course, the high point of Howard Carter's life—more of an escarpment than a peak, a plateau that lasted ten years. At 59, in early 1933, he completed the removal of the more than 2,000 objects he found in the hypogeum.

Like most men, Carter had plans that never materialized. He reconsidered his plan to explore Ethiopia; but, perhaps influenced by the gold he had found, he announced that he would instead search for the tomb of Alexander the Great. Carter was convinced that it was located in the environs of Alexandria, Egypt's great port city whose very name evoked memories of that imperishable conqueror. Many scholars were skeptical; unimaginatively, they argued that even if the tomb were found, no important relics would be recovered. According to tradition, the tomb was rifled first by Cleopatra to settle her debts and then by her Roman paramours, Caesar and Antony. But, just as Carter had been certain that Davis had not found Tutankhamen's tomb and that the Valley of the Tombs was not exhausted, he was convinced that Alexander's lost tomb could be uncovered. And he forecast that Alexander would be found entombed in a "coffin of pure gold."

But when the work in Tutankhamen's tomb was finished, as if on signal from Osiris, Carter took grievously ill. For the next six years he suffered in great torment and agony. On March 2, 1939, on the eve of his sixty-sixth birthday, a year that is best remembered for marking the outbreak of World War II, he died. The press, with whom he had feuded for years, was charitable. In death, he was universally characterized as a "great Egyptologist."

In truth, however, Carter was not thus accepted by the archaeological establishment of his time. He lacked formal training; he was self-taught. He had no old school tie. In the class-conscious Victorian and Edwardian England in which he reached his majority, his origins worked against him—he never truly came up from downstairs. After all, his father had painted animal pictures for the fox-and-hound crowd, who thought of him on a level only slightly above that of their stableboys.

Like his father, Howard Carter also was in the employ of the nobility. But it was not only his lack of formal education and his class origins that worked against him—it was also his explosive personality. Carter was essentially a self-contained loner, fiercely proud, fiercely independent of mind and sharp of tongue. He did not make friends easily.

In one respect, Carter's plight resembled that of Heinrich Schliemann, who unearthed the gold of Troy. Through archaeology, both men groped for social status. But Schliemann, the extrovert, was a crafty, worldly trader and skilled public relations practitioner in an age before the term was invented. Schliemann, who, perhaps more than any other individual, had a right to the sobriquet of "founder of modern archaeology," made certain that he was rewarded for his finding of fabled Troy. He was dined and wined by the kaiser in his native Germany and lionized in England, where he was a guest at No. 10 Downing Street and where he was accorded a doctor of canon law degree by Oxford University and was made an honorary fellow of Queen's College. By contrast, Carter never enjoyed an audience with either his king or prime minister, and no university in Britain bestowed upon him even an honorary degree.

The attitude of the Egyptological and English establishments is best mirrored in the assessment of Carter by his friend and colleague, Sir Wallis Budge, keeper of Egyptian antiquities at the British Museum. Sir Wallis said he possessed "very special qualifications for the work he undertook for Lord Carnarvon, namely, a good knowledge of colloquial Arabic, great experience in dealing with the natives [sic] and the 'antica' dealers in the country, [and was] skilled in the practical work of excavation." Budge also paid him the high compliment of being "a gentleman." But then Budge put him down forever, although he probably never thought of it that way. Carter, Budge said, possessed a "keen interest in Egyptian archaeology." So much for Carter's work over a span of forty-plus years in Egypt. He was not an Egyptologist.

Among the Egyptians, Carter fared no better with the elite than in his own country. In the Cairo Museum, the corridors are lined with busts of great and small Egyptologists, the giants and those "keenly interested in Egyptian archaeology," Brugsch, Mariette, Lepsius, Wilkinson, Maspero, and many others. Carter is conspicuously absent.

When I inquired about a bust of Carter (and of Carnarvon, who, if nothing else, most assuredly was "keenly interested"), I was told by an important Museum official, "Ah, the busts on display were all made before 1922." Perhaps. But in the courtyard I noticed, as I left the threadbare, rundown building, the latest addition to the collection, the bust of Zakharia Gnomeim, the splendid Egyptologist who died suddenly in 1959 at the age of 48, apparently a suicide.

Of even greater interest, on the second floor of the Museum, where the treasures of Tutankhamen are on display in a shabby and dingy setting—reflecting the economic strains and stresses through which Egypt passed during the turbulent Nasser period—a placard in three languages, Arabic, French, and English, retells the story of the discovery and excavation of the pharaoh's tomb. The names of Carter and Carnarvon do not once occur.

Egypt's treatment of the English explorers is explicable, given the spirit of troubled nationalism that has possessed the Nile for the past half century. But for England, a nation of explorers, the failure to honor one of its indefatigable sons is not so readily explicable.

Carter died at home, in physical agony but in peaceful surroundings, amid Egyptian artifacts, at Albert Court in the southwestern section of London. His last days attracted no such attention in the press as Carnarvon's had. At his death, the king sent no message.

In the retrospect of millennia, there was perhaps no one richer in experience nor more suited than Carter to have managed the excavation of the tomb; for that, Tutankhamen's ka should at least be grateful, even if Carter was the instrument of fate in shattering the hopefully eternal peace of its corporeal mold. It was as if thousands of years had to pass before the world produced a Carter to undertake the task of locating and restoring to Aten's rays the artistic triumphs of Tutankhamen's epoch. That it took Carter a decade to complete the excavation of the tomb is proof of his thoroughness, patience, and sincerity.

Four days after his death, on March 6, Carter was laid quietly to rest at Putney Vale Cemetery, a burial place now largely forgotten. Among those few on hand was Lady Evelyn Beauchamp, who had not forgotten. She remembered him well as the tempestuous figure from her girlhood, when she was her father's constant companion on his forays into Upper Egypt.

By coincidence, a month after Carter's death, following a silence of more than three thousand years, Tutankhamen's trumpets reverberated around the world. At the Cairo Museum, in an experiment that was broadcast live to every continent, the two trumpets Carter had found in the tomb, one of silver and the other of copper, were played. Described as shrill and piercing by those in attendance, in a poetic sense the three short blasts on each bugle were, fittingly, taps—Tutankhamen's farewell to Carter above the earth and his welcome to Carter below.

Carter's *ka*, eternally hovering in the twilight zone between light and darkness, was probably pleased.

AUTHOR'S NOTE

Manifestly, in the putting together of the story of Howard Carter's search and discovery of Tutankhamen's tomb, his own three volumes were the starting point. These are *The Tomb of Tut-ankh-amen: Discovered by the late Earl of Carnarvon and Howard Carter*, 3 volumes (London: Cassell, 1923, 1927, 1933). Volume 1 was written in collaboration with A. C. Mace, with photographs by Harry Burton; Volume 2 contained appendices by Douglas E. Derry, A. Lucas, P. E. Newberry, Alexander Scott, and H. J. Plenderleith, with photographs by Burton; and Volume 3 contained appendices by Derry and Lucas and, again, photographs by Burton. Somewhat pathetically, the title pages of Volumes 2 and 3 list Carter's only academic credentials, an honorary doctorate from Yale University and his appointment as "Correspondent," Real Academia de la Historia, Madrid; in Volume 2 particularly, they are lost in the alphabet soup of his collaborators.

Several editions have appeared since the original publication of his work. In 1963, Cooper Square Publishers, Inc., New York, reissued a complete set. In 1972, E. P. Dutton, New York, published an incomplete but ambitious set, with magnificent color plates (there were no color plates in the original edition), under the title *The Tomb of Tutankhamen*.

Since Carter's death in 1939, the copyright to his work has been held by Phyllis J. Walker, a niece. I sought to contact her through the Ashmolean Museum, Griffith Institute, Oxford, where Carter's files on the tomb are deposited. But the effort ended in failure. Helen Murray, a member of the Museum's staff, explained, "Miss Walker is still alive but, sadly, she is not able to conduct her own affairs any more."

Carter's index files and his accompanying field notes have had an ironic fate. In the very first line of Volume 1 of *The Tomb* . . . , Carter wrote: "This narrative of the discovery of Tut-ankh-amen is merely preliminary: a final record of purely scientific nature will take some time, nor can it be adequately made until the work of investigation of the tomb and its vast material has been completed." More than fifty years later, the final record is yet to be published.

In 1926, Carter estimated that its publication would cost about $150,000. In 1961, the aging Sir Alan Gardiner put the figure at $300,000. Today the production costs would probably be double that. And so, despite the tomb's being the richest find in the history of archaeology, no individual or institution has come forward to publish the final record. (What seems truly appalling is that the material is not even on microfilm for safekeeping.)

Although Carter's three volumes are a thousand pages in all, they are wholly inadequate as a record of the commotion surrounding the discovery. As he himself said, "This [is a] narrative of the discovery. . ." Indeed, it is. A very private person, he wrote little about the search and even less about the aftermath. It was as if he sought to expunge both from his mind just as Harmhab purposefully sought to obliterate the distinctive cartouches and ellipses of Tutankhamen.

Carter meant his work to be a monument not only to himself, but also to Lord Carnarvon. "I dedicate this account of the discovery of the tomb of Tut-ankh-amen to the memory of my beloved friend and colleague, Lord Carnarvon, who died in the hour of his triumph," he wrote in Volume 1. Carnarvon's effort to extend the knowledge of Egyptology, Carter concluded, "will ever be honoured in history, and by me his memory will always be cherished."

For an appreciation of Carter's trials during the search and his tribulations during the aftermath, I looked elsewhere.

Glimpses of him as a young man appear in Sir Flinders Petrie's *Seventy Years in Archaeology* (London: Low, Marston, 1931) and in the memoir Newberry wrote for the *Journal of Egyptian Archaeology*, XXV (1939). Early clues about the existence of the tomb of Tutankhamen turn up in two books by Theodore M. Davis, for whom Carter worked: *The Tomb of Thoutmosis IV* (Westminster: Constable, 1904), which Carter, Newberry, Gaston Maspero, and G. Elliot Smith coauthored, and *The Tombs of Harmhabi and Touatankhamanou* (London: Constable, 1912), coauthored by Maspero (now Sir Gaston), George Daressy, and Lancelot Crane. The latter volume contains Davis's famous declaration that he had found Tutankhamen's tomb and that the Valley of the Tombs of the Kings "is now exhausted."

Useful insight into a young Carter is also found in Carter's "Report on the Robbery of the Tomb of Amenhophis II, Biban-el-Moluk," which appeared in *Annals du Service des Antiquités de l'Egypte*, Volume III (Cairo, 1902). And material on Carter during World War I shows up in two papers Carter wrote for the *Journal of Egyptian Archaeology* as follows: "Report on the Tomb of Zesser-Ka-Ra Amenhetep I, Discovered by the Earl of Carnarvon in 1914" (Volume III, 1916) and "A Tomb Prepared for Queen Hatshepsut and other Recent Discoveries at Thebes" (Vol. IV, 1917).

Other primary material on Carter is found in *Pioneer to the Past: The Story of James Henry Breasted, Archaeologist* (New York: Scribner's, 1943) by Charles Breasted, who, like his father, was a close friend of Carter. *The Lost Pharaohs* by Leonard Cottrell (New York: Holt, Rhinehart and Winston, 1961) contains two chapters on Tutankhamen, including portions of a lengthy Sir Alan Gardiner interview about Carter and Carnarvon.

As for Carnarvon, the only material extant in his own hand is in his series of articles in *The Times* of London. These appeared between December 1922 and April 1923. Carnarvon's private papers were largely destroyed in the Blitz in 1940, a year after Carter's death. Lady Evelyn's biographical sketch of her father appeared in the original edition of Volume 1 of Carter's work, and a wealth of material about Highclere Castle appeared in the three-volume biography of Carnarvon's father, *The Life of Henry Howard Molyneux Herbert, Fourth Earl of Carnarvon* (London: Oxford, 1925) by Sir Arthur Hardinge.

For general works on Egyptology, in addition to the works listed above and in the text, the author is indebted to the authors and publishers of the following: *The Geography of Strabo* by Strabo, translated by Horace Leonard Jones and John Robert Sitlington Sterrett (Cambridge, Mass.: Harvard University Press, 1895); *The History of Herodotus* by Herodotus, translated by George Rawlinson (Chicago: University of Chicago Press, 1952); *Travels in Egypt, Arabia Petraea and the Holy Land,* Volume I, by the Rev. Stephen Olin (New York: Harpers, 1843); *Egypt as It Is* by J. C. McCoan (London: Cassell Petter & Galpin, 1877); Amelia B. Edwards's classics, *A Thousand Miles Up the Nile* (New York: Caldwell, 1878) and *Egypt and Its Monuments* (New York: Harpers, 1891); *The Literature of the Ancient Egyptians* by Adolf Erman, translated by Aylward M. Blackman (London: Bloom, 1927); the works of the extraordinary American Egyptologist James Henry Breasted, especially his five-volume *Ancient Records of Egypt* (Chicago: University of Chicago Press, 1906), *Development of Religion and Thought in Ancient Egypt* (New York: Scribner's, 1912), and *Dawn of Conscience* (New York: Scribner's, 1934); the prolific writings of Sir Ernest A. Wallis Budge, many of whose classics from the turn of the century are currently available in paperback from Dover, New York, including *Osiris and the Egyptian Resurrection, Egyptian Magic, Gods of the Egyptians*; Sir Charles Leonard Woolley's *Digging Up the Past* (London: Penguin, 1937); H. R. Hall's *The Ancient History of the Near East* (London: Methuen, 1963, 11th ed.), a comprehensive survey of the region to the battle of Salamis; *Ancient Egypt: Its Culture and History* (New York: Dover, 1970) by J. E. Manchip White; *Egypt of the Pharaohs* by Sir Alan Gardiner (London: Oxford, 1961); *The World of Archaeology*, Volume II by Marcel Brion, translated by Neil Mann (New York: Macmillan, 1961); and M. Zakaria Gnomeim's *The Lost Pyramid* (New York: Rhinehart, 1956).

As for the books that deal specifically with Tutankhamen, among the best are *The Shrines of Tut-Ankh-Amon* by Alexandre Piankoff (New York: Harpers, 1955), which contains a translation of the hieroglyphics that covered the shrines found by Carter in the tomb; *When Egypt Ruled the East* by Georg Steindorff and Keith C. Seele (Chicago: University of Chicago Press, 1942), which lists objects found in the tomb; *Tutankhamun's Treasure* by Penelope Fox (London: Oxford, 1951); *Tutankhamen* by G. Elliott Smith (London: Routledge, 1923); *From Joseph to Joshua* by H. H. Rowley (London: Oxford, 1950); *The Date of the Exodus* by J. W. Jack (Edinburgh: Clark, 1925); and *Tutankhamen and Egyptology* by Samuel A. B. Mercer (Milwaukee: Morehouse, 1923); *A Century of Excavation in the Land of Pharaohs* by James Baikie (London: Religious Tract Society, 1974); *A Brief Description of the Principal Monuments, The Egyptian Museum* (Cairo: Institut Français d'Archéologie Orientale, 1931); *A Brief Description of the Principal Monuments, The Egyptian Museum* (Cairo: General Organization for Government Printing Office, 1968), which contains a complete list of the objects from the tomb on display today at the Cairo Museum; *Lights on the Royal Mummies in the Egyptian Museum* by Ahmed Ragab Mohamed (Cairo: Dar el-Kita el-Arabi, 1964); and *A Brief Study of Mummies and Mummification* by H. S. K. Bakry (Cairo: Al-Takaddum Press, 1965). In Upper Egypt, I found *The Latest Pocket Guidebook to Luxor and Environment* [*sic*], including *Tut-Ankh-Amen* (Luxor: Gaddis, 1973) especially useful.

In *Gods, Graves and Scholars* by C. W. Ceram (New York: Knopf, 1951), the author quoted from a monograph of Georg Steindorff refuting the legend of the mummy's curse. In vain I searched for a copy; in a private letter, Dr. R. Krauspe, Fachgruppe Ägyptologie, Karl Marx Universität, Leipzig (the former University of Leipzig), wrote that the university's bibliographic index did not list any such monograph, which, according to Ceram, was written in the early thirties.

Others besides Dr. Krauspe have come to my rescue with answers to queries. Among them are Professor Edward F. Wente, Egyptologist, University of Chicago, who replied to a query on a Breasted reference to Carter; Christine Lilyquist, curator, Department of Egyptian Art, Metropolitan Museum of Art, who uncovered the original exchange of cables between Carter and the Museum when the former appealed for help in 1922; Dr. R. G. Harrison, Department of Anatomy, the University of Liverpool, who sent me a copy of his provisional reports on the reexamination of Tutankhamen's mummy in 1968; Mary Kohn, indefatigable reference librarian, Ruth A. Haas Library, Western Connecticut State College, where I serve on the adjunct graduate faculty; the library's director, Robert M. Blaisdell, who permitted me on several occasions to remove microfilm for photographic purposes; my editor, Margaret B. Parkinson; and my typist of many years, Isabelle Bates. Newspapers were an indispensable source of information, especially on the aftermath, particularly Egyptian, British, and American journals. To the Egyptian press, I am especially grateful for the assistance I received in Cairo from Talat Ibrahim, chief of periodicals, National Library of Egypt.

I am also grateful to the following for permission to quote from their copyright: *The Times* of London, which permitted me to use the Carnarvon-Carter dispatches, and Scribner's, New York, which permitted me to quote from *Pioneers of the Past*, 1943, which contained the Breasted correspondence. Cassell, London, was the original publisher of Carter's work and suggested I use the material "giving our edition acknowledgment as the source, with an additional note stating that you endeavored to trace the copyright owner but were unable to do so." The explanation is that Cassell's archives were destroyed during the Blitz and "it is, therefore, impossible for us to establish the copyright situation."

Researching the subject would have been incomplete without a visit to Luxor, where I lodged in the old Winter Palace Hotel; took the S. S. *Abu El Haggag* across the Nile to the west bank; visited Carter's house; walked around Carnarvon's locked-up house; traveled along the sinuous road, glistening with white marble chips, that led into the Valley of the Tombs of the Kings; and, ultimate of ultimates, descended the sixteen white steps, now protected by wooden scaffolding, into the tomb of Tutankhamen, crossing in life into the world of the dead. There I gazed on the rose-colored sarcophagus and mummiform coffin that contained the mummy of the young king. During this phase of my journey I was fortunate to have the company of Nasif Bestauros Jounan, a retired history teacher and Egyptology hobbyist who possesses a working knowledge of hieroglyphics. A Coptic (a Christian descendant of the native Egyptians), he was especially eloquent on the relationship between Egyptian religion and the Old and New Testaments.

None of the individuals listed above or quoted below are in any way responsible for what I have written.

Despite Carter's discovery and the endless inquiry into Tutankhamen's Eighteenth Dynasty, the world today knows as much about Tutankhamen, his life, and times, as the day Carter unwrapped the mummy—virtually nothing. When and where Tutankhamen was born is not known. Nor is the identity of his father known. When and how he died is also unknown. This ignorance points up the biggest disappointment in Carter's work: the failure to recover so much as a shred of papyrus from the hypogeum. As a consequence, nothing substantive was added or subtracted from contemporary knowledge about Tutankhamen except that he represented the transition from the worship of Aten to a return to the worship of Amen and the other gods and that the Eighteenth Dynasty was already into the Iron Age. In particular, nothing was added to our knowledge about Akhenaten's heresy and the relationship, if any, between Akhenaten and Tutankhamen and between them and the Exodus of the Old Testament.

In 1923, Samuel Mercer, a professor of Semitic languages and Egyptology at Trinity College, Toronto, mirrored the general dismay of scholars. "The objects so far discovered in Tutankhamen's tomb have never before been equalled in richness and . . . called forth the wonder and admiration of the world. But with all their value and artistic worth, they have not added one word to our historical knowledge of ancient Egypt. Not one inscription of any value has been found, not a single papyrus has come to light."

But that same year, in a book dedicated to the late Lord Carnarvon, *Tutankhamen: Amenism, Atenism and Egyptian Monotheism* (New York: Dodd, Mead, 1923), Sir Wallis Budge hinted that papyri may have been found in the tomb. In an extract from a letter Carnarvon wrote him from Egypt on December 1, 1922, the earl said he wanted to write "one line just to tell you that we have found the most remarkable 'find' that has ever been made, I expect, in Egypt or elsewhere." Enthusiastically, Carnarvon described what he had seen in the first two chambers. "I have not opened the boxes, and don't know what is in them," he said, "*but there are some papyri letters*, faience, jewelry, bouquets, candles in ankh candlesticks. All this is in [the] front chamber, besides lots of stuff you can't see." (Italics added.) Commenting on the letter, Budge observed that ". . . the tomb of Tutankhamen and its contents include no new historical facts."

And then he added speculatively, "Lord Carnarvon may have obtained from the tomb information that would amplify our knowledge of the reign of Tutankhamen, but if he did so he did not publish it."

Did Carter and Carnarvon find papyri in the tomb? If so, did they suppress them? This hardly seems likely, given Carter's obsession with integrity. For Carter to suppress a discovery would have been wholly, inexplicably out of character. For that matter, the same may be said of Carnarvon. One must assume, therefore, that in the general excitement of discovery, articles that appeared to be rolls of papyri were simply something else. Yet the Carnarvon letter is intriguing, for all the other objects he listed were found in the tomb and later exhibited.

But if, just for the sake of discussion, something were suppressed, what could it conceivably have been? The only plausible material of a highly combustible nature would be evidence about the relationship between the two great monotheists of that millennium, Akhenaten—Tutankhamen's father and/or father-in-law—and Moses (as discussed later).

Carter's failure to recover papyri from the tomb has not tempered, however, the imaginative license of researchers. In her *Life and Death of a Pharaoh: Tutankhamen* (New York: Graphic Society, 1963), Christiane Desroches-Noblecourt provides a breathtaking display of erudition that leaves the reader exhausted—and confused. On the one hand, she observes that the death of Tutankhamen's predecessor, Smenkhare, was "preceded or followed" by the death of Akhenaten, exhibiting understandable doubt in the face of a lack of hard evidence; a page later she employs such phrases as "it was certain" and "there is no doubt" in developing a grandiose complot between Tutankhamen's grand vizier, Ay, and the pharaoh's general, Harmhab, both of whom later ascended the red-and-white, cobra-and-vulture throne as kings. Yet there is not a scrap of evidence to support her thesis of a plot.

But if Desroches-Noblecourt, an eminent Egyptologist, is swept away by her mind's eye, Immanuel Velikovsky's *Oedipus and Akhnaton* (New York: Doubleday, 1960) is overwhelmed by imagination. Velikovsky concludes that the Oedipus of the Greek legend, the parricide who sired children by his mother, was none other than Akhenaten and that Tutankhamen was his son and that by marrying Ankhesenpaaton, Tutankhamen married his sister or half sister. Queen Tiy, according to this version, is Akhenaten's mother and Ay's brother. Further, Smenkhare and Tutankhamen were brothers, sired by Akhenaten and his mother. Thus, Smenkhare is the Polynices of the Greek legend and Tutankhamen the Eteocles. Accuracy aside (and who can truly say?), Velikovsky's work is nothing short of intellectually dazzling.

Six years after Velikovsky's thesis was published, R. G. Harrison, professor of anatomy, the University of Liverpool, undertook the anatomical reexamination of the remains of a body found by Theodore Davis in the Valley in 1907. Davis and others thought it to have been the remains of Akhenaten. But Derry later concluded that the remains bore such a striking similarity to those of Tutankhamen, whom he X-rayed in the tomb, with Carter at his elbow, that he suggested that the remains were those of Smenkhare, and not Akhenaten, and that Tutankhamen had been his brother.

Following his own examination, Harrison confirmed that "the reconstructed remains bore a striking resemblance to Tutankhamen as depicted on the mummiform coffins, but no resemblance whatsoever to Akhenaten in the art of the period." This meant that Tutankhamen and Smenkhare may have been brothers after all and that Akhenaten is yet to be discovered. "A reappraisal of the anatomical and radiological features of Tutankhamen is urgently necessary, and it is to be hoped that such an investigation may be made possible in the not-too-distant future," Harrison wrote in the *Journal of Egyptian Archaeology* (Vol. LII, 1966).

Impressed with Harrison's conclusion, Cairo granted him permission for the reappraisal, on the condition that Tutankhamen's remains not be removed from the tomb. Thus, on December 4, 1968, for the first time since 1926, when Carter and Derry replaced the mummy in the outermost coffin, living men again gazed on the features of Tutankhamen.

When Carter had returned the coffin to the sarcophagus forty-two years earlier, he replaced the cover of the sarcophagus with a protective sheet of glass 6 mm. thick. Just as Carter had struggled within the confines of the tomb to disassemble the shrines and coffins, Harrison and his team reported that removing the sheet of glass "was no mean task in the confines of the small tomb." During the operation, one corner of the sheet was broken off; a British firm replaced the glass free of charge with a sheet of its 10 mm. armor-plate glass.

When Harrison and his colleagues finally opened the lid of the coffin, they found that Carter had left his calling card, a quaint discovery, impish and out of character.

The fresh linen bandages with which Carter rewrapped the mummy were removed. Harrison's people were a bit surprised. "It was immediately obvious that the mummy is not in one piece," he reported. The head and neck were separated from the trunk and the limbs were detached from the torso and broken in many places, perhaps as a result of trying to pry the mummy free from the sticky black resin that originally stuck it fast to the coffin. The resin, Harrison observed, still exuded, after almost 3,500 years, a sweet odor. The remains were X-rayed; in addition, a radioisotope, I_{125}, suggested by the British Atomic Energy Commission, was injected into the mummy's lip as a tracer.

Derry had postulated that Tutankhamen probably died from tuberculosis, but this was not borne out by radiology. There were rumors that Harrison discovered a small hole in the cranium and suspected Tutankhamen died of foul play or an accident. In a private communication last spring, Harrison wrote: "There was no hole to be discovered in the cranium of Tutankhamun [*sic*] but the radiological appearances suggest that there is a healed depressed fracture in the left temporal region, which could have resulted from an accident such as falling from a horse or chariot."

An analysis of the tissues of Tutankhamen and the 1907 remains, by serological micromethods, showed conclusively that both mummies possessed the same blood groups. Harrison's team concluded that there was between the two remains "a relationship sufficiently close as to suggest that the two pharaohs are brothers." This, of course, was Velikovsky's speculation. In any event, in a coauthored preliminary report that appeared in *Antiquity* (XLVI, 1972), Harrison and Dr. A. B. Abdalla, professor of anatomy at the University of Cairo, wrote of Tutankhamen, "All present at the exposure of the king's remains agreed with Howard Carter's description of a 'refined and cultured face' and a 'serene and placid countenance.' "

As technology improves, archaeologists and historians may be compelled to make major revisions in the chronology of the Egyptian king lists. This was demonstrated most recently in *X-Raying the Pharaohs: The most important breakthrough in Egyptology since the discovery of Tutankhamen's tomb* by James E. Harris and Kent R. Weeks (New York: Scribner's, 1973), a preliminary report based on the University of Michigan's expeditions to Egypt. X-rays proved that the previous calculations of the ages at which various pharaohs died are incorrect and that "therefore parts of the chronology of ancient Egypt will have to be altered, in some cases drastically." The misleading subtitle notwithstanding, the expedition has not yet examined the mummy of Tutankhamen.

In retrospect, the two most important results of Carter's exploratory activities were in bringing to light the fantastically exquisite art of Egypt's Eighteenth Dynasty and in focusing renewed attention on Akhenaten's heresy and a possible relationship between Akhenaten and Moses.

As for art, on January 18, 1923, Sir Wallis Budge, a facile writer, said of the articles Carter recovered from the tomb: "Their beauty is unique and indescribable." Since then, the appraisal has not changed.

In 1974–1975, art critic Diana Loercher of *The Christian Science Monitor* asked directors of some of the world's major art museums a challenging question: "If you could have any five of the world's art treasures for your personal collection, which ones would you choose?" The first respondent, Thomas P. F. Hoving of New York's Metropolitan Museum, put the bust of Nefertiti, Tutankhamen's mother-in-law, up front. "It's impossible, of course, to choose only five, but if I must I must," he said.* In the same *Monitor* series, René de Roo, the director of Brussels' Royal Museums of Art and History, selected among his five pieces the solid gold funerary mask of Tutankhamen: "Because of its perfection this mask represents to me all the qualities of Egyptian art," he said.

As for the Akhenaten-Moses relationship, Carter's discovery rekindled a volatile debate among archaeologists, Biblical scholars, and historians. The core issue was ostensibly the relationship, if any, between Tutankhamen and Exodus; but it soon gave way to a more heated dispute over that between Akhenaten and Moses. In the long run, the Tutankhamen discovery merely served to widen divergence among the three major schools of thought on the matter.

The traditional school rests its case primarily on two pieces of evidence. (1) In Exodus 1: 11, the Israelites are said to have built the "treasure cities" of Pithom and Rameses during their sojourn in Egypt. References to these cities suggest that the Israelites were still in bondage during the reign of Rameses in the Nineteenth Dynasty. (2) In 1896, Petrie found the pharaoh Merneptah's victory stele, on which the name *Israel* was mentioned for the first and only time in Egyptian annals; Breasted cautioned that this was perhaps an "accident of preservation." Merneptah, a successor of Rameses II, ruled circa 1290/1233 B.C. "Unless we deny the historical accuracy of Ex. 1: 11," wrote A. H. Sayce, the Oxford scholar, "the date of Exodus is definitely fixed." But to accept the Bible's accuracy, as do many other authorities, including the *Jewish Encyclopaedia*, is shattering. Akhenaten and Tutankhamen, of course, belonged to the Eighteenth Dynasty. If the Old Testament is accurate, Akhenaten, the heretic pharaoh who preached monotheism, was the precursor of Moses.

Out of this startling conclusion arises a second school of thought whose most eloquent champion is Breasted. In his *Dawn of Conscience*, referred to previously, Breasted directed attention to the striking parallels between Akhenaten's hymn to the sun and Psalm 104, and to other parallels between Egyptian religious texts and the Old Testament, notably the Proverbs. Breasted then drew the revolutionary conclusion that Akhenaten was the pathfinder in the recognition of one God, a universal Creator of all men.

"In a world where might had always made right and power was the supreme word, the Egyptian social dreamer looked beyond actual conditions and dared to believe in an age of ideal justice," Breasted wrote. "When the Hebrew prophet caught the splendor of this vision and rose to a higher level he was standing on the Egyptian's shoulders." Thus, Breasted concluded, "Our moral heritage therefore derives from a wider *human* past enormously older than the Hebrews, and it has come to us rather *through* the Hebrews than *from* them." (Breasted's italics.)

Another Egyptologist, of lesser authority, Arthur Weigall, took the analysis further. He

---

*The bust of Nefertiti was excavated in Egypt by Ludwig Borchardt, the German Egyptologist, in 1912, while Carter and Carnarvon were searching for Tutankhamen's tomb. It became the centerpiece of the Berlin Museum, rivaled only by the gold of Troy found by Schliemann. On March 28, 1945, the sculpture was spirited out of Berlin and hidden in a coal shaft near Helmstedt. After the war, it reappeared in a Dahlem museum and was later moved to the museum at Charlottenburg. When Naguib and Nasser overthrew the Egyptian monarchy in 1952–1953, while rummaging through the treasures collected by ex-King Farouk, they came across the diamond-studded baton of Field Marshal von Brauchitsch, former commander in chief of the German armies during World War II. Egypt offered to swap the baton for the bust, but the West Germans declined the trade. Last year, the East Germans demanded that the bust be handed over to them because the Berlin Museum was located in the city's eastern sector. Bonn balked.

linked Exodus with Akhenaten's revolution and believed the Israelites were driven out of Egypt at the end of Tutankhamen's reign by Harmhab, the general who later proclaimed himself pharaoh. Weigall's case is stated in his *Tutankhamen and Other Essays* (London: Butterworth, 1923) and *The Life and Times of Akhenaton* (London: Blackwoods, 1923). According to Weigall, the Israelites were not only implicated in Akhenaten's heresy, but may even have caused it. When the old religion of Amen and the other gods was restored at Thebes under Tutankhamen and secured more drastically under his successors, notably Ay and Harmhab, the Israelites were ill-treated, persecuted, and ultimately "thrust out of Egypt" (Exodus 12:39). "I need not point out how wide an area of thought is opened up by this supposition that Moses lived through the Aton heresy," Weigall wrote in his *Tutankhamen*, "for the question as to what connection there was between the Hebrew monotheism and this earliest known monotheism of the Egyptians will at once present itself to the reader."

Agreeing with this school was Sigmund Freud. In his last book, *Moses and Monotheism* (New York: Knopf, 1939), Freud described himself as thinking the unthinkable. Moses, the liberator of the Israelites, who gave them their religion and laws, was, Freud speculated, an Egyptian who had formerly been an aide to Akhenaten.

Freud reasoned that with Akhenaten's death, the old priesthood at Thebes, which Akhenaten had suppressed, vented their fury on his memory. The Aten religion was proscribed; Akhenaten's capital city, Akhetaton, was leveled. The pharaoh's reforms seemed to be but an incident in Egyptian history, doomed to be forgotten. At this juncture, Freud gave rein to imagination. He believed Moses was a zealot who looked to Akhenaten for inspiration and leadership. In disappointment and loneliness at the turn of events, Moses addressed himself to the strangers (Israelites) dwelling in Egypt and sought in them a compensation for what he had lost when Akhenaten died and his religious concept was mercilessly crushed. "He [Moses] chose them for his people and tried to realize his own ideals through them," Freud suggested. He gave them the Aten religion, which the Egyptians had just discarded. "With an astonishing premonition of later scientific knowledge he [Akhenaten] recognized in the energy of the sun's radiation the source of all life on earth and worshiped the sun as the symbol of his God's power," Freud said. "He gloried in his joy in the Creation and in his life in Maat [truth, i.e., harmony]. It is the first case in the history of mankind, and perhaps the purest, of a monotheistic religion."

Thus, Freud expressed the opinion that Exodus occurred during the Eighteenth Dynasty—Tutankhamen's—and not the Nineteenth Dynasty of the Old Testament. Parenthetically, it should be noted here that Breasted, Freud, and others of this school expressed alarm at putting their thoughts to paper in the thirties, as the manic Hitler consolidated his murderous rule. "In a world in which anti-Semitic prejudice is still regrettably evident, it seems appropriate to state that the book was not written with the slightest anti-Semitic bias," wrote Breasted, who taught Hebrew in university classes and had among his students many future rabbis. "On the contrary, the author's admiration of Hebrew literature, which began in his boyhood, has always been such that his judgment of it was much more likely to be affected by a favorable bias than otherwise."

Just as the first school of thought, deriving its strength from the Old Testament, gave rise to the second school, the latter in turn gave rise to a third, the best summary of which appears in J. W. Jack's *The Date of the Exodus: In the Light of External Evidence* (Edinburgh: Clark, 1925). According to Jack, the Exodus did take place during the Eighteenth Dynasty, but at its outset, in 1445 B.C., rather than at its end. This would have been during the long reigns of Tuthmosis II and his son, Amenhotep II, a view in general agreement with such standard works as the late H. R. Hall's *The Ancient History*. . . . This conclusion is based on letters found at Akhenaten's capital city and the attack on Egypt by nomadic tribes called Habiru [Hebrews?] during this period. But Jack is not dogmatic about it. "This does not mean that the Exodus may not have taken place shortly before or after." If this school of thought is correct, Moses was the precursor, rather than the follower, of Akhenaten.

Some Biblical scholars and Egyptologists modify one or the other of the principal theories. They conclude that the Exodus took place over a long period—perhaps, as Mercer observed in his *Tutankhamen*—in the course of 200 years, "as such movements of people do." The Hebrews left Egypt as the occasion offered itself, the main body departing in the time of Merneptah, which is in accord with known archaeological facts. Mercer concluded that "there is, therefore, a general sense in which it may be that Tutankhamen was *a* pharaoh of *an* exodus of Hebrews from Egypt." But, he added, "the 'Pharaoh of the Exodus' as we know him in the Old Testament was not at all Tutankhamen but Merneptah, the son and successor of Rameses the Great." In Mercer's view, Akhenaten came before Moses; he described the Egyptian ruler as "endowed with poetic fancy and religious zeal . . . a great religious reformist."

A generation later, in 1950, in *From Joseph to Joshua*, Rowley also rejected the view of a single Exodus. He believed Joseph entered Egypt during the reign of Akhenaten, under whom he rose to high office in 1370 B.C. The oppression was more severe under Rameses II, and Moses, who was born in 1290 B.C., led the main body of Hebrews from Egypt in 1230 B.C. Rowley's view of Akhenaten is sympathetic: "No pharaoh would be more ready to welcome ministers from unusual sources than Ikhnaton [Akhenaten], and more than one indication in the Joseph story points to this age."

J. Marquat, the Semitic linguist, pointed out that the name of the wife given to Joseph by the pharaoh was, according to the Old Testament, Asenath. He speculated that it might have been a corruption of the name of Akhenaten's second daughter, Ankhesenpaaton, who later became Tutankhamen's wife.

Obviously, there is much work to be done in sorting out the pieces.*

Yet it is interesting to note that in some quarters of contemporary Egyptology, Akhenaten is so denounced as a "criminal" that one would think we were still living in ancient Egypt. Cyril Aldred, who has written extensively on Akhenaten, in *The Egyptians* (New York: Praeger, 1961) regards his reforms as "disastrous" and "insane." William C. Hayes, in *The Scepter of Egypt*, Volume II (Cambridge, Mass.: Harvard University Press, 1959), which provides background for the study of Egyptian antiquities at the Metropolitan, describes Akhenaten as "physically weak and unprepossessing, with a frail, effeminate body and an emaciated, lantern-awed face . . . nothing of either the soldier or the statesman." Hayes further contended that "with little or no ethical content, it is difficult to see how the Aten cult can be presumed to have been a forerunner of Judaism and Christianity," and he dismisses Akhenaten as a "religious fanatic" whose monotheist vision contained no significance in the history of world religion. In a related assessment, the French Egyptologist Georges Lefebvre put down Akhenaten as a transvestite. The aforementioned Hall, former keeper of Egyptian antiquities at the British Museum, wondered aloud if Akhenaten was not demented. "Certainly Akhenaten was the first doctrinaire in history," he wrote, "and, what is much the same thing, the first prig." Velikovsky, who appeared dismayed at the suggestion that Akhenaten may have been the forerunner of Moses, in *Ages of Chaos: From the Exodus to King Akhenaten* (New York: Doubleday, 1952) thought the confusion surrounding the date of the Exodus resulted from the failure of Egyptologists to recognize that "Egyptian history must be revised and moved forward more than half

---

*And the sorting out continues. On February 21, 1976, in a spectacular development, Prof. Donald B. Redford, the Canadian director of the University of Pennsylvania's Ikhnaton Project, announced the discovery—after nine years of research and exploration—of the foundation stones of an Akhenaten temple built at Thebes in the name of Aten, the masterbuilder of the universe. This may prove man's first monotheistic house of worship. One day, I believe, Egyptologists will recover Akhenaten papyri whose contents will outrival the Dead Sea scrolls.

a thousand years." In Velikovsky's bid to demolish Akhenaten, he out-Freuded Freud. "Were it possible for King Akhnaton to cross the time barrier and lie down on an analyst's couch," Velikovsky wrote in *Oedipus and Akhnaton*, "the analysis would at an early state reveal autistic or narcissistic traits, a homosexual tendency, with sadism suppressed and feminine traits coming to the fore and a strong, unsuppressed Oedipus complex." In baseball, that would be known as touching all bases.

In contrast, Sir Alan Gardiner, the impeccable Egyptologist, characterizing Akhenaten as a "genuine monotheist," wrote: "It is in the moral courage with which the reformer strove to sweep away the vast accumulation of mythological rubbish inherited from the past that his true greatness lay."

Taking a mid-position, Sir Wallis Budge may have been closest to the truth. "It was fortunate for Egypt that she only produced one king who was an individualist and idealist, a pacifist and religious 'reformer' all in one," he wrote in *Tutankhamen: Amenism, Atenism and Egyptian Monotheism*. "Amenhotep IV [Akhenaten] attempted to establish a positive religion, and as a religious innovator he spoke and acted as if he were divinely inspired and had a divine revelation to give men, and in every way he tried to depart from the traditions and religious instincts and susceptibilities that already existed among the Egyptians, and because he would not tolerate the traditional forms in which their spiritual feelings were embodied."

Akhenaten's remains are yet to be found, or, if found, they have yet to be identified. The same is true of other important figures from the Eighteenth Dynasty, from Tutankhamen's lovely wife, Ankhesenpaaton, to Ay and Harmhab. Meanwhile, speculation continues.* In *Pensée* (Vol. 2, No. 2, May 1972), a journal that promotes Velikovsky's theories, Lewis Greenberg, who teaches the history of art at Franklin and Marshall College, endorsed Velikovsky's controversial thesis that the planet Venus, as a comet, joined the earth's solar system at the time of Akhenaten's rule. Greenberg went on to say that Akhenaten's representation of Aten, the solar disk, shows rays emanating in arcuated fashion from one side only, as with a comet's tail, and raised the question of "whether this suggests the existence of linguistic and cosmological relationships between the name Aten and that of the Greek tutelary deity, Athena, herself associated with Venus." And in his latest book, *Akhenaten and Nefertiti* (New York: Viking, 1974), Aldred suggests that Akhenaten's wife Nefertiti was viewed by the ancient Egyptians as a Venus figure.

Clearly, up to now the story of Tutankhamen and the great Eighteenth Dynasty is incomplete, inadequate, and unsatisfactory. The conflicting theories set out above cannot and will not be reconciled until further hard evidence is forthcoming. That evidence must come, can only come, from below the earth, from archaeology. Beneath the protecting sands, the answers surely await the spade: Other tombs? Other treasures? Papyri?

As the tools and techniques of archaeology improve, present-day Egyptologists increasingly echo the confidence of Amelia Edwards, who wrote in 1891: "The mine [Egypt] is never exhausted. I will go yet further and say that this mine is practically inexhaustible."

"We cannot say the Valley is exhausted," Abdulkadir Selim, the director general of the Cairo Museum told me in an interview in 1975. "There is always the possibility of a new find." Dr. Francis Abdul Malik Ghattas, an Egyptologist at the Center of Documentation, appropriately located on Cairo's Rameses Street, endorsed Selim's sentiment: "Who can say what may happen in the future—we live in a mysterious world. Most finds are by accident."

---

*And so does the uneasy fate of the Tutankhamen treasures in today's world. With the outbreak of World War II and the Nazis at the gates of Cairo, the Tutankhamen sarcophagus, jewels, and other art objects were packed in forty cases and hidden in bombproof cellars thirty feet underground to protect them from destruction. In 1973, during the Yom Kippur War, with Israel then at the gates of Cairo (shades of Merneptah!) the treasures were repacked and "removed to a safe place for protection."

Dr. Gamal Eddine Moukhtar, secretary of state in the Egyptian ministry of culture and president of the Egyptian Antiquities Organization, told me, "I think there are still kings of the new empire whose tombs have not yet been discovered," a remark that prompted a colleague, Professor Abdulbaker of Cairo University, to interject, "We want to think there are other tombs in the area, if not of kings, then surely of princes and other members of high nobility." And a leading authority on the Valley, Dr. Labib Habachi of the Institute of Egypt, said, "I do not think the Valley is exhausted. If systematic work is done, something may yet be found."

In Upper Egypt, close by the Valley itself, where Tutankhamen continues to sleep in his outer mummiform coffin, Mohammed el-Sakher, who holds the job Carter once had as inspector of antiquities for Upper Egypt, pondered the question I put to him. "The chances of a new discovery? One per cent. It depends on luck. That is the great dream of all the people who work here—to make another Tutankhamen discovery." Similarly, the inspector of antiquities for Karnak, Abdul Hamid el-Daly, who inherited Carter's bleak house on the west bank of the Nile, said, "Really, no one knows whether or not the Valley is exhausted."

At this writing, one Egyptologist has received permission to excavate in the Valley under the tomb of Rameses IX. As Habachi put it, "He thinks there is reason to believe that there is something under the Rameses tomb." Tutankhamen's tomb, of course, was found situated beneath the tomb of Rameses VI.

The Color Plates

3. Burial Chamber, east wall: the royal catafalque on a sledge
   drawn by court officials in ceremonial procession.

4. Burial Chamber, west wall: the solar boat, divinities, and squatting baboons evoking Thoth, god of the moon and magic.

The Shrines

15. Shrine IV, the innermost, in the form of the primitive coronation Sanctuary of the North, *Per-Nu*, the House of Flame.

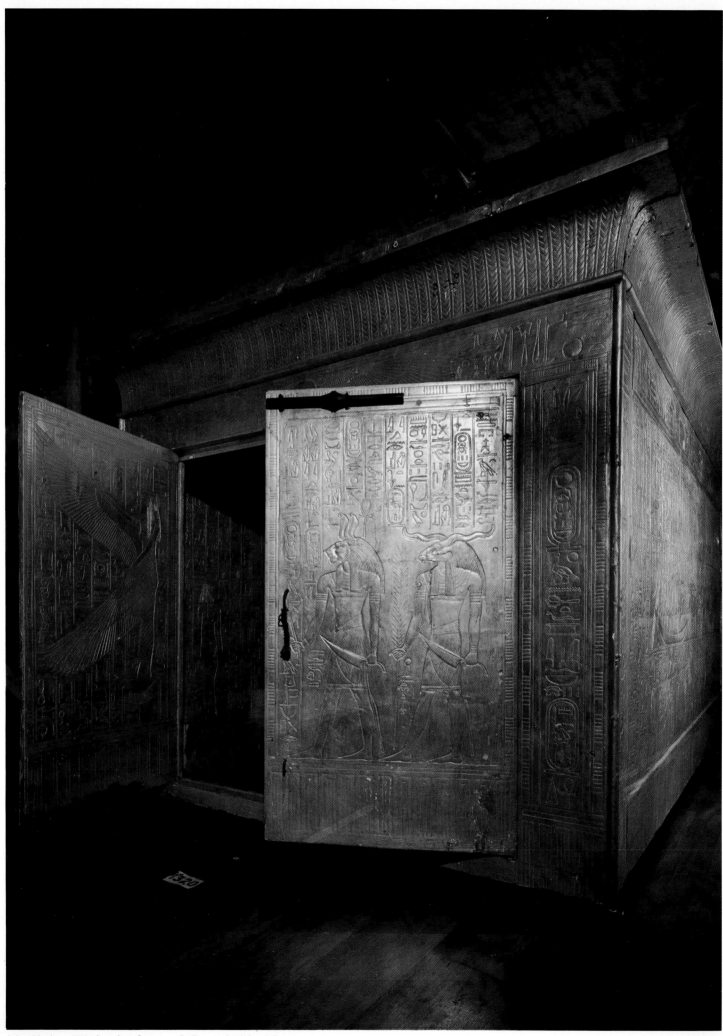

16. Shrine III, in the form of the primitive Sanctuary
of the South, *Per-Wer*, the Great House.

17. The goddesses Isis and Nephthys, on interior rear
    panel of Shrine III.

18. Guardian divinities, on exterior left door of Shrine III.

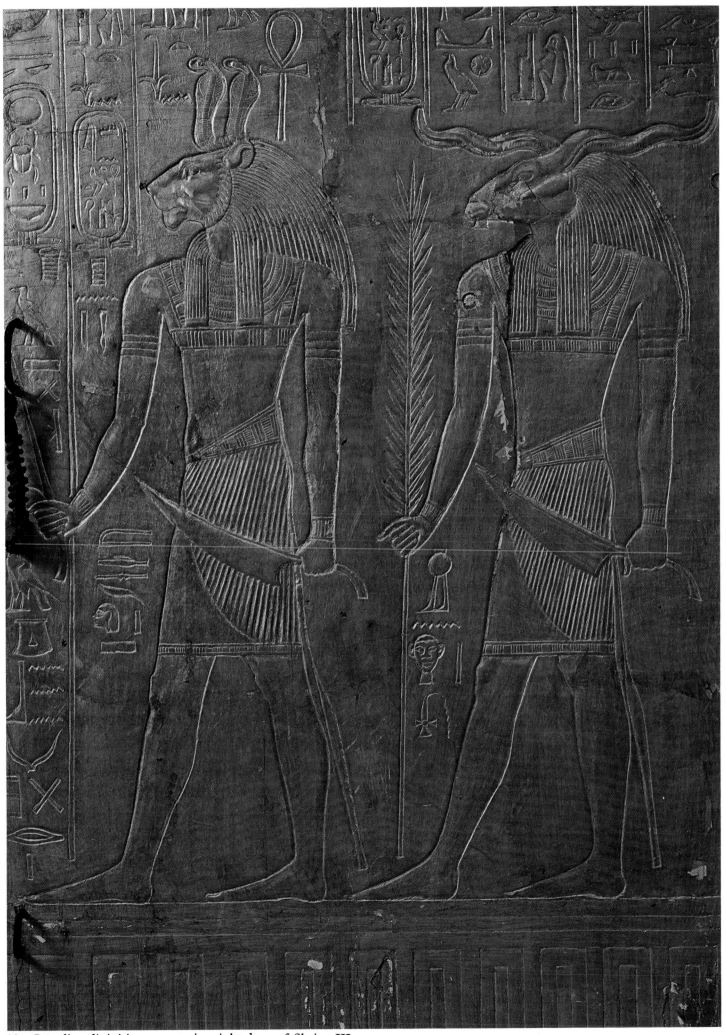

19. Guardian divinities, on exterior right door of Shrine III.

20. Thoth, god of magic and wisdom, Shrine III.

21. The sacred scarab and the symbol of the goddess Hathor,
    in procession of boats preceding the Solar Bark, Shrine III.

22. Running figures carrying the Sign of the Year, Shrine III.

23. The Solar Bark, from the *Book of Am-Duat*, Shrine III.

24. Symbolic attributes of royalty, and royal divinities, Shrine III.

25. Shrine II, in the form of the primitive Sanctuary
of the South, *Per-Wer*.

26. Text from Chapter 17 of the *Book of the Dead*, interior
rear wall, Shrine II.

27. The King before Osiris, Lord of Eternity, Shrine II.

28. The King before the god Re-Harakhti, Shrine II.

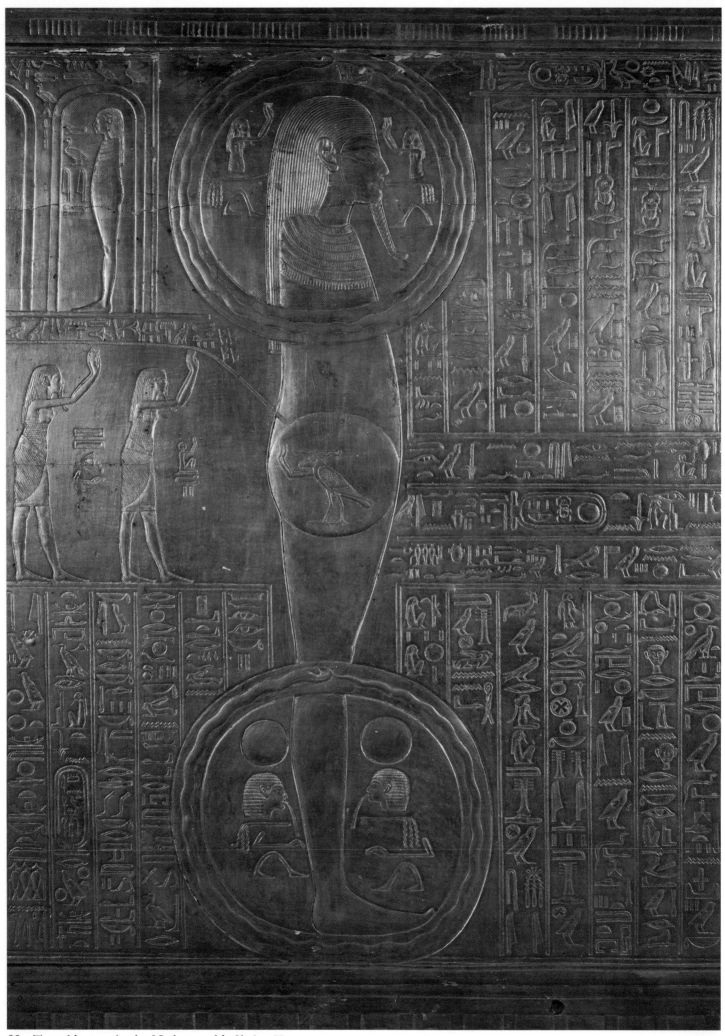

29. Tutankhamen in the Netherworld, Shrine II.

30. Transformation of divinities, Shrine II.

31. Rebirth in the Netherworld, Shrine II.

32. Regeneration of the sun god, Shrine II.

33. The solar disk recharged with fire as it passes through the night, Shrine II.

34. Life-giving goddesses, Shrine II.

35. Stages of rebirth, Shrine II.

36. Stages of rebirth, Shrine II.

37. The goddesses Isis and Nephthys, exterior rear panel, Shrine II.

38. Shrine I, in the form of the Sanctuary of the Feast of Sed.

39. The Divine Cow, rear interior panel, Shrine I.

40. Osiris of the Horizon, left door of Shrine I.

Notes to the Plates

The Tomb

1. *The Valley of the Kings.*

The Valley of the Kings in the forbidding region behind the western cliffs of Thebes, where Tutankhamen lies buried, was the area chosen by the pharaohs of the Eighteenth Dynasty for their tombs. Abandoning the ancient custom of building pyramids, Tuthmosis I was the first to dig a rock-cut hypogeum at the foot of the Qurna (Horn) peak, which rises like a natural pyramid from among the last outcroppings of rock at the edge of the Libyan desert. This was also called "Mountain of the West," evoking the sun god's descent into the Primordial Night on his voyage toward the dawn of eternal rebirth. Secrecy and seclusion to avoid the incessant plundering of tombs had been the original aim of the underground tombs, which were continued there by all the kings of the Eighteenth, Nineteenth, and Twentieth Dynasties. But the ransacking continued, and it was largely because rubble from the excavation of Rameses VI's tomb nearby had completely covered the entrance of Tutankhamen's tomb that the latter was saved for some 3,300 years from the depredations of grave robbers. In this plate, Tutankhamen's tomb is visible at lower right.

2. *Burial Chamber, north wall: in foreground, the outermost coffin lying in the sarcophagus.*

Tutankhamen's mummy now lies in its outermost gilded wood coffin in the massive quartzite sarcophagus, in the Burial Chamber. Originally, the sarcophagus had a porphyry lid and was completely covered under four gilded shrines fitting closely over each other. When in place, these shrines—now in the Cairo Museum—filled the whole chamber, shrouding from view the wall paintings representing episodes of Tutankhamen's afterlife.

The north wall shown here is divided into three scenes. At right, Tutankhamen, metamorphosed as Osiris, is being ritually given new life by his successor, the "Divine Father" Ay, wearing the leopard skin of a *setem* priest and performing the ceremonial Opening of the Mouth. In center, the goddess Nut is greeting Tutankhamen as a son. At left, still wearing the striped *nemes* headdress of royalty and accompanied by his *ka* (spirit), Tutankhamen is embracing the god Osiris.

3. *Burial Chamber, east wall: the royal catafalque on a sledge drawn by court officials in ceremonial procession.*

The painting on the east wall of the Burial Chamber commemorates the transportation of Tutankhamen's body to its eternal destination. The King, now in Osirian form, lies headfirst on his leomorphic bed under an enormous catafalque composed of two superimposed shrines. The whole is mounted on a funerary boat guided by Nephthys in the bow and Isis in the stern. The boat itself rests on a sledge which is being drawn overland by twelve courtiers, favorites of the King, all wearing the headband of mourning. The three nearest the boat may be identified by their dress, the first possibly as Horemheb, commander-in-chief of the army, and the two in front of him as the viziers of Upper and Lower Egypt.

4. *Burial Chamber, west wall: the solar boat, divinities, and squatting baboons evoking Thoth, god of the moon and magic.*

The west wall of the Burial Chamber is covered with representations of divinities and texts from the First Division of the *Book of Am-Duat* ("What there is in the Beyond"). In the upper register, at right are five deities; and at left in the solar boat, the scarab Khepri, creator of life, is being worshiped on both sides by Osiris, god of the Netherworld. Below, the space is divided into twelve compartments, in each of which are quotations from the *Am-Duat*, each presided over by a squatting baboon, an animal sacred to Thoth, god of magic and wisdom. The twelve divisions, probably representing the twelve hours of the night, contain spells to absolve the deceased from misdeeds committed during life.

5. *Burial Chamber, south wall: the goddess Hathor giving life to the King.*

In the succeeding scene, on the south wall of the Burial Chamber, the goddess Hathor, patroness of cosmic regeneration, is applying the sign of life (*ankh*) to Tutankhamen's nostrils, while the jackal-headed Anubis, protector of tombs and patron of mummification, touches his shoulder in approbation. Tutankhamen, wearing the royal headcloth *afnet*, with the royal cobra uraeus affixed to his brow, holds his arms down with the back of his hands turned forward, a deferential attitude in the presence of the goddess similar to that found in representations of the king Akhenaten approaching a temple.

6. *Burial Chamber, north wall, detail: the goddess Nut welcoming Tutankhamen into the realm of the gods.*

The goddess Nut, in this detail of the north wall of the Burial Chamber, is shown welcoming Tutankhamen as he starts on his nocturnal journey through the Netherworld. Still wearing a headband to which is affixed the royal uraeus, the King holds in his left hand the sign of life (*ankh*) and a symbolic mace to ward off evil spirits, and in his right a staff fitted with a handrest in the shape of a papyrus flower. The scene can be interpreted as Tutankhamen's initiation into the world of the gods.

Gold Mask and Coffins

7–9. *The gold mask.*

The gold mask of Tutankhamen was made of several sheets of beaten gold, with ceramic and semiprecious stone inlays. This portrayal of the Pharaoh faithfully resembles the young King as he looked at the time of his death, at age nineteen. It bears the characteristic features of Tutankhamen's thin, slightly tilted nose, the delicate nostrils, and the full lips. Accents of lapis-lazuli are set around his eyes and extended to the temples, according to the ancient tradition. The earlobes are pierced, but they were covered with strips of gold when the mask was found. The neck has two folds, a reminiscence of Amarnian art. The King wears the traditional *nemes* headdress, with blue and gold stripes recalling the sun god Re, whose body was of gold and hair of lapis-lazuli. The eyes are also symbolic, the left eye representing the moon, and the right eye the sun. The two divinities associated with royalty, the vulture of the South, and the cobra uraeus of the North, scintillate on the King's forehead—lapis-lazuli for the beak of the vulture, and white and black painted quartz for its eyes; while the uraeus is likewise inlaid with carnelian, lapis-lazuli, and turquoise. The King's shoulders are covered by a wide collar made of lapis-lazuli, quartz, and green feldspar segments, terminating in two inlaid falcon heads on the shoulders. The engraved hieroglyphic inscription on the back of the mask, in ten columns from the right to the left shoulder, quotes Chapter 531 of the text of the sarcophagi of the Middle Kingdom. This text dates from five hundred years before Tutankhamen, and later was incorporated in the *Book of the Dead*. The passage is a salute in poetic terms to the beaming face of the young King, now covered with its golden mask of glory made out of the incorruptible flesh of the gods. The highest gods of Egypt—Ptah-Sokar-Osiris, Anubis, Horus, the gods of the Ennead—are actually materialized in the elements of the mask, and the royal head retains its eternal youth. Osiris-Tutankhamen has now triumphed over the companions of Seth.

Height: 21 inches; width at shoulders: 15$^1/_2$ inches.

10. *The innermost coffin, of solid gold.*

The innermost coffin was found wrapped in a linen shroud upon which had been laid a garland of flowers, fruit, and faience beads attached to a sheet of papyrus. This coffin, in which rested the King's bejeweled mummy covered by its mask, was made of solid 22-carat beaten gold, weighing 2,448 pounds.

Tutankhamen's flesh was thus endowed with the everlasting brilliance of gold, enabling the King to become as immortal as the gods. Once again his features are faithfully reproduced on the face of this mummiform coffin, following the Amarnian tradition. But here the King's empty eyes and the absence of blue stripes on the *nemes* headdress confer on Osiris-Tutankhamen the glaring immobility of the Netherworld. In Tutankhamen's hands are his royal emblems, the crook *heka* and the flail *nekhekh*, of the Southern and Northern Osirian Kingdom. The uraeus Wadjet, goddess of Lower Egypt, and the vulture Nekhbet, goddess of Upper Egypt, are attached to his headdress. His chin is adorned with the long symbolic beard of the gods. Tutankhamen is also wearing the double necklace of gold and faience beads commemorating military feats. This is laid over a wider collar made of successive bands of faience incrustations similar to the ones dealt with later in this book. Contrasting with the powerful and deadening brilliance of the blank gold surfaces of the coffin, two winged deities in cloisonné work, representing once again the uraeus Wadjet and the vulture Nekhbet, wrap their protective wings around the King's mummy; and the goddesses Isis and Nephthys are engraved across the legs to restore life to the dead King.

Length: 76 inches; width: 20 inches; depth: 20 inches.

11. *The intermediate coffin, wood with gold and cloisonné inlays.*

The second mummiform coffin was also found covered with a linen shroud. A small wreath of flowers was placed around the shrouded forms of the vulture and the cobra, while larger garlands had been placed around the King's shoulders. The coffin fitted so closely into the shell of the outermost coffin that it was very difficult for Carter to extract the silver tongues and gold-headed pins that fastened the lid to the shell. The coffin was made of wood, covered with a sheet of gold adhering to it with a light coat of plaster. Osiris-Tutankhamen is again wearing the *nemes* headdress and his royal attributes, but the yellowish tone of his skin and of the cornea of his eyes accentuate the image of suffering and death. The feather decoration of this coffin is encrusted from head to foot with polychrome glass and semiprecious stones, separated by long strips of hieroglyphic inscriptions running from the mummy's hands and middle of its shoulders to its foot. In place of the winged figures of Isis and Nephthys on the innermost coffin, this one is protected by the vulture Nekhbet and the serpent Wadjet.

Length: $80^2/_5$ inches; width: $26^3/_4$ inches; depth at foot: $30^7/_8$ inches.

12. *The innermost coffin, detail.*

This detail of the upper part of the gold innermost coffin shows Tutankhamen now likened to the god Osiris. The pure gold surface confers a precision and delicacy on the royal features, heightening the sense of majesty and divinity as the young Pharaoh is yet further removed from the world of humans.

13. *Foot of the innermost coffin.*

Under the foot of the innermost mummy, the goddess·Nut, symbolizing the starry vault of heaven, is stretching out her winged arms to protect Tutankhamen as he makes his journey through the Netherworld.

14. *The intermediate coffin, detail of cloisonné inlays.*

This detail of the glass-inlaid surface of the intermediate coffin shows the particular technique, loosely called cloisonné, employed by the Egyptians of the Middle and New Kingdom. A sheet of gold was first applied to the carved wood base of the coffin, to which it adhered by means of a thin coat of plaster. To this were soldered thin gold ribs in the chevron-shaped or circular cells which formed the design, and these were filled with pieces of colored glass. This procedure differs from true cloisonné, in which different colored powders are put into the cells (*cloisons*), and heated to form a unified glazed surface.

The Shrines

The four sepulchral shrines which fitted closely into each other over Tutankhamen's stone sarcophagus are now in the Cairo Museum. They are the only examples of the kind known, although it is believed that other royal sarcophagi of this period were similarly encased. Covered inside and out with hieroglyphic inscriptions and mythical representations, they served a highly important religious function in promoting the afterlife of the King. They resemble in many ways the decorations painted on the walls of tombs in the Valley of the Kings and are often enigmatic and difficult to interpret. Based on ancient rituals and texts, such as the *Book of the Dead*, they convey to the deceased the dangers to be encountered in the Netherworld and offer magic spells and protection to overcome them.

When first discovered in Tutankhamen's tomb, these shrines were described in the order in which they were opened by Carter, that is from the outermost Shrine I to the innermost Shrine IV, next to the sarcophagus. However, as the sequence of texts and magic spells inscribed on them runs from the innermost to the outermost, representing the course of the cosmic cycle in the deification of the deceased King, this order is observed here. The descriptions and quotations from texts rely heavily on the published work of Alexandre Piankoff, in *The Shrines of Tut-Ankh-Amon* (Bollingen series XL.2, Princeton University Press, 1977).

15. *Shrine IV, the innermost, in the form of the primitive coronation Sanctuary of the North,* Per-Nu, *the House of Flame.*

Shrine IV, the innermost of the series, is shaped to symbolize the archaic palace of the Northern Kings, called *Per-Nu,* or "House of Flame," recalling the sanctuary where the King had been crowned with the divine uraeus. The roof is characterized by a low barrel-vault, terminated at each end by a projection on which is displayed the winged solar disk. On the architrave under the flaring cavetto cornice, the winged solar·disk is again represented. On the doors themselves and also on the back panel are depicted the figures of Isis and Nephthys, flapping their wings to give the breath of life to the King. The interior walls are inscribed with Chapter 17 of·the *Book of the Dead,* a monologue of the sun god Re describing his emergence from the Watery Abyss, the primeval god Nun, who is portrayed on the ceiling with arms and wings outspread.

16. *Shrine III, in the form of the primitive Sanctuary of the South,* Per-Wer, *the Great House.*

Shrine III, in the form of the primitive Sanctuary of the South,

Per-Wer, the "Great House," in which resided the vulture goddess Nekhbet, protectress of Upper Egypt. Architecturally, the building is distinguished from the previous shrine by the shape of the roof, which slopes back from a bulging front. Beneath the roof on all four sides and projecting outward is the cavetto cornice, the same as on all four shrines. On the right exterior door are two guardian divinities, and on the left interior door can be seen the goddess Nephthys spreading her protective wings. Inside at one end of the ceiling is represented the winged sun disk; then, in superimposed registers, seven vultures with wings outspread, all holding the sign of infinity in their claws, and one with the head of a cobra. Below them, also with wings outspread, is a falcon, symbolizing the King. The inscription below contains a description of Aten, the god of Akhenaten: "The rays of the Disk are a protection over thee, their hands carry health and life. . . ."

17. *The goddesses Isis and Nephthys, on interior rear panel of Shrine III.*

As on the inside of the doors of Shrine III, the interior rear panel shows the goddesses Isis and Nephthys standing on signs of gold, their outspread wings flapping to sustain the deceased. The inscription recording the words spoken by Nephthys, daughter of Nut, is quoted from the Pyramid texts describing the birth of Nut: "I have been powerful in the body of my mother Tefnut on the day of my birth. I have come, I present Osiris, Lord of the Two Lands Neb-Kheperu-Re, the justified one, with life, stability, and prosperity, so that he will not die. . . ."

18, 19. *Guardian divinities, on exterior doors of Shrine III.*

On the outside of the two doors of Shrine III are four guardian divinities with animal heads on human bodies. On the left door, one identified with the head of a bubalis, the other with a crocodile head, both armed with knives, are respectively identified in the accompanying inscription as "He who repulses the wicked" and "Great Voice." On the right door, the lion-headed divinity with the double uraeus and the *ankh* sign of life is named "He who slaughters a head," and behind him, the ram-headed figure, "He who brings to the fire." The accompanying inscription of the incantation to be spoken reads: "Osiris, King, Lord of the Two Lands Neb-Kheperu-Re, He who dams the flood, who separates the Two Fellows, has come. . . ." here referring to the deadly struggle between Horus and Seth.

20. *Thoth, god of magic and wisdom, Shrine III.*

In the center of the exterior right panel of Shrine III, immediately in front of the Solar Bark, the seated baboon-headed divinity holding an ibis in his outstretched hand is an incarnation of the spirit of Thoth, resulting from the legendary partnership between the baboon and the ibis. Thoth, god of wisdom and magic, was indispensable for every divine action, and this may explain his strategic position here, immediately in the front of the Solar Bark as it makes its way in the Netherworld. The accompanying inscription reads:

"Thoth, who stands before the Lord of those in the Netherworld." It is known that it was Thoth, with his magic command over calculations, who presided over the weighing of tribute to be carried down the Nile from Nubia to Thebes.

21. *The sacred scarab and the symbol of the goddess Hathor, in procession of boats preceding the Solar Bark, Shrine III.*

One of the boats preceding the Solar Bark, in the exterior left panel of Shrine III, carries in its center a huge symbol of the goddess Hathor, between two legs. In the bow of the boat, Khepri, the sacred scarab, symbol of "the becoming," is represented with legs outstretched, while the upturned stern of the boat terminates in the head of a king wearing the Feather Crown and the symbolic beard of royalty.

22. *Running figures carrying the Sign of the Year, Shrine III.*

The four running figures in this detail from the exterior left panel of Shrine III are part of a long procession of deities below the Solar Bark. Three of them carry the "year" sign and the fourth a knife. The accompanying inscription reads: "The gods are like this, they acclaim this Great God with the symbols of the year, they acclaim him with branches which they hold in their hands, while the Great God gives them orders. . . . He grants them the plants which are in their fields . . . the green plants of Urnes to the Gods in the following of Re to eat . . . who bring water to the spirits. . . ."

23. *The Solar Bark, from the* Book of Am-Duat, *Shrine III.*

The exterior right panel of Shrine III, containing descriptions from the Sixth Division of the *Book of Am-Duat* ("What there is in the Beyond"), deals with the Solar Bark and the divinities encountered on the journey as it progresses through the Netherworld. In the upper register of this detail, four of nine divinities seated on invisible thrones, identified by attributes on their heads, are named as follows (from left to right): the first, with a loaf of bread and a jar of beer on his head, "Contentment which is in the Netherworld"; the second, wearing the Crown of the North, "Isis of the Dead"; the third, with a beard, "Osiris, He in the heart of the gods"; the fourth, with a falcon head, "Horus, in front of his Net."

Near the center of the Solar Bark, the sun god with the head of a ram (Amen-Re?) stands in a little shrine. In front of the shrine is a goddess with a disk between two horns (Hathor?), and behind the shrine is a falcon-headed god (Horus?). There are nine gods in the boat, which corresponds to the number in the Ennead, the hierarchy of gods who represented the elemental forces in the universe.

24. *Symbolic attributes of royalty, and royal divinities, Shrine III.*

In this detail from the exterior right panel of Shrine III showing seven of a series of nine crooks, symbols of royalty, three are surmounted by the Crown of Upper Egypt, three by the Crown of Lower Egypt, and one by a cobra. The accompanying text reads:

"Decree of the majesty of this great god [to] the Kings of Upper Egypt and [to] the Kings of Lower Egypt who are in the Netherworld: Lift up the White Crowns, wear the Red Crowns in the midst of your subjects. . . . May your majesties be just, your throats breathe. . . ."

Below, the series of twelve Osirian mummiform figures precede the Solar Bark (Pl. 23), two wearing the Crown of the North, two with the Crown of the South, others without crowns, and all having the beard of Immortality.

25. *Shrine II, in the form of the primitive Sanctuary of the South,* Per-Wer.

Shrine II, the second of the two shrines symbolizing the Palace of the South where resided the goddess Nekhbet, is architecturally similar to the previous one, with a roof sloping back from a bulge in front. Its decoration is however strongly influenced by Amarnian art, with many references to the sun god. The lintel under the cornice is decorated with the winged solar disk, and on the doors Tutankhamen is confronted by the two deities who were to constitute his present and future being, Osiris and Re-Harakhti. Inside on the ceiling, again under the winged solar disk, the sky goddess Nut, standing on the sign of gold, spreads her winged arms, uttering the words: "I stretch myself over this son of mine, Osiris, in my name of Nut. I will not be far from this son of mine, Osiris, King, Lord of the Two Lands Neb-Kheperu-Re, bodily son of the Sun, beloved by him, Tut-Ankh-Amen, ruler of Heliopolis of the South."

26. *Text from Chapter 17 of the* Book of the Dead, *interior rear wall, Shrine II.*

The whole of the interior rear panel of Shrine II is devoted to Chapter 17 of the *Book of the Dead*, which first appeared during the Middle Kingdom, in the nineteenth century B.C. This text consists of a monologue of the sun god Re, followed by allusions to various myths, including rebirth in the Watery Abyss, and prayers to be pronounced by the deceased. One invocation reads: "O Ra in his egg, who shivers in his disk, who appears on his horizon, who swims in his copper [firmament], he who has not his second among the gods, who travels on the Lifted One of Shu [the sky], who makes wind with the hot breath of his mouth, who makes brilliant the two banks with his rays—may thou save Osiris, King Neb-Kheperu-Re, Son of the Sun, Tut-Ankh-Amen, living forever, from this god, whose forms are mysterious, whose two eyebrows are the scale beams on that night of judging the evildoers!"

27. *The King before Osiris, Lord of Eternity, Shrine II.*

The King before Osiris, on the left door of Shrine II, is wearing the double crown of Upper and Lower Egypt, and holding the crook and the flail, Osirian emblems of sovereignty. Facing him is Osiris in the image and likeness of the King, also holding the crook and the flail. Between them there is a small offering table on which stands a vase with lotus flowers. The inscription above Osiris reads:

"I grant thee to be a living god at my side, every day, like the father Horus, the son of Isis. . . ." Between the table and Osiris are the words: "Refreshment, wine, milk." Standing behind the King is Isis, who pronounces the words, "Thou art my son, from my body, my beloved one, Lord of the Two Lands Neb-Kheperu Re, the justified one, before the Great Ennead who are in the Netherworld."

28. *The King before the god Re-Harakhti, Shrine II.*

The King before the falcon-headed god Re-Harakhti, on the right door panel of Shrine II, is wearing a crown with ram's horns and ostrich plumes, over which is the disk of the sun. Behind the King stands Maat, the goddess Truth. Re-Harakhti holds the *was* staff of dominion and the *ankh* sign of life, and the huge disk over his head has a uraeus. The inscription above him reads: "Welcome, thou comest in peace, my beloved son, Lord of the Two Lands. I make thy seat in the Necropolis to be as that of one of the gods, the Lords of the Netherworld."

29. *Tutankhamen in the Netherworld, Shrine II.*

The gigantic figure of Tutankhamen as an Osirian mummy, in this central detail of the exterior left panel of Shrine II, is described as "He who hides the hours." It is part of a cosmological composition dealing with the ancient belief—still held by the Greek philosopher Heraclitus in the sixth century B.C.—that the sun loses its heat by day and is replenished during the night by fumes from the earth which become ignited at dawn. In this image, the figure seems to be immobilized by circles around both the head and the feet by the serpent Mehen, the Enveloper. In the center of the mummy, the disk containing a ram-headed bird with human arms raised in adoration symbolizes the night sun. It is being pulled from the body with a rope held by the figures of deities at left with arms raised, an action which is believed to mark the passing of the night hours.

30. *Transformation of divinities, Shrine II.*

The row of mummiform divinities in this detail from the exterior left panel of Shrine II symbolizes the different transformations undergone by the sun god on his passage through the Netherworld. In the accompanying hieroglyphic inscriptions, these enigmatic appellations (from left to right): "Cat. Terrible One. Fat Face. Turned Face. The One belonging to the Cobra. He in the Netherworld." An inscription above reads "These gods are like this in their caverns, which are in the Netherworld. Their bodies are in darkness."

31. *Rebirth in the Netherworld, Shrine II.*

Still more explicitly than in the preceding plate the transformations undergone by the sun god while passing through the Netherworld are pictured in this detail from the exterior left panel of Shrine II. In the row of deities, the ram-headed and human-headed mummiform figures at far left correspond exactly with the two with human bodies wearing kilts at far right. However, the upper torsos of the latter are in the form of a scarab whose legs extend on either side of their heads. The parallel with the metamorphosis in the life cycle of the scarab is thus made clear, the two mummiform deities representing the inert chrysalis stage in which the features are recognizable, followed by the fully developed final stage. The mummiform counterparts of the two middle figures are not included in this detail.

32. *Regeneration of the sun god, Shrine II.*

In this grandiose but enigmatic composition, which is a detail of the exterior right panel of Shrine II, four pairs of arms—two rising out of the ground, and two descending from the sky, support two disks each enclosing a ram-headed bird with human hands raised in adoration. Between the enclosing arms are bovine torsos, two above and two below, each with a standing goddess between their horns. A serpent above and below follows the interior line of the arms and encircles a mummiform figure of Osiris at top, and a bent arm at bottom. Included in the long inscription in center is Tutankhamen's cartouche.

33. *The solar disk recharged with fire as it passes through the night, Shrine II.*

The recharging of the sun's heat as it passes through the night is the theme in this detail from the exterior right panel of Shrine II, in the section immediately to the right of the preceding plate. The sun itself is pictured by the little disk on legs, moving towards the right, at the right end of the middle register. A group of four lion-headed divinities (not shown in this detail) belches fire toward it. The inscription above reads: "These gods are like this; the rays of Re penetrate their bodies; they praise when they see his soul." A stream of rays of fire enclosing a serpent descends from the disk of the sun and seems to communicate with the prone figure at left who raises his arms in offering to the disk with a bird at far left (part of the detail in the preceding plate). Gigantic cobras in the upper and lower registers belch fire toward mummiform figures creating a stream of fire which is communicated to others.

34. *Life-giving goddesses, Shrine II.*

Six standing female divinities, three in this detail from the exterior right panel of Shrine II, belch fire towards disks before them, and shed water or fire from their hands onto the heads of serpents emerging from the ground. A star and a disk are inscribed on the body of each figure, and in front of each are an arm and walking legs. An inscription identifies the divinities as "She who adores. She who lights up," etc. Before each serpent rising from the ground are written the words "Evil Face."

35, 36. *Stages of rebirth, Shrine II.*

These enigmatic images, details from the upper and lower register of the exterior right panel of Shrine II, schematize the mystical regeneration in the Netherworld. In the upper register (Pl. 35), before a seated cat whose hindquarters are hidden in the ground, six headless mummiform figures stand with their severed heads before them, each surmounted by a star and resting on a disk from which descend lines of fire communicating with an undulating serpent below. The heads are identified as "Head of Horus," "Face of Horus," "Neck of Horus," etc.

In the lower register (Pl. 36), a lion in profile to the left, with hindquarters hidden in the ground, faces six ram-headed mummiform figures, only four of which are seen here, each with the sign of walking legs above the horns. Before each figure a disk surmounted by a star projects rays of fire to the ground. An inscription above the lion reads: "The gods are like this: they pour on what is hidden . . . they see. . . ."

37. *The goddesses Isis and Nephthys, exterior rear panel, Shrine II.*

The goddesses Isis and Nephthys, sisters of Osiris, standing on the sign of gold, wave their wings across the back of Shrine II, to make air for the departed soul to breathe. Inscription of words spoken by Isis: "I have come to be thy protection, thou art my son, my beloved Horus, I have taken away the veil above thee, from him who acted against thee. Mayest thou lift thy head to see Re, to stand on thy feet, to walk about in the forms thou likest to move as before. . . ."

Words spoken by Nephthys: "I have come to protect thee from behind, my brother Osiris, King, Lord of the Two Lands Neb-Kheperu-Re. I have established thy head on thy neck, Anubis has gathered for thee thy bones, he has restored thy limbs to health, he has removed all evil, he has caused all sorrow to depart. Thou shalt not decay!"

38. *Shrine I, in the form of the Sanctuary of the Feast of Sed.*

Shrine I, the outermost of the four sepulchral shrines, differs from the others in having a concave roof sloping inward from bulges at each end. The form symbolizes the Sanctuary of the Feast of Sed, for the jubilee celebrations wherein an aging king had to restore his vital powers by a ceremonial simulacrum of death to gain a renewal of life. In contrast to the other three shrines the exterior panels are decorated with an overall pattern of gilded *djed* columns in pairs alternating with pairs of *tat* amulets against a background of blue enamel. On the doors this pattern is interrupted by two gilded rectangles with figure and hieroglyphic inscriptions.

39. *The Divine Cow, rear interior panel, Shrine I.*

On the rear inside wall of Shrine I, visible through the wooden struts which held the star-studded pall over Shrine II, can be seen the Divine Cow representing the goddess Hathor, incarnation of the primordial ocean, the Watery Abyss through which the deceased had to pass before reaching rebirth. As depicted here, the image follows closely the instructions given in the *Book of the Divine Cow* for proper representations of her to insure the effectiveness of the magic incantations to be recited before her. Her belly is lined with stars symbolizing the firmament, held up by the raised arms of the god Shu who stands below, accompanied by Heh deities, gods of eternity. Above, next to the cow's haunch, is a small Solar Bark in which the sun god Re is standing. An inscription at the side reads: "Come, son of my body, my beloved one, Lord of the Two Lands Neb-Kheperu-Re. Be with thy father Re as one of these gods who are in his following at the side of the Great Flood [the Cow]. . . ."

40. *Osiris of the Horizon, left door of Shrine I.*

In a gold panel on the left door of the entrance to Shrine I, Osiris, wearing a crown with ram's horns surmounted by the solar disk and two ostrich feathers, is seated in an attitude of watchfulness, holding the sign of life, *ankh*. The inscription at right reads: "I have repelled, I have killed, I have beheaded, I have cut the legs of the enemies of Osiris. They are fallen! They will not survive! All the enemies of Osiris, King Neb-Kheperu-Re, are fallen!"

The Young King

41. Painted wood head of Tutankhamen as a child, emerging from a lotus.

42. Painted wood half-length effigy of Tutankhamen.

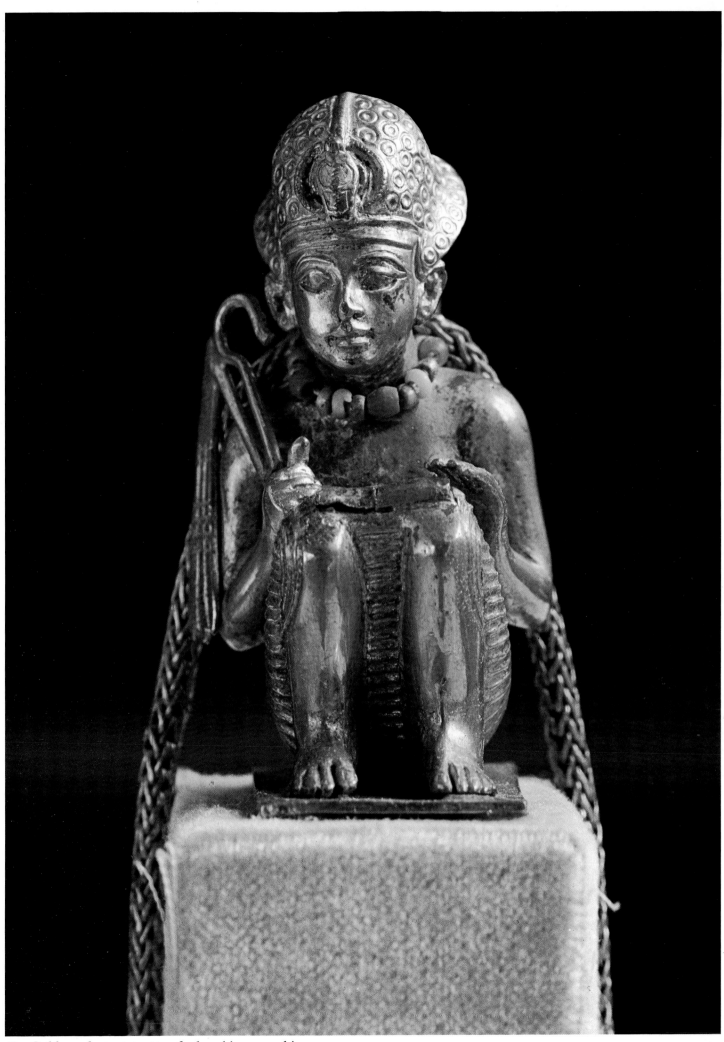

43. Gold pendant, statuette of a boy king crouching.

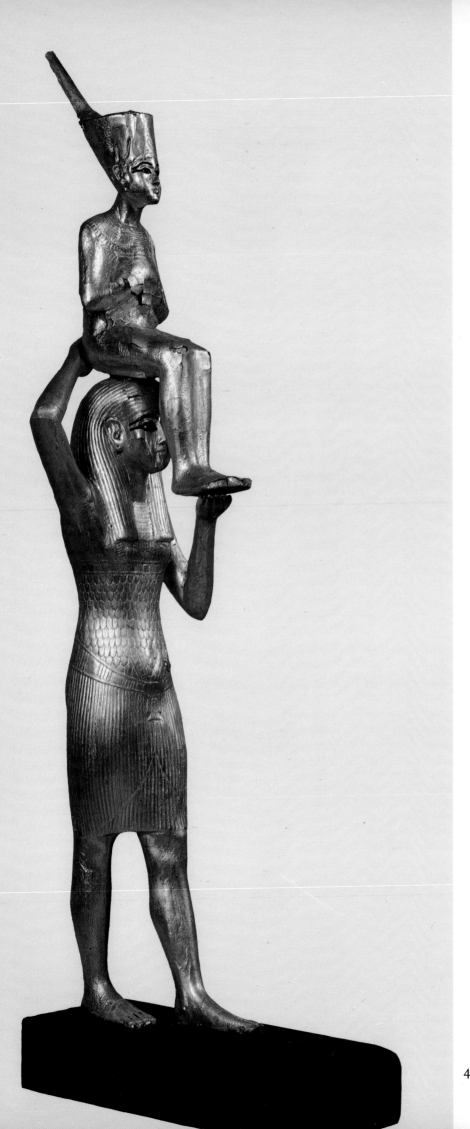

44. The goddess Menkheret carrying the body
of the King wrapped in a shroud.

45. Gilded statuette of the King with a flail and a long crook, wearing the Red Crown of Lower Egypt.

46. The Queen bringing unguents and flowers to the
King, detail of small gilded shrine.

47. The King in a ritual hunting scene, assisted by the
Queen, detail of small gilded shrine.

48. Tutankhamen and Ankhesenamen in a garden,
    painted ivory plaque from the lid of a chest.

49. Back panel of the King's throne.

Burial Apparatus

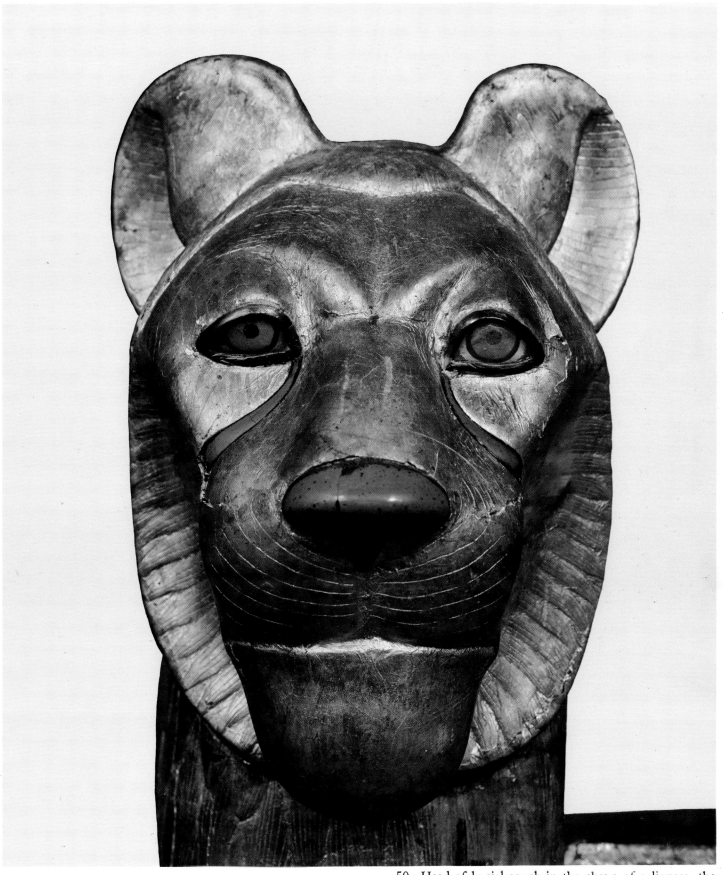

50. Head of burial couch in the shape of a lioness, the
goddess Sekhmet.

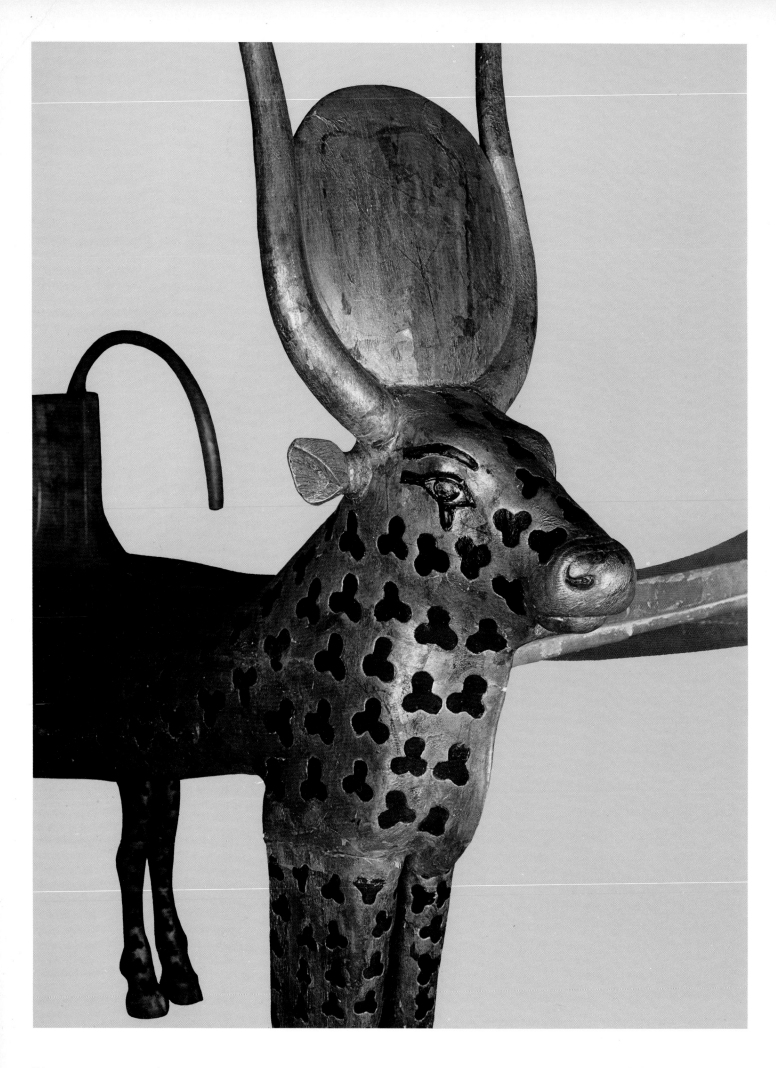

51. Head of burial couch in the form of the Divine Cow,
    with the solar disk between her horns.

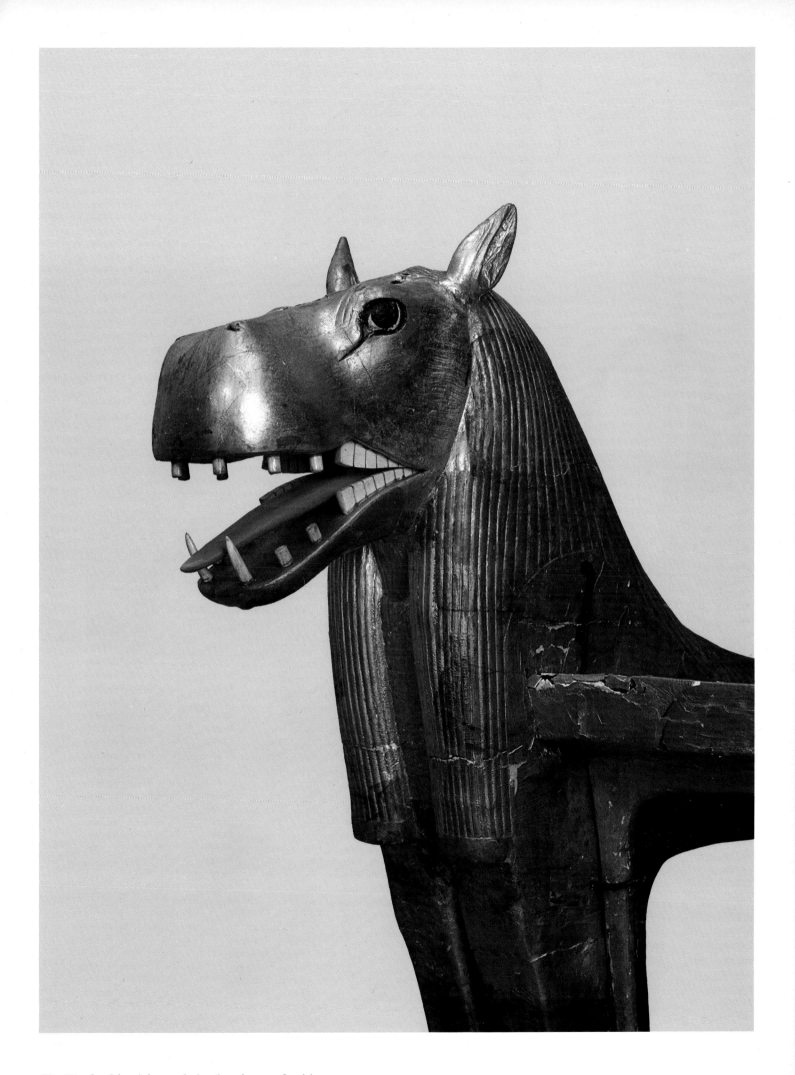

52. Head of burial couch in the shape of a hippopotamus, the goddess Thueris.

53. The burial couch in the form of the Divine Cow.

54. Burial couch with hippopotamus heads.

55. Burial couch in the form of the Divine Cow, profile view.

57. Life-size effigy of Tutankhamen's royal *ka*, as guardian of the Burial Chamber.

◁ 56. Tutankhamen's royal *ka* (spirit), detail.

58. Gilded cow's head, here associated with the goddess Hathor.

59. The god Anubis, Guardian of the Dead, on the pylon-shaped
shrine at the entrance to the tomb Treasury.

The Keys to Eternal Life

60. Gilded wood canopy and shrine, with Isis and Selkhet, two of the four guardian goddesses protecting the alabaster canopic chest within.

61. The alabaster canopic chest containing the four
miniature coffins for Tutankhamen's internal organs.

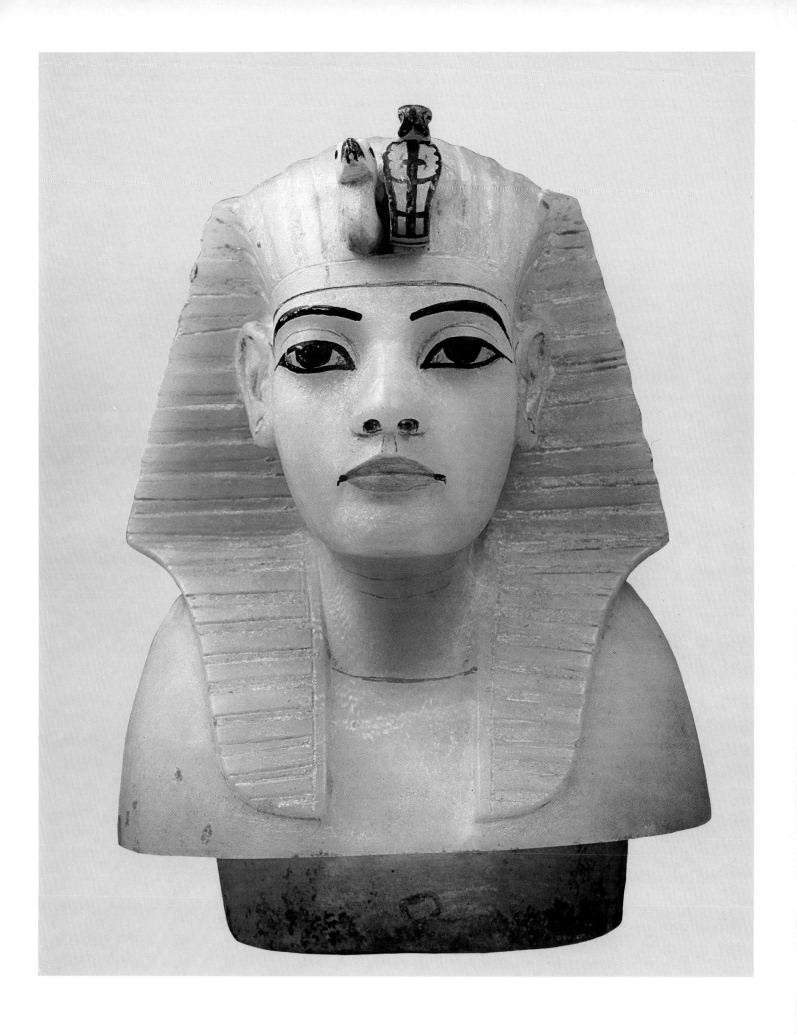

62. One of four alabaster portrait heads of Tutankhamen used
as stoppers to close the compartments in the canopic chest.

63. One of four miniature mummiform coffins containing
the embalmed organs of the King.

64. Gold sheaths used to cover the finger and toe tips of
Tutankhamen.

65. Two of the king's *ushabty* figures; the larger figure carrying
two flails, the smaller one wearing the *nemes* headdress.

66. Two gilded *ushabty* figures, both wearing the Red
    Crown of the North.

67. Model of the Pharaoh's boat, with mast and rigging.

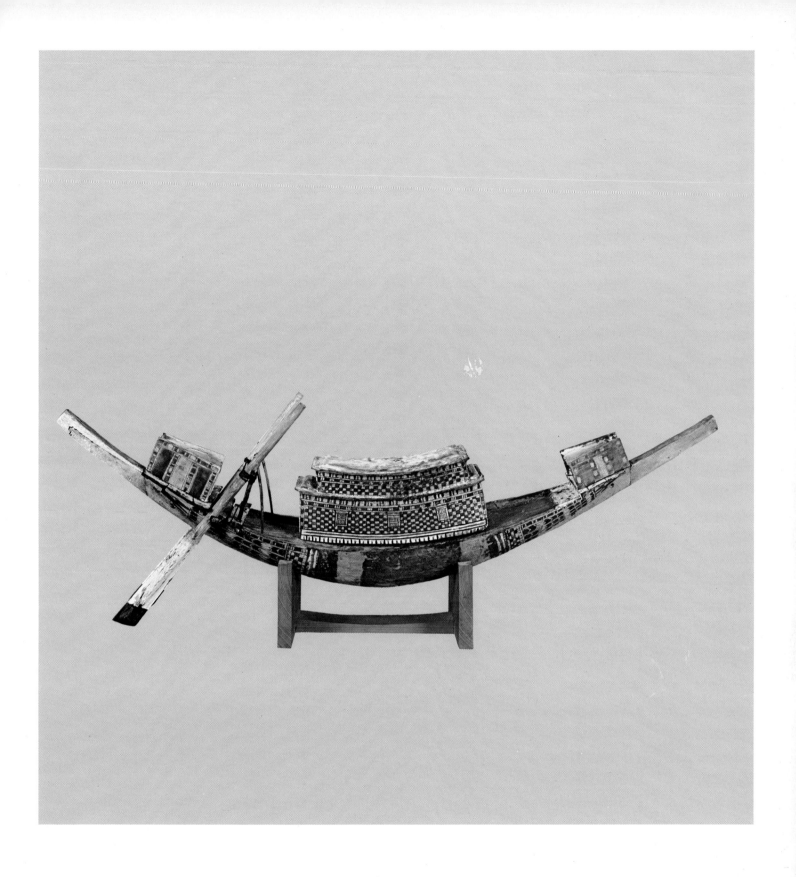

68. Model of a royal bark, one of seven found in the Treasury.

69. Carved wood image of the mummified King on his
lion-headed funerary bed, flanked by two soul birds.

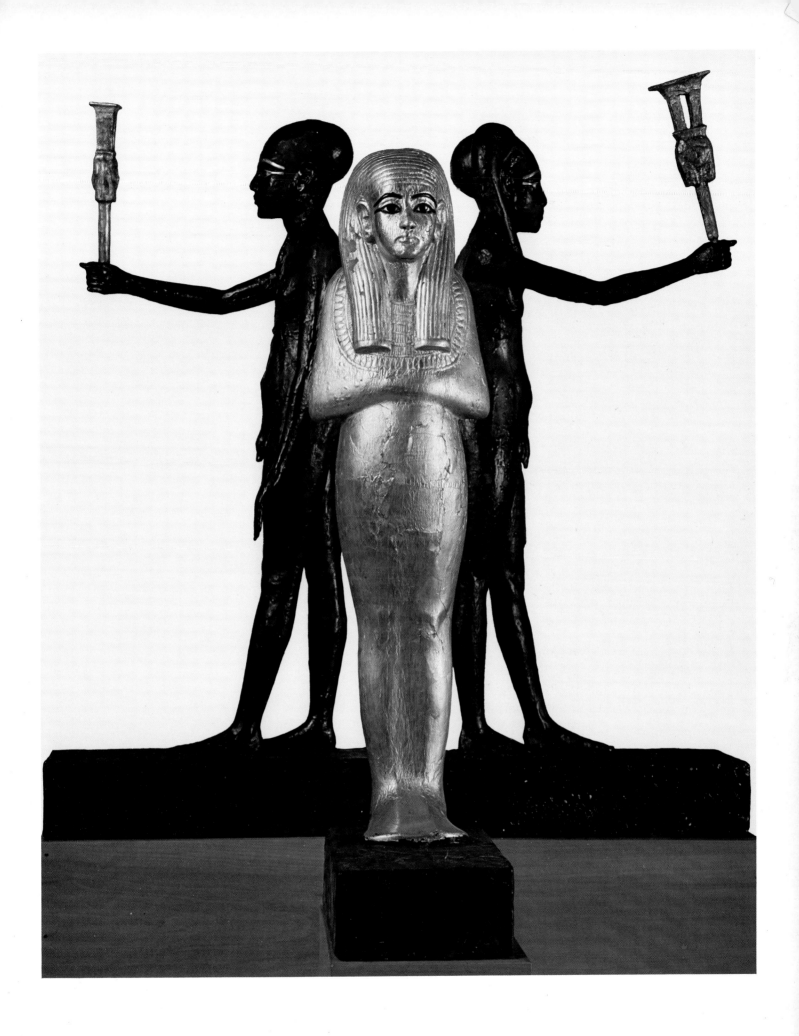

70. Gilt-wood statuette of the god Atum, in front of
    two statuettes of the god Ihy playing a sistrum.

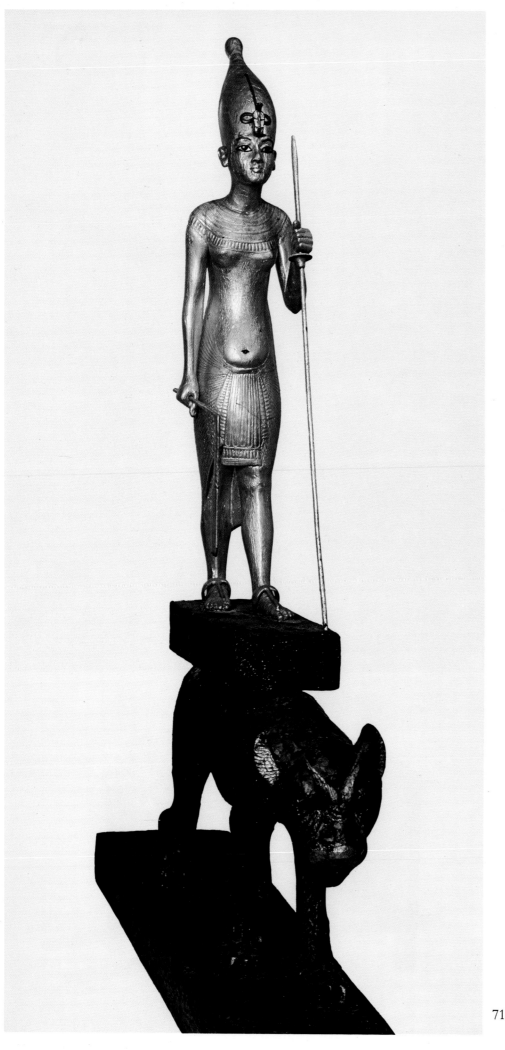

71. Gilded statuette of Tutankhamen
on a black leopard.

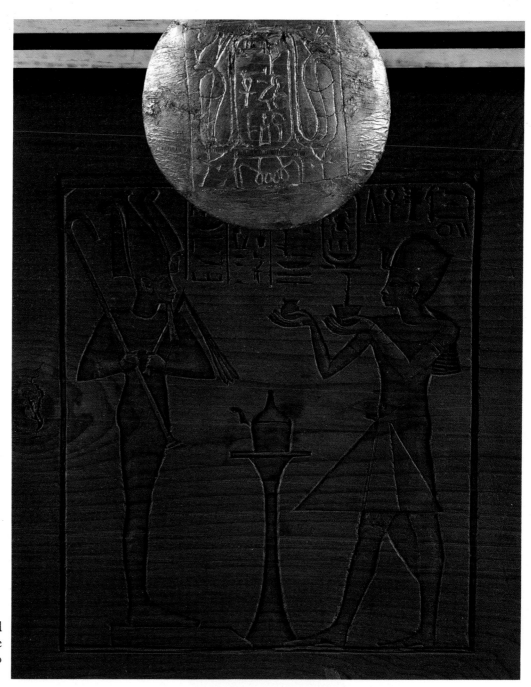

72. Detail of portable redwood funerary chest, showing the King making an offering to Osiris.

73. Portable redwood funerary chest.

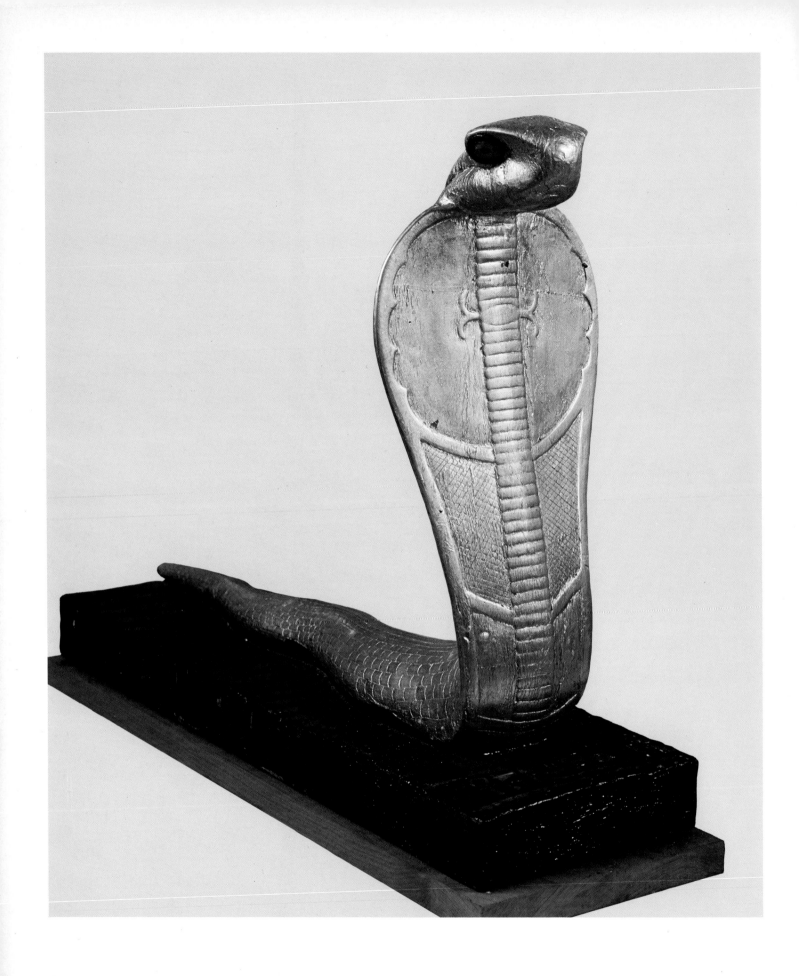

74. The serpent divinity Neter-Ankh.

75. Gold-plated standard of the falcon Gemhesu.

76. The god Ptah, wrapped in a robe of feathers.

Notes to the Plates

The Young King

41. *Painted wood head of Tutankhamen as a child, emerging from a lotus.*

Painted in gesso over carved wood, this portrayal of Tutankhamen displays the chubby features of a child. He is shown on a sculptured base in the form of the blue lotus (*nefer*) of Lower Egypt, evoking his rebirth at dawn from the primordial Abyss, as expressed in the concluding phrase of the mummification ritual: "You live again, you live again forever, now you are young once more forever." The ears are pierced for the earrings of youth, and the eyes and eyebrows are strongly accented with dark blue. But the shaving of the head is an anomaly, and the elongation of the skull is typical of the Akhenaten-Amarnian physiognomy.

42. *Painted wood half-length effigy of Tutankhamen.*

This half-length effigy of the King, wearing the Crown of Lower Egypt truncated to resemble Queen Nefertiti's, but with the royal uraeus affixed, shows Tutankhamen at the time of his adolescence, seemingly near his death at the estimated age of nineteen. The face, with its marked resemblance to other portraits of the young king, is strongly individualized in the firm set of the mouth and the protruding chin, the latter recalling the profile of his half-brother, the heretic king Amenhotep IV, Akhenaten. Contrasting with the attributes of kingship on his head, the simple white tunic in which he is dressed and the absence of arms (which never seem to have been added) raise questions as to the meaning or function of this image. It has been suggested that it may have been linked to the exercise of sympathetic magic in order to promote the process of rebirth of the King.

43. *Gold pendant, statuette of a boy king crouching.*

The *kepresh* crown with the uraeus on the head of this diminutive statuette of solid gold and the crook and flail he is holding immediately identify the crouching figure as that of a king. The statuette was found in the Treasury, wrapped in a piece of linen within a miniature mummiform gilded coffin together with two other smaller gilded coffins, one inside the other, the innermost one bearing the title of Queen Tiy, wife of Amenhotep III, and enclosing a lock of her hair. This association has been considered as conclusive evidence that the statuette represented Amenhotep III, and that these carefully preserved objects were inherited heirlooms, proving that Amenhotep III and Queen Tiy were Tutankhamen's parents. However, questions have been raised which seem to indicate that the statuette represents Tutankhamen. His name is inscribed on the second of the small coffins, and that one is in the image of Tutankhamen; and the fact that the ears are pierced, a custom which did not begin until Akhenaten, would seem to exclude the identification as Amenhotep III.

44. *The goddess Menkheret carrying the body of the King wrapped in a shroud.*

This singular gilded group of Tutankhamen being carried on the head of the divinity Menkheret is one of the statuettes placed in black wooden shrines in the Treasury to promote the reintegration of the King's body for his resurrection to eternal life. Tutankhamen, in Osirian form and wearing the Crown of Lower Egypt, is wrapped in a winding sheet, which emphasizes the lethargy of death. The goddess Menkheret, holding the King protectively on her head, is shown in exactly the same pose as in a wall painting in the tomb of Sethos II, in the Valley of the Kings, reflecting an ancient, obscure ritual by which in the mystical pilgrimage the King was raised high to enable him to meet the sun god. The black color of the shrine in which this statue was found, and the pedestal painted black on which it stands, both allude to the fertile soil from the Nile inundation.

45. *Gilded statuette of the King with a flail and a long crook, wearing the Red Crown of Lower Egypt.*

From among as many as thirty-two ritual statues found by Howard Carter enclosed in twenty-two rudimentary wooden shrines placed along the wall of the Treasury of the tomb, this gilded figure is one of seven representing Tutankhamen. Wearing the Red Crown of Lower Egypt, a bead collar, a pleated kilt and sandals, he holds the symbolic flail in one hand, and in the other a long *awet* crook, which resembles the *heka* insignia of Southern royalty. The eyes are made of glass, and the uraeus of bronze. While the general stance, with the left leg forward, follows the ancient convention of Egyptian sculpture, the general style of the figure—the girdle dipping low on the abdomen, the development of the breasts, and the gilding itself alluding to the brilliance of the sun—is characteristic of Amarnian art.

46. *The Queen bringing unguents and flowers to the King.*
47. *The King in a ritual hunting scene, assisted by the Queen.*

Both of these plates are details from a small gilded shrine with shallow reliefs depicting the life of Tutankhamen and Ankhesenamen. The shrine itself, with double doors, is a small-scale model of a sanctuary of the vulture goddess Nekhbet, of Upper Egypt. When found, it was empty except for a pedestal with marks for the King's feet, providing evidence that the shrine must have contained a statuette of the King, and probably also of the Queen, both of gold, which had been stolen when the tomb was opened by ancient tomb robbers. The shrine was thus a ritualistic shelter for the couple. In the scene shown on Plate 46, the King is seated, wearing the blue *khepresh* crown; before him, the Queen in sumptuous dress of pleated linen is reaching out her hand to anoint him with perfume from an unguent jar which she is holding in the other hand along with lotus blossoms. Plate 47, another panel on the same shrine, shows the King seated on a folding stool with his tame lion beside him. He is drawing his bow, aiming an arrow at the water fowl rising from a papyrus swamp, while the Queen, seated on the ground at his feet, is handing him an arrow. The vulture Nekhbet hovering behind the King's head would seem to indicate that this is a ritual hunting scene, the birds symbolizing foes in the Netherworld.

48. *Tutankhamen and Ankhesenamen in a garden, painted ivory plaque from the lid of a chest.*

One of the most seductive works of art in the tomb is the chest in the form of a cabin-shaped shrine decorated with a veneer of ivory inlaid with a marquetry of ebony, faience, and colored glass. The top, which is reproduced here, shows the youthful King and Queen in the enchanted surroundings of a grove of tall papyri and mangroves. Tutankhamen, leaning slightly forward on a long staff, is raising his hand to receive bunches of papyri and lotuses being tendered to him with both hands by Ankhesenamen. Both are wearing pleated linen garments with flowing sashes. Only in the Amarnian period is an Egyptian pharaoh represented in the company of the Queen with such informality, but here this intimate, idyllic setting is in a style which can be called "Tutankhamenesque."

49. *Back panel of the King's throne.*

Among the objects from the tomb not immediately related to the ritual of burial yet intimately connected with the life of the young King is the royal throne (see Pl. 123). Overlaid from top to bottom with gold plate, combined with inlays of multi-colored glass, faience, and semiprecious stones, the dazzling decoration is permeated with the style and motivation of Akhenaten-Amarnian art. In the scene on the back panel of the throne, Ankhesenamen is reaching forward to anoint Tutankhamen with unguent from a container held in her other hand. The informal pose of the King and the intimacy of the scene contrasts with the splendor of the setting, which appears to be in the hall of a palace, where—despite Tutankhamen's official renunciation of the cult of Aten—the sun shines down through an opening in the roof with the rays terminating in life-giving hands, as in the days of Akhenaten's reign. The Queen's and King's robes are of silver and the exposed portions of their bodies of red glass. The wide collars around their necks, composed of inlays of colored glass, carnelian, and calcite, represent the elaborate necklaces of real flowers worn on state occasions. The necklace on a stand at the right is intended as a replacement for when the one worn becomes faded.

50–55. *Burial couches in the form of sacred animals.*

An important part of the burial apparatus in Tutankhamen's tomb are the three large zoomorphic beds, found in the Antechamber. One is in the form of a lioness, another in the form of the Sacred Cow, and the third half hippopotamus and half crocodile. It is clear from the height of these beds that they could not have been used by the King in his lifetime. Of a form previously known only from tomb paintings, these are the first actual examples of this type discovered in an Egyptian tomb, and there is no doubt that they served a magical purpose. They were in fact intended to be symbolic vehicles to carry the deceased to the Netherworld.

The lioness (Pl. 50) is an evocation of the goddess Sekhmet, who had sanctuaries wherever lions came to drink, notably in the region of Memphis. This goddess was regarded as a manifestation of the Eye of Re in rage, destroyer of the enemies of the Sun. But her worship became connected with the practice of medicine, which by "appeasing Sekhmet" was able to heal and preserve from disease. The streak of blue enamel sloping down from the eyes of the lioness's head suggests a tear of commiseration for the suffering of the afflicted.

The disk of the sun between the lyre-form horns of the Divine Cow (Pls. 51, 53, 55) clearly identifies that animal as the goddess Hathor, or her alternate form, the goddess Mehturt (meaning "the Great Flood"), symbolizing the primordial waters across which the sun god had to travel. By reclining on the cow bed, Tutankhamen could be transported across the Abyss to the morning of a new life. The inscription in a cartouche on this bed reads: "May the good god live, may he be one who lives forever, the Lord of the Two Lands who holds the sovereignty of Re, Osiris, King of Upper Egypt Neb-Kheperu-Re. . . ." The elongated body of the cow, with its trilobed pelt marks, symbolizes the vault of the night sky identified with the goddess Nut.

The third bed (Pls. 52, 54), with the ferocious head of a composite animal, both hippopotamus and crocodile, is an evocation of the goddess Thueris. This divinity, often represented bearing a crocodile on its back and, as here, having the paws of a lion, was patroness of birth and child-bearing, protecting both the living and the dead. Her invocation here is thus insurance for the rebirth of the king to eternal life.

These beds are made of wood, coated with gesso and gilded, with accents generally picked out in dark blue paste. The teeth and tongues of the hippopotamus heads are of ivory, with the tongues stained red. All three beds consist of four detachable members, two sides in the form of elongated bodies, a string-mesh mattress, and the footboard. The beds could thus be taken apart for carrying into the tomb and reassembled. Their height of almost 3 feet indicates that they might have been used in the preparation of the mummy with the accompanying ritual.

56, 57. *Tutankhamen's royal* ka.

One of two almost identical statues found facing each other in the Antechamber, on each side of the entrance to the Burial Chamber, is this effigy in the likeness of Tutankhamen. He is represented wearing the striped *nemes* headdress out of which springs the uraeus on his brow, symbol of sovereignty. Picked out against the black of the face, the eyebrows, eyelids and kohl marks extending from the eyes consist of gilded bronze inserts. The eyes themselves are composed of crystalline white alabaster, with black obsidian for the pupils.

The figure, which measures 5 feet 6 inches in height—corresponding almost exactly to the length of Tutankhamen's mummy—is shown in the conventional pose with left leg forward. In the left hand he holds a long staff fitted with a stop in the shape of a lotus; and in the right he carries a mace as a symbolic protective weapon. From the collar which covers his chest, a shrine-shaped pectoral is depicted, like those found on the King's mummy. All of his attire, including the girdle around the waist and the pleated triangular apron, is gilded, in stark contrast to the black of the bare parts of the body. As in other statues from this tomb, and generally in Egyptian art, black was the color of regeneration, directly associated with the fertile black soil from the inundation of the Nile, the source of Egypt's plant life. The application of black resin to these statues conferred magical powers which would assure the rebirth of the deceased King. The statue itself represents the King's *ka*, or guardian spirit, which became separated from the body at death but followed him and watched over him in the hereafter. An inscription on the panel of the apron reads: "The good god of whom one may be proud, the Sovereign of whom one boasts, the Royal *Ka* of Harakhti, Osiris, King, Lord of the Two Lands Neb-Kheperu-Re." Statues like these had previously been found in other tombs, but it was not until the discovery of the pair in the Antechamber of Tutankhamen's tomb that their function as sentinels of the Burial Chamber became identified.

58. *Gilded cow's head, here associated with the goddess Hathor.*

The head of the cow Hathor—eye of Re—gilded over a wood base is seen emerging from the papyrus swamps; only her head is visible. The same black varnish which is painted over the base covers her elegant horns made of wood plated with bronze. It is the black and fertile soil coming from the annual flood of the Nile which thus covers these statues and enables them to participate in the rites of the Osirian rebirth. The eyes of Hathor are made of alabaster and obsidian; they are outlined together with the eyebrows, with a thin stripe of black glass.
Height: 36 inches.

59. *The god Anubis, Guardian of the Dead, on the pylon-shaped shrine at the entrance to the tomb Treasury.*

The god Anubis, resting on his gilded wooden shrine, was placed at the entrance of the room called the Treasury. He is made of wood heavily painted with black gesso. The pectination of his ears, his eyelids, eyebrows, and collar are covered with gold. His toenails are made of silver while his eyes are filled with pieces of alabaster set around pupils of obsidian. The statue of Anubis was draped in a fringed piece of cloth dating from the seventh year of the reign of Akhenaten, about the time of Tutankhamen's birth. Around Anubis' neck was placed a floral collar and a scarf. Anubis, the wild dog that roams around the dead—the black god who according to the legend had first embalmed Osiris—presided over the embalmment ritual. As a recumbent animal, placed on the gilded chest, decorated with *djed* and *tat* signs, symbols of eternity and life, Anubis becomes "He who presides over the Secrets."

Height of Anubis: $23^1/_2$ inches. Height of shrine: $21^1/_4$ inches; length: $37^1/_2$ inches.

60. *Gilded wood canopy and shrine with Isis and Selkhet, two of the four guardian goddesses protecting the alabaster canopic chest within.*

The Keys to
Eternal Life

This great gilded shrine is contained within a gilded wood canopy held by four pillars at each angle covered with hieroglyphs. Both the shrine and the canopy are surmounted by a magnificent frieze composed of uraei carrying the solar disk. The shrine itself contained the canopic chest with Tutankhamen's lungs, liver, intestines, and stomach, corresponding in this way to the gilded shrines which contained the stone sarcophagus and the three coffins with the King's mummy. This shrine was made of wood subsequently gilded; the walls are covered with hieroglyphic inscriptions; however, the most surprising and delightful motif of this part of the burial ritual is the group of four guardian goddesses extending their arms on each side of the shrine, so as to protect its contents: Nephthys, Ncith, Isis, and Selkhet, the latter with the scorpion on her head, symbol of magic and of healing. These statuettes are all draped in long, pleated dresses and are placed in most natural poses with a slight turn of the head. Their eyebrows and eyes, painted black with white corneas, contribute to the lively aspect of these gilded statuettes which are so reminiscent of the earlier Amarnian style.

Height: $78^1/_4$ inches.

61. *The alabaster canopic chest containing the four miniature coffins for Tutankhamen's internal organs.*

This alabaster canopic chest replaces the four canopic vases which we traditionally find in Ancient Egypt. It is painted with black pigment and is decorated with hieroglyphs evoking the words pronounced by each of the four goddesses placed at each angle. This alabaster chest is divided into four hollow compartments made to contain four miniature mummiform coffins for the king's organs and covered by alabaster stoppers. This chest for the viscera thus corresponds to the great stone sarcophagus containing the whole mummy. Here, the four goddesses, which we have already encountered standing in front of the gilded shrine on each side, are figured naked and in low relief at the angles. They are now joined by the four spirits, sons of Horus, who care for the royal body: Isis is

joined by Imset at the southwest corner to protect the liver; the baboon-headed Hapi is coupled with Nephthys to take care of the king's lungs at the northwest corner; Khebesenuf, the falcon-headed spirit, guards the viscera with Selkhet; and the dog-headed Duamutef is taking care of the stomach in the company of Neith. The base was decorated with *djed* pillars of eternity alternating with the knot of Isis, and was placed on a gilded sledge. The massive sloping lid was attached to the chest by little sealed cords tied to gold rings.
Height: 34 inches.

62. *One of four alabaster portrait heads of Tutankhamen used as stoppers to close the compartments in the canopic chest.*

Four heads of this kind were carved out of alabaster coming from the quarries of Hatnub. They were placed facing each other in the alabaster canopic chest over each of the four compartments containing the miniature gold coffins. These stoppers were inspired by the features of Tutankhamen at the time of his death. He is wearing the *nemes* headdress and the animals of royalty, the vulture and the uraeus. The Pharaoh's eyes are here slightly less made up than on the great coffins and on the mask: the black outline of the eyes and eyebrows is extended towards the temples by finer brush-strokes. The irises are painted black and a thin black line follows the folds of his eyelids and of his neck; his ears are pierced in the Amarnian tradition, while his full red lips evoke the promised regeneration. Traces of unguent can be found on the *nemes*.
Height: 9$^1/_2$ inches.

63. *One of four miniature mummiform coffins containing the embalmed organs of the King.*

These precious containers were modeled like the second of the King's coffins and are made likewise of two parts, the shell and the lid. On the outside, these objects are made in the now familiar technique of Egyptian glass cloisonné and semiprecious stone inlays. Inside, the coffin was lined by a thick gold sheet covered with inscriptions except on the hands and face of the mummy. From these inscriptions, it appears that the name of Tutankhamen was substituted for others, probably Smenkhare's, Akhenaten's co-regent and brother or half brother of Tutankhamen. As both kings probably resembled each other, one of the current hypotheses supports the idea that these coffins, along with a group of other artifacts found in this tomb, were first made and intended for Smenkhare. On the exterior of these miniature coffins, the Pharaoh is shown wearing the *nemes* headdress and the two royal animals. He is holding the Osirian scepter and flail in his hands. On the back of this mummiform coffin, two vulture goddesses are crossing their wings while clasping the hieroglyphic sign for eternity, *shen*, in their claws. The body of the mummy is covered with feathers as on the second of the large coffins.
Height: 15$^3/_8$ inches.

64. *Gold sheaths used to cover the finger and toe tips of Tutankhamen.*

The King's fingers and toes were left free of the last layer of the mummy wrappings and were covered by gold sheaths, after having been individually bandaged. As in the royal mask, they were meant to liken Tutankhamen's features and flesh to those of the gods. Seal rings were found on the middle and ring fingers of the King's left hand. The sheaths were delicately modeled so as to imitate nails and knuckles. A pair of gold sandals (Pl. 150) was slipped on to his gold-sheathed toes.

65. *Two of the King's* ushabty *figures; the larger figure carrying two flails, the smaller one wearing the* nemes *headdress.*

The first little funerary figures of this kind were called *shawabty*, from the word for wood, *shawab*, out of which they were made during the Middle Kingdom. In the New Kingdom, they were called *ushabty*, from the verb *ushab*, to answer; these statuettes were placed in the tomb in order to answer for the King when asked to participate in certain activities. The simple citizens possessed *ushabty* carrying the instruments of their trade, but the King's bore the instruments of power, and for 413 *ushabty* found in this tomb, 1,866 miniature instruments were also identified. Tombs were supposed to contain at least 365 *ushabty*, one for each day of the year. The most handsome *ushabty* of Tutankhamen show different headdresses and instruments; some are in alabaster, others more simply in enameled pottery. They were placed in tall black boxes in the shape of shrines coated with bitumen, and were stacked in the Treasury.

These two gilded *ushabty* of Tutankhamen were probably made of a kind of redwood (cedar?). The larger *ushabty* is wearing a short Nubian headdress and carries two flails—it was only during the ceremony of the Jubilee that the Pharaoh carried two flails. Its arms and shoulders are left free of the mummiform envelope which is engraved with a hieroglyphic inscription. A broad gilded collar is placed on its shoulders. The second *ushabty*, the smaller one, seems to have lost its instruments as well as the royal animals on its forehead. This figure is also wrapped in a mummiform envelope and a *nemes* cloth is placed around its head, held by a gold band. Its face is delicately made up in order to give life to the figure: red lips and eyes in which the black iris is surrounded by the white of the cornea.

66. *Two gilded* ushabty *figures, both wearing the Red Crown of the North.*

These two figures are wearing the tiara of Northern Egypt. The one on the left is wearing the cobra uraeus of the reigning king; it was probably entirely gilded but for the uraeus, its hands, and the face, which was delicately made up. The figure is carrying a crook in its right hand—it is the crook which was carried by the pharaohs during their lifetime—but it appears to have lost whatever it was carrying in the left hand. The second *ushabty*, on the right, is also entirely gilded, and the text of Chapter 6 of the *Book of the Dead* referring to the *ushabty* is engraved on the mummiform body. The crown is adorned with both the uraeus and the vulture; it is carrying the two royal scepters, the crook and the flail.
Height: about $25^1/_4$ inches.

67. *Model of the Pharaoh's boat, with mast and rigging.*

Many boats were found in the so-called Treasury room: they were intended most probably for the mystical voyage of the king in his afterlife, as he went in the wake of Re and Osiris. This particular boat is undoubtedly similar to the one the King must have used in his lifetime. A large rectangular sail was probably raised on the double mast and rigging. A central cabin, decorated with a mosaic of colorful and lively check pattern is framed at the bow and stern by two little shrine-shaped cabins decorated with the royal sphinx at the bow and with the bull (also representing the Pharaoh, sometimes called the bull of his mother) at the stern. This type of shrine-like construction is also depicted on the exterior wall of Shrine III, where the Solar Bark is depicted accompanied by a flotilla of smaller boats.

Length: $8^5/_8$ inches; height: $3^7/_8$ inches.

68. *Model of a royal bark, one of seven found in the Treasury.*

One of seven found in the tomb, this model of a royal boat is brightly painted and decorated. The ship is steered by two large oars which are firmly held by a crossbar. This boat was probably meant to be towed during the funerary procession or during one of the mystical voyages of the afterlife. Windows and doors are painted on the central cabin. Screens for the crew were placed on the bow and stern of this ship, which must have been intended for mourners.

69. *Carved wood image of the mummified King on his lion-headed funerary bed, flanked by two soul birds.*

This effigy was found in its wooden coffin. It was carved out of a single piece of cedar (?) wood. The reclining figure of the mummified King wearing the *nemes* headdress is adorned with the uraeus alone, indicating that he has not yet begun his voyage into the Netherworld. The two scepters which the King held in his hands have disappeared. On either side of the mummy two birds extend their protective wings. On the right, the falcon-headed bird symbolizes the regeneration after the King's trip through the Netherworld; it is Horus, the son conceived by Osiris after his death. On the left, the human-headed bird represents the soul which belongs to the past, Osiris. The mummy lies on a lion-headed bed similar to those found in the tomb. The little lions can be associated with the ones placed on each side of the ivory headrest (see Pl. 130); they symbolize the Eastern and Western horizon. Four hieroglyphic strips envelop the mummy from one side to the other: they invoke the sons of Horus, Hapi, Khebesenuf, Imset, and Duamutef, along with Osiris, Horus, and Anubis. Running from his hand to his feet another inscription refers to the goddess Nut, asking for her protection during the mummy's long trip through the starry Heaven and the Netherworld. Last but not least, a third hieroglyphic inscription runs under the feet of the mummy and along the bed between the two lion paws: it refers to Maya, the "Chief of Works in the Magnificent Place on the West Bank, the Superintendent of

241

the Treasury." This very high official may have been among those who saved Tutankhamen's tomb after the two earlier violations by robbers.

Length: 16⁵/₈ inches.

70. *Gilt-wood statuette of the god Atum, in front of two statuettes of the god Ihy playing a sistrum.*

The two statuettes of the god Ihy are in the shape of the young King entirely naked, wearing the long braid linked to childhood and agitating the sistrum of Hathor, a gesture traditionally associated with women. But for his gilded eyes, the young god is entirely covered with black bitumen; he is the incarnation of Tutankhamen, now stripped bare of his mortal form and hiding in the swamps of Chemnis. He has become the son of Hathor, and while he is still in the dark, he is calling the great goddess with the sistrum, the sound of which imitates the rustle of papyri in the wind. His left hand is slightly raised in respect. All the statuettes of this kind were entirely covered except for the face by pieces of linen woven in the city of Akhenaten and often even bearing a date. These statuettes are all reminiscent of the Amarnian style, with their natural poses and the slightly androgynous aspect of their bodies. Tutankhamen as Ihy, or as seen later in the gilded statuettes of the King standing on a feline or spearing hippopotami from a reed boat are all projections of the King, often still irradiated by the sun, seen while he is accomplishing the different deeds associated with his trip through the Netherworld.

The gilded statuette of the god Atum shows him wearing the symbolic collar. He is wrapped in a shroud, and as all the little gilded statuettes which were found in these black shrine boxes, he was probably also meant to help Tutankhamen in his voyage through the Netherworld.

71. *Gilded statuette of Tutankhamen on a black leopard.*

The gilded statuette of Tutankhamen standing on a leopard also belongs to this series of projections of the King as seen through the different stages of his transformation in the Netherworld. This wood statuette is entirely gilded, as Tutankhamen is still irradiated by the sun god. He is wearing the Crown of Upper Egypt and the uraeus alone, worn by the Pharaoh during his actual reign, as well as a flail and a long stick made of gilded bronze. The slightly effeminate gestures of the King as well as the natural and relaxed quality of his pose are reminiscent of the late Amarnian style. As a matter of fact, some of his facial features and the prominent breasts seem to have been also associated with his half-brother Smenkhare, and, as for a couple of other objects found in this tomb, it is not known whether this statuette was meant for Smenkhare or for Tutankhamen. The statuette is standing on the black leopard, the animal of night. There were two statuettes of this kind in Tutankhamen's tomb and they can be compared to a painting in the later tomb of Sethos II, where the Pharaoh is depicted in his afterlife, standing on a lion.

Height: 33¹¹/₁₆ inches.

242

72, 73. *Portable redwood funerary chest and detail, showing the King making an offering to Osiris.*

This chest was found stripped of its original contents on the floor of the Antechamber of the Treasury. Because of its sober elegance it remains one of the most beautiful chests of the tomb. Similar objects were also depicted in earlier Fifth Dynasty mastabas, and the classical sobriety of this chest recalls the traditional canons of aesthetics of the two earlier kingdoms. With its four retractable poles, it is perhaps the ancestor of our traveling trunk. But this delicate framework made out of ebony and set around inner panels of lighter cedar wood, these ivory strips, gilded knobs and accompanying inscriptions were definitely intended to be part of the King's afterlife. The feet are capped in bronze. The funerary character of the chest is clearly expressed by the gilded inscription engraved on the ebony framework: offerings and utterances of the gods Thoth, Geb, Harendotis, Harakhti, and Ptah-Sokar-Osiris, telling the Pharaoh of his future regeneration and satisfactions. The name of the Great Royal Spouse Ankhesenamen, Mistress of the Two Lands, is linked on the lid, as on the semicircular chest, to the titles of Tutankhamen. The gilded knob placed on the coffer is engraved with the name and title of Tutankhamen, regent of the Southern Heliopolis. The only carved panel of this chest is placed just beneath the knob: it further enhances the funerary meaning of the chest. Tutankhamen is draped in a simple kilt and is wearing the customary *khepresh* with the uraeus. He is offering wine and a burning lamp to Osiris. The god is wrapped in his shroud, wearing the *atef* crown flanked by ostrich feathers and the uraeus. Osiris is holding the flagellum and a long crook recalling the royal *heka*. His artificial beard is exceptionally long. Between these two figures a pedestal has been placed supporting a libation cup terminated by an ostrich feather symbolizing Truth, the goddess Maat, for in the weighing of the souls, the dead had to be as light as a feather. An inscription is placed over the scene, referring to the god as Unen-Nefer, Great God leading the West, Lord of the Necropolis, and Tutankhamen is called Osiris Neb-Kheperu-Re, of the True Voice, both titles referring to his afterlife; the sign for heaven dominates the scene.
Height: 25 inches.

74. *The serpent divinity Neter-Ankh.*

This gilded serpent is identified by an inscription on its pedestal. Neter-Ankh was one of the five serpents which, along with the five vultures, were found as amulets in the coffins of the Middle Kingdom. This is a larger version of the many other amulets of the kind found in the King's wrappings.
Height: 22$^1/_4$ inches.

75. *Gold-plated standard of the falcon Gemhesu.*

The gilded wood standard of the falcon Gemhesu is carrying the flail and is adorned with collarettes and counterpoise. His name, Gemhesu, is inscribed on the pedestal: "He who espies himself." Gemhesu also bore the epithet, "He who gives Light with his two eyes." The falcon was commonly used as an emblem on standards. This standard can be compared to the two forms of the falcon standard of the ancient 20th Nome of Lower Egypt. A second standard with a falcon, but this time crowned with two feathers, Sopd, was also found in the tomb. Both probably represented districts; Sopd, the one which is not illustrated here, was associated with a district in the Delta.

76. *The god Ptah, wrapped in a robe of feathers.*

One of the twenty-five black shrines piled up in the Treasury room contained the wood statuette of the god Ptah, wrapped in linen. His body was gilded with an alloy of gold and copper while his face seems to have been gilded with a purer sheet of gold. The skull cap is made of blue faience and his eyes are inlaid with glass. He is wearing a symbolic bronze beard and holds in his two hands the scepter *was*, symbolizing dominion, surmounted by the *djed* pillar of eternity, the *ankh* knot for life, and the animal head belonging traditionally to the *was* scepter and identifying it. The figure is standing on a base whose form recalls Maat, Truth, which is inscribed with a dedication to Tutankhamen, beloved of Ptah. The body is wrapped in feathers and Ptah is wearing the broad collar and back pendant, *mankhet*. Ptah was the most important god of Memphis, the capital of the Ancient Kingdom before it was transferred during the Middle Kingdom to Thebes, the city of Amen-Re. Ptah was held responsible for mankind, for, according to his priests, by uttering the names of the living beings, he had brought them into existence. The name Egypt itself derives from the Greek Aegyptos, which means the Shrine of Ptah, referring thus to Memphis, the ancient capital.
Height: $20^3/_4$ inches.

Hunting and War

77. Gilded statuette of the King as the god Horus, spearing from a reed boat.

79. Tutankhamen's second State Chariot.

◁ 78. Detail of the second State Chariot.

80. Tutankhamen defeating the Syrians, detail from the
side of a painted chest.

81. Gold flabellum, detail showing the King hunting
ostriches.

82. The King's ceremonial footstool, showing the
enemies of Egypt carved in sunk relief.

83. Ceremonial shield showing the King as a sphinx trampling on the foes of Egypt.

84. Ceremonial shield showing the King slaying lions.

85. The two daggers from the King's mummy and their sheaths.

Ceremonial Jewelry

86. The Royal Diadem from the King's mummy, with the vulture of the South and the cobra of the North.

87. The crook and the flail, Tutankhamen's royal attributes.

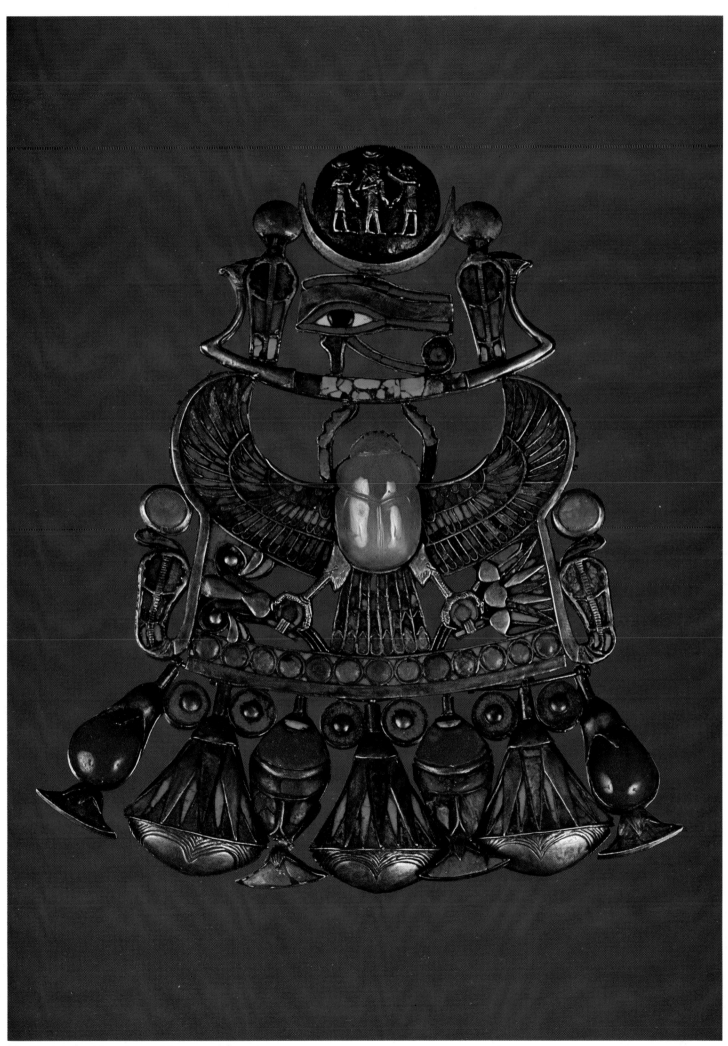

88. Pectoral with solar and lunar emblems.

89. Shrine-shaped pectoral with winged scarab supported by Isis and Nephthys.

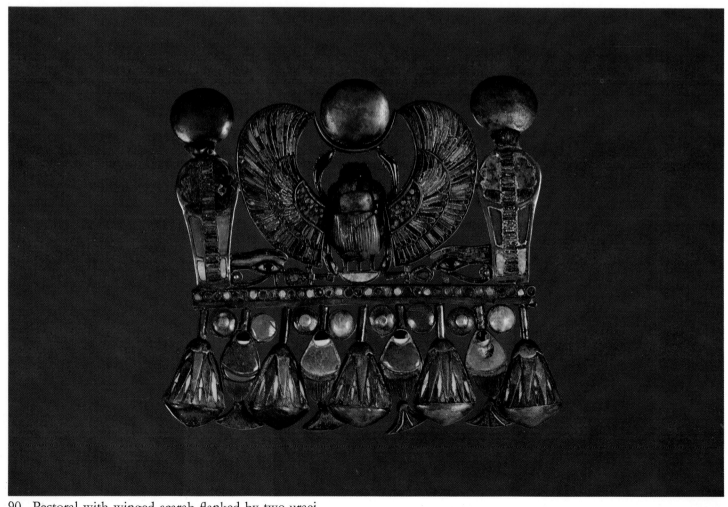

90. Pectoral with winged scarab flanked by two uraei.

91. Pectoral in the shape of a shrine with *djed* pillar
    protected by Isis and Nephthys.

92. Pendant of a necklace with the scarab as Rising Sun
    between two baboons.

93. Gold unguent box with double royal cartouches.

94. Gold inlay necklace and pendant with scarabs.

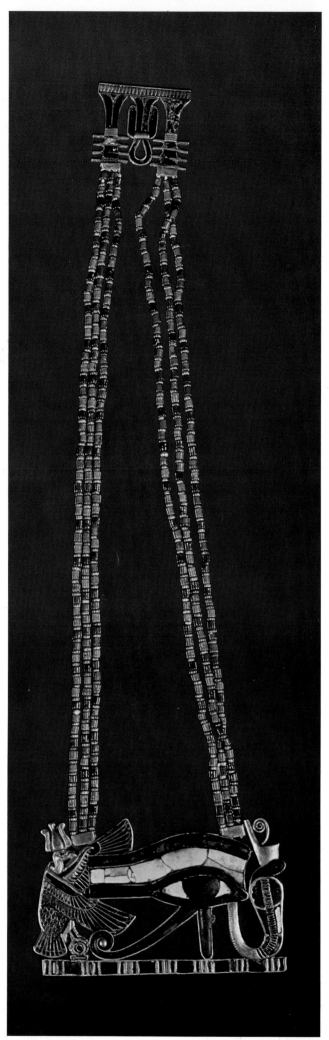

95. Pectoral with three scarabs.

96. Pectoral with *udjat* eye protected by the vulture and the uraeus.

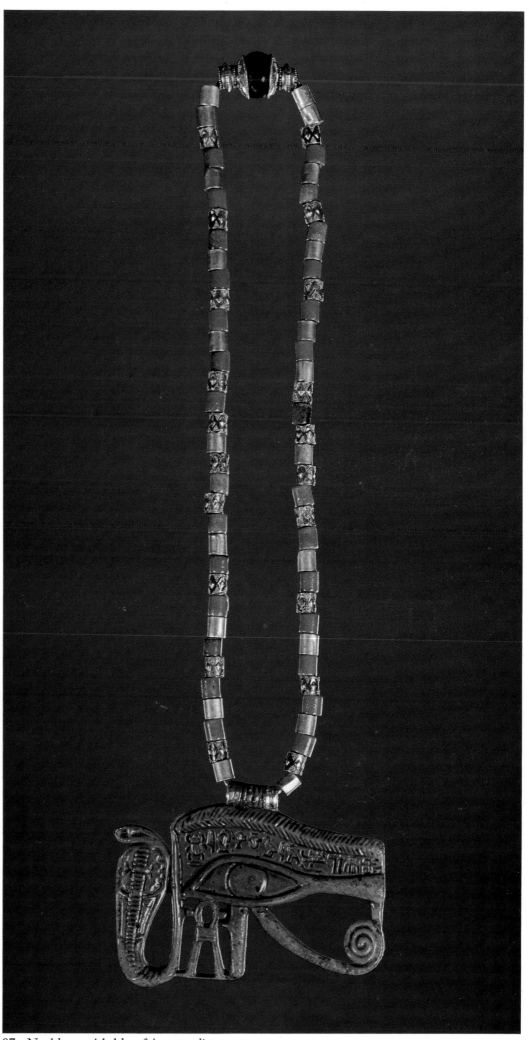

97. Necklace with blue faience *udjat* eye.

98. Earrings in the shape of falcons with ducks' heads.

99. Earrings with gold filigree and stone beads.

100. Earrings with an effigy of the King between two uraei.

101. Royal scepter, used for offerings, detail.

102. Gold filigree ring bracelet with turquoise-type stone.

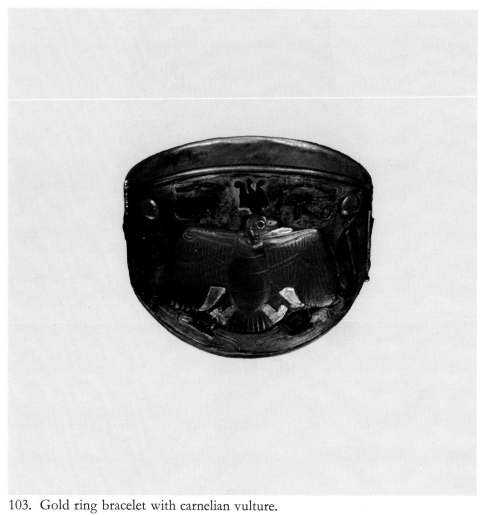

103. Gold ring bracelet with carnelian vulture.

104. Band bracelet with three lapis-lazuli scarabs.

105. Band bracelet of three scarabs, one white, with
clasps showing the King's cartouches.

106. Four bracelets with beads and semiprecious stones.

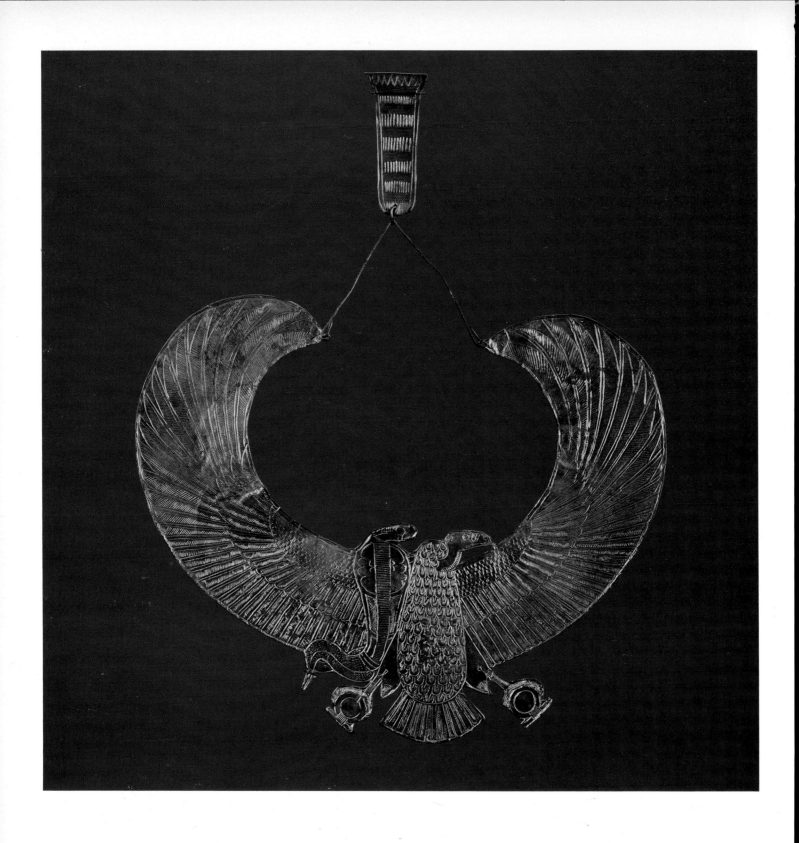

107. The collar of Nebti, chased sheet gold, with the
Nekhbet vulture and the Buto uraeus.

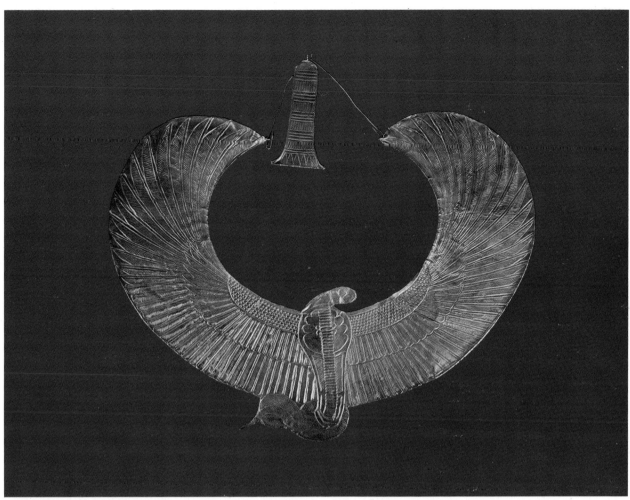

108. The collar of Buto, chased sheet gold, with the uraeus.

109. The collar of Horus, chased sheet gold, with the falcon.

110. Collar of cloisonné work terminating in falcon heads.

111. Broad "floral" bead collar.

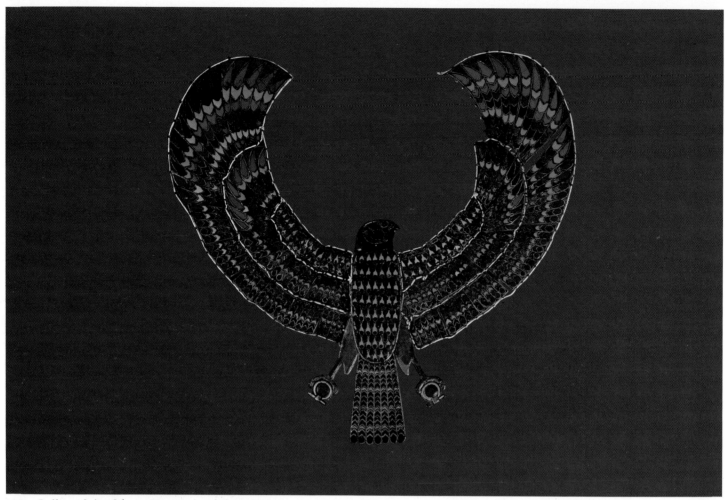

112. Collar of the falcon Horus, in cloisonné.

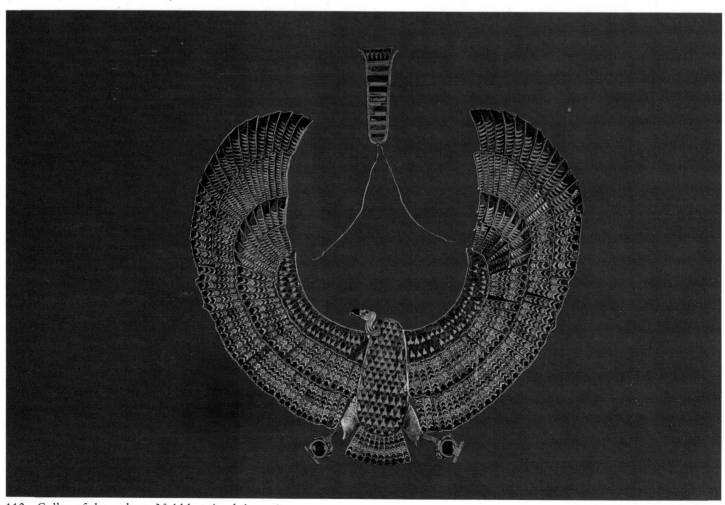

113. Collar of the vulture Nekhbet, in cloisonné.

114. Scarab pectoral with cloisonné wings.

115. Pectoral of Horus, in cloisonné, holding the symbols of Life and Eternity in his claws.

116. (above left) Pectoral of the vulture in cloisonné, with the *atef* crown.

117. (above right) Pectoral of the vulture in blue cloisonné.

118. (below left) Pectoral of Horus in cloisonné.

119. (below right) Pectoral of Nekhbet in cloisonné.

120. Six gold amulets, five of which are inlaid with glass
and semiprecious stones.

Objects of Royal Life

121. Religious throne and foot stand.

123. The gilded throne.

124. Child's chair with ebony and ivory inlays.

125. Crosslegged stool with imitation leopard-skin seat.

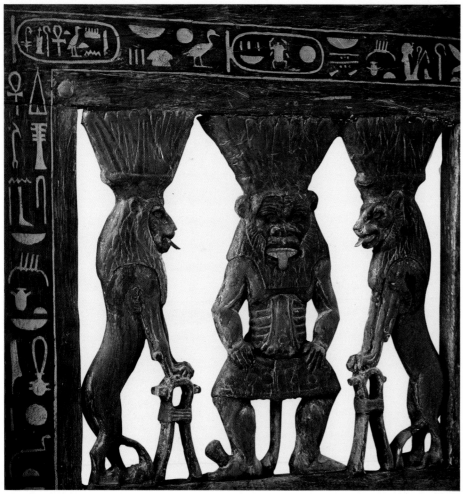

126. Bed stand with the god Bes, detail of the bed in the following plate.

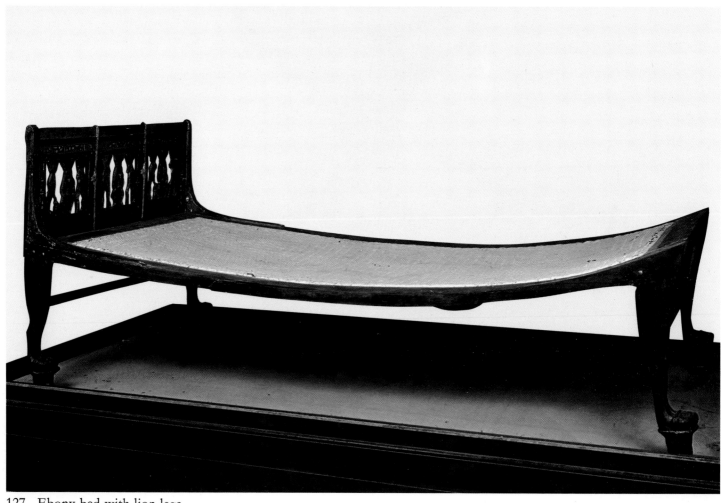

127. Ebony bed with lion legs.

128. Headrest of lapis-lazuli blue glass.

129. Headrest ornamented with heads of the god Bes.

130. Symbolical ivory headrest with the god Shu as support.

131. Chest in the form of a shrine, with gold plaques
and blue faience inlays.

132. Coffer with gilded openwork decoration.

133. Painted alabaster coffer.

134. Chest with ivory inlays.

135. Wood cabinet on legs with decorative openwork.

136. Semicircular box with royal gold cartouche over *sma-tawy* symbol.

137. Alabaster chalice in the form of a lotus flower.

138. Alabaster unguent container in the form of a ceremonial boat.

139. Triple alabaster lamp in the shape of a lotus plant.

140. Perfume vase with Hapi deities holding papyrus and lotus plants.

141. Alabaster unguent jar with a lid in the shape of a recumbent lion.

142. Alabaster flask with decorative inlays.

143. Unguent jar in the form of a standing lion.

144. Silver vase in the shape of a pomegranate.

145. Lid of an alabaster jar showing a bird on its nest.

146. Ostrich feather fan with ivory handle.

147. Ceremonial flabellum with colored glass inlays;
the royal cartouches protected by vultures.

148, 149. Three ceremonial canes showing the adversaries of Egypt.

150. Gold sandals.

151. Wooden sandals with gilded inner soles showing figures of captives.

152. Left to right: ivory smoother for papyrus, Princess Meritaten's
palette, and ivory and gold palette with brushes.

Notes to the Plates

77. *Gilded statuette of the King as the god Horus, spearing from a reed boat.*

The King, standing on a small papyrus boat with arm raised to throw a harpoon, is represented as Horus hunting hippopotami in the marshes of the Nile delta. The action commemorates the search to avenge the murder of Osiris by the confederates of his brother Seth, who had transformed themselves into hippopotami. Carved in wood, the statue is coated with gesso and gilded. The King is shown wearing the Red Crown of Lower Egypt, a bead collar, and a pleated linen kilt. The eyes are of glass set in bronze in copper sockets; also of bronze are the uraeus, sandals, harpoon, and the coil of rope in his left hand, all gilded except for the rope. The unnatural development of the breasts and the billowing kilt reflect the Amarnian style, as also the gilding itself, symbolizing the brilliance of the sun. The piece is an exceptional example in Egyptian sculpture of the human figure realistically poised at a moment of action.

78, 79. *The second State Chariot.*

Of four chariots found in the tomb, the extraordinary ornamentation on this one and another identifies them as vehicles used by the King for ceremonial occasions, standing in the open-back chaise behind richly caparisoned horses. Sturdily built of wood, the body of this chariot is covered with a sheet of gold embossed with bands of an allover feather design, rosettes and running spirals alternating with inlays of polychrome glass. Low down on the side (Pl. 78), an oculus of semiprecious stones encloses an *udjat* eye, symbol of the protective sky god Horus; and at its side is the cobra goddess Wadjet, symbolizing royal authority. The curving frame of the body consists of a single piece of wood bent semicircular to form the sides and front. The back is left open for easy access in and out. A long yoke pole provided the attachments for two horses.

80. *Tutankhamen defeating the Syrians, detail from the side of a painted chest.*

This triumphant battle scene showing Tutankhamen in his chariot attacking a tumultuous horde of Syrian enemies is of a type which

301

can be seen elsewhere on chariot fronts and pylon walls. Similar versions have also been found in mural paintings of the succeeding dynasty, notably depicting the battle of Kadesh under Rameses II. But it is unlikely that the young King ever waged war, and this painting must be regarded as a symbolic representation of the Pharaoh's invincible power. It is one of the sides of a wooden chest decorated all over with paintings in varnished gouache over gesso. The other side shows the king overcoming black Africans, and on the lid is a lion hunt, with ostriches, antelopes, hyenas, and other desert animals in flight. Notable in this detail showing the Syrian foe in close-quarter fighting is the depiction of anguish and pain in the faces and attitudes of the combatants. Such realism and freedom of expression is characteristic of Amarnian art from the period when Tutankhamen was born and lived his early years, in the capital built by his predecessor, the heretical King Akhenaten.

81. *Gold flabellum, detail showing the King hunting ostriches.*

This semicircular panel measuring $7^1/_4$ inches across and 4 inches high is a feather holder for a ceremonial fan of ostrich feathers on the end of a gold handle 37 inches long. It is made of wood covered, with sheet gold, embossed on each face with a scene of the King hunting ostriches. Holes on the curved perimeter still show the stumps of feathers which protruded from the holder; and an inscription on the handle states that the fan is made of "ostrich feathers obtained by the King when hunting in the desert east of Heliopolis." On the front face the King is shown riding in his chariot at a rapid pace and aiming an arrow at ostriches on the ground ahead. Under the galloping horses is a hound in hot pursuit. The King is wearing the blue *khepresh* crown with the uraeus, and following on the ground behind the chariot the *ankh* sign of life, animated with arms and legs, is holding the staff of a feather fan like the one described here. The long handle terminates, where it is attached to the fan, in a stylized papyrus or lotus flower. This fan was found in Tutankhamen's Burial Chamber between the last two shrines nearest the sarcophagus, near the level of the mummy's head, symbolically conferring shade and a breath of air on the Pharaoh.

82. *The King's ceremonial footstool, showing the enemies of Egypt carved in sunk relief.*

Among the frequent representations of alien types depicting the peoples with whom Egypt had to contend, these carvings on a ceremonial footstool enabled the Pharaoh symbolically to tread his enemies underfoot. Clearly recognizable are several racial types. In the upper register are the adversaries of Egypt's northern borders —a Syrian with his curly beard, the disk-pendant hanging from his neck, and wearing a tassellated skirt; and a Libyan, nude except for his loincloth, with plaited hair to which are affixed two ostrich feathers. In the lower register are represented a Nubian and a Sudanese as the adversaries of the South. Their clothing is identical, but their facial characteristics are vividly distinguished, and the Nubian has a feather in his hair. Between each pair is a large bow. On the front of the stool (not shown here) are represented these four types, conquered and bound as captives under the yoke of the Pharaoh, in an arrangement of lotus and papyrus stems tied in a central knot, which is a variation of the hieroglyphic sign for the Unification of the Two Lands (i.e., Upper and Lower Egypt).

83. *Ceremonial shield showing the King as a sphinx trampling on the foes of Egypt.*

Of eight shields found in Tutankhamen's tomb, this one and the following (Pl. 84) are clearly ceremonial in character, almost heraldic in design. Here the King is represented as a sphinx wearing the double crown of Upper and Lower Egypt and treading on two dark-skinned enemies. A winged sun disk symbolizing Horus carrying the reborn sun fills the arched top, while a falcon—again as the god Horus—grasping the hieroglyphic sign for eternity (*shen*) in his claws, hovers protectively over the sphinx. Behind the sphinx, upright on a pole, stands a ceremonial fan with ostrich feathers. The two victims, both African negroes, are each wearing kilts, and one has an arrow in his head. A decorative band forming the base of the shield has a design suggesting dunes in the desert. The shield, measuring 30 inches in height, is made of carved wood in high relief, gessoed and gilded.

84. *Ceremonial shield showing the King slaying lions.*

Just as the previously described example, this shield is clearly ceremonial in character, although here the young King is depicted in human form. He is shown as no more than a boy, with arm raised, holding a scimitar-shaped sword, about to strike two lions he is holding by the tails. Such a feat would be beyond the capability of the youthful Tutankhamen, who was only nine at his accession, and the scene probably commemorates the exploits of hunting prowess performed by kings in their coronation festivities. The shield probably is intended to depict the ritual gestures which the young King made on that occasion. He is shown wearing the *atef* crown with ram's horns and the sun disk of the god Re, and behind him is the vulture goddess. These associations with Upper Egypt recall the close bond of the Amarnian family with Nubia which persisted through Tutankhamen's reign. But the hieroglyphic inscription at right compares the strength of the King to the god Montu, the warlike Lord of Thebes.

85. *The two daggers from the King's mummy and their sheaths.*

As protection against the demons of the Netherworld, Tutankhamen was provided with these two prestigious daggers, one with a blade of hardened gold, the other with an iron blade, weapons truly worthy of a pharaoh. The workmanship of the gold dagger and particularly its sheath reflects technical skill of a very high order. The back of the sheath shows an overall feather pattern with cloisonné inserts, terminating at the point with a jackal's head. But along the full length of the front is an extraordinary procession of animals in combat. Lions, a cheetah, and dogs—animals considered friendly to man—are shown attacking evil and ferocious beasts, such as ibexes and bulls. The theme is clearly symbolic in showing triumph over evil forces, and it conferred magical power on the sheath, rendering the blade invulnerable. This animal style appears foreign to Egyptian art, suggesting Syrian or Asiatic influences, which however have been absorbed in integrated design. The hilts of both daggers, with their geometric designs in granulated gold and cloisonné, are very similar except for the pommels, that of the gold dagger bearing the King's cartouche on its top and protective falcons holding the sign of eternity on its underside, while that of the iron dagger has a pommel of rock crystal. The iron blade, in pristine condition when found, was of an extremely rare metal then. Only two or three other objects in the tomb were of iron, one being an amuletic headrest placed under the head of the mummy.

86. *The Royal Diadem from the King's mummy, with the vulture of the South and the cobra of the North.*

Ceremonial Jewelry

This magnificent fillet was discovered circling the head of Tutankhamen after the gold mask and several layers of linen wrapping were removed from his head. Since it was impossible to place the gold mask over the vulture and the uraeus, these two objects were detached from the fillet and were found separately on the mummy. The cobra was found lying on the left thigh, the vulture on the right. Each is provided with grooves which fit perfectly into T-shaped tongues on the fillet proper.

The gold fillet itself imitates a ribbon. The series of circles along this ribbon are made of carnelian whose centers contain bosses of gold. At the rear, serving as a clasp, are two lotus blossoms horizontally springing from a sun disk, from which descend obliquely two streamers. Two additional streamers, somewhat shorter in length but wider, fall at an acute angle from each lotus blossom. Each of these last two streamers is decorated with a massive gold uraeus, the royal cobra, along its outer edge.

The crowning glory of this fillet is the representation of the vulture and of the cobra, the two primeval symbols of Upper and of Lower Egypt. Since the mummy of Tutankhamen was lying in its coffin with its head oriented to the West, the vulture was oriented towards Upper Egypt in the South. Such an orientation is consistent since the vulture, still abundantly found today in Nubia, symbolized Nekhbet, the titulary deity of Upper Egypt whose sanctuary was at Elkab. The eyes are made of obsidian. The cobra, symbolizing Wadjet, the titulary deity of the Delta, was associated with the site of Buto. The fillet thereby indicated that King Tutankhamen was truly the Lord of the Two Lands because Nekhbet and Wadjet, the titular deities of Upper and Lower Egypt respectively, were united over his head in the fillet.

87. *The crook and the flail, Tutankhamen's royal attributes.*

Although often illustrated together, this crook and flail are not likely to have been made as a pair. Both were found in different parts of the tomb: the crook in the Antechamber and the flail in the so-called Treasury. Also, on the round base of the crook's handle, the king's name appears in its original form, Tutankhaten, indicating that this royal scepter was fashioned early in his reign, perhaps at the time of his coronation at Tell-el-Amarna. The flail, however, shows the ruler's later designation, Tutankhamen, and was thus made after the court abandoned Akhenaten's city approximately two years after the young King's accession.

The use of the crook and flail as divine and royal insignia can be traced back to the Predynastic Period, before the invention of writing or the establishment of the Egyptian state. In that primordial time, the shepherd's crook was associated with Andjety, a local god of the eastern Delta. Eventually, Osiris superseded Andjety and adopted his most characteristic attribute. Since the Egyptians felt that all dead monarchs were assimilated with the essence of the god Osiris, the crook evolved into a royal symbol as well. Indeed, the Egyptian word "to rule" (*heka*) was written with a hieroglyph in the form of a crook.

The origin of the flail, however, is less perfectly understood. The device was composed of three swingles or streamers attached to a whip-like handle. Like the crook, the slender flail enjoyed an early association with Osiris, but the god's benevolent nature cannot be easily reconciled with a whip. For this reason, much current opinion favors viewing the flail as a *ladanisterion*, an implement used to gather ladanum, an aromatic gum secreted by the cistus shrub and used in the manufacture of perfumes and medicinal unguents. Both the crook and flail are made of alternating gold and blue glass cylinders mounted, in the case of the handles, on a bronze core. The swingles of the flail, however, have a wooden core.

88. *Pectoral with solar and lunar emblems.*

This pectoral was found, not on the mummy proper, but in one of the chests. It symbolizes the journey of the sun and the moon across the heavens. Its central motif is a scarab, the dung beetle, which was associated by the Egyptians with the sun. This scarab, of chalcedony, forms the body of a falcon whose outstretched wings, talons, and tail are done in cloisonné. The falcon and scarab, each a distinct natural form, have here been united into one composite beast with such skill that the spectator is hardly aware of the dichotomy. This harmonious union of such disparate elements characterizes Egyptian design and sets its artists apart from those of other cultures.

The falcon-scarab holds in each talon the *shen* sign, symbolizing eternity, to which on the left is tied the open lily and on the right the lotus flower and buds. These plants symbolize Upper and Lower Egypt. Along the outer edge of each wing is a uraeus, whose gold body forms a convenient frame into which the above elements are placed. Beneath the border of alternating circlets is a series of pendants in the form of lotus, papyrus, and poppy flowers.

The scarab pushes a *wia* bark, which itself is the hieroglyph for the verb *djai*, "to sail," strictly applied to the divine journeys of the Sun. The *wia* bark, whose prow and stern are in the form of bundled papyri, carries two uraei, each crowned with a sun disk, which flank the *udjat* eye. This eye, representing the left eye of Horus, which is associated with the moon, supports a crescent and a moon. Within the moon, made of silver, are three figures of gold representing, left to right, Thoth, the ibis-headed moon god, Tutankhamen, and Re-Harakhti, the falcon-headed god of the Two Horizons.

89. *Shrine-shaped pectoral with winged scarab supported by Isis and Nephthys.*

This pectoral, made of gold inlaid with carnelian and various colors of glass, was found with several other pectorals in a shrine upon which was a black varnished image in wood of a jackal, representing Anubis, the god of embalming. Unlike many of the other pectorals, this example was intended to be worn by stringing the corners with four ribbons or straps which have not survived. Its rectangular format is intended to recall a façade of an Egyptian shrine whose cornice is here replaced by a winged sun disk, representing the falcon-headed god Horus the Behdet. He was a solar deity whose epithet was "the one of colorful plumage." The corners are again, as in Plates 88 and 90, filled with uraei crowned with sun disks.

The main scene represents two goddesses, Nephthys, left, and her sister, Isis, right, who symbolize two of the four quadrants of the Egyptian universe. Their outstretched arms support the wings of the scarab, representing the sun god in his manifestation as Khepri, the dawn. He is made of a greenish stone; the back of his gold mount is inscribed with a spell from the *Book of the Dead* which urges Tutankhamen's heart not to bear false witness against the boy king at the last judgment.

The two cartouches, royal rings symbolizing ropes, by which the hieroglyphs comprising the royal names are tied together, contain the nomen, *Tutankhamen heka On resey*, "Tutankhamen [The living image of Amen], the ruler of the southern [city of] On [Thebes]." The second cartouche contains this King's prenomen, *Neb-Kheperu-Re*, "The god Re is the Lord of Forms." The remaining six columns of inscriptions contain assertions of the protection of Tutankhamen by the goddesses Isis and Nephthys.

90. *Pectoral with winged scarab flanked by two uraei.*

This pectoral is analagous in its meaning to that of Plate 88, but is simpler in its design and less complex in its symbolism. Comparison between these two pectorals reveals the versatility of the Egyptian artisans to adapt similar motifs to different designs.

The main register is once again framed by two uraei, each crowned with a sun disk. Here, however, the serpents are in front view, whereas in Plate 88 they are in profile. The principal motif is the scarab, the dung beetle of Ancient Egypt. This insect was observed to roll a ball of dung across a field, an activity which the Egyptians soon associated with the forces responsible for propelling the sun across the sky on its daily journey.

In each corner is an *udjat* eye, representing the left and right eyes of the falcon god Horus which symbolized the sun and the moon. These are confronted with horizontally oriented *ankh* signs, representing in actuality sandal straps, and signifying the words "to live," "life."

The central motif is a rebus or pun consisting of the hieroglyphs in the prenomen of Tutankhamen. These signs are the disk, *Re*, the beetle itself beneath which are three vertical lines which when taken with the beetle form the plural *Kheperu*, and the blue semicircular sign, itself representing a basket, and read *Neb*. Taken together these signs read *Neb-Kheperu-Re*, "Re is the Lord of Forms." By combining his name into the central motif of the sun's symbol, Tutankhamen becomes associated with the sun; his rebirth is thereby assured.

91. *Pectoral in the shape of a shrine with* djed *pillar protected by Isis and Nephthys.*

Complex pectorals of this type were a common ornament for kings as well as private persons from the Middle Kingdom on. The Egyptians wore them as breast ornaments, suspending them from the neck on a bead, linen, or gold chain. Egyptian pectorals are characterized by extensive use of openwork and complex compositions, usually religious in nature.

This example, somewhat tame in comparison to other more garish examples from Tutankhamen's tomb, takes the form of a shrine capped by a heavy cavetto cornice. The two goddesses, Isis on the right and Nephthys opposite her, spread their great feathered wings over a *djed* pillar (the symbol of stability), capped by a golden sun disk. Two cartouches, or name rings, one containing Tutankhamen's throne name, the other his personal name, flank the pillar. A pair of uraeus cobras, adorned with the Red and White Crowns of Lower and Upper Egypt, hang from the cartouches.

Isis was the sister of Nephthys and the wife of the god Osiris. Early Egyptian texts relate that Osiris fell victim to the treachery of his brother Seth, who murdered him and mutilated his body. The ever-faithful Isis, with the assistance of Nephthys, succeeded in magically restoring Osiris to animate existence, though since he had died he could never again be truly "alive." The myth of Isis, Nephthys, Osiris, and Seth became the model for all Egyptians—king and commoner alike—who hoped to be reborn again after death into an everlasting state.

92. *Pendant of a necklace with the scarab as Rising Sun between two baboons.*

This necklace is dominated by a delicately executed openwork pectoral of gold and semiprecious stones. The ends of the pectoral take the form of *was* scepters, hieroglyphs meaning "dominion." They support the "sky" hieroglyph, composed of a band of rich blue lapis-lazuli with fourteen inlaid five-pointed stars. Likewise, the lower edge of the pectoral features a lapis strip with gold inlays. But their zigzag pattern identifies the composition as water. The divine Solar Bark, with its characteristic recurved prows, rests upon the water. Amidships appears the sun god as Khepri, a glorious lapis scarab beetle, standing on a tiny *shen* (eternity) sign while elevating the glorious solar disk carved from a single piece of carnelian. Two baboons, squatting on golden shrines, flank the image of Khepri. Wearing a sun disk and lunar crescent atop their heads, they raise their forepaws in a gesture of veneration.

Baboons wearing coiffures such as those supported by this pair symbolize Thoth, the moon god, who often accompanied the sun on its daytime journey across the heavens. Yet, as was typical in Egyptian iconography, a second allusion is being made in this scene. The ancient Egyptians observed that certain animals, such as the hedgehog and the baboon, greeted the morning sun with excitement often capped by piercing shrieks. Although it would be an oversimplification to say that the Egyptians viewed this behavior as a form of sun worship, they did come to associate some creatures, particularly apes, with the sun.

93. *Gold unguent box with double royal cartouches.*

Two small boxes, each surmounted by twin ostrich plumes and a sun disk, carved in the form of royal name rings called cartouches, have been combined in an ornate gold case resting on a silver base. Traces of a brown substance preserved within one of the boxes indicate that in antiquity the chest contained some variety of unguent, perhaps used for magical or medicinal purposes. The presence of two cartouche-shaped compartments may have accommodated different varieties of unguents or they may simply refer to the two cartouches that surrounded the ruler's throne name and personal name.

On this example, however, the cartouches contain not names but images of the King squatting on a hieroglyph meaning "festival" (*heb*), and holding the crook and flail to his chest. He wears a full-length pleated cloak, broad collar, and a skullcap with a uraeus and sidelock, the latter an emblem of youth. Above the King appears a yellow sun disk encircled by a pair of uraeus cobras with *ankh* (life) signs suspended from their necks.

The reverse of the case shows two images nearly identical to those just discussed. But in one of the cartouches Tutankhamen appears with a dark head and neck, rather than the light color of the other representations; this may be an allusion to Osiris or Min, deities often shown with black skin, symbolizing the cool dark Egyptian soil from which new life springs forth each year.

The artist responsible for these complex designs made extensive use of polychrome glass imitating semiprecious stones: red for jasper, blue-green for turquoise, and blue for lapis-lazuli. The sun disk and the King's body, however, are quartz or calcite, and bits of jasper and lapis may have been used in the royal collars and *heb* hieroglyphs.

The outer edges of the cartouches show kneeling figures of Heh, the god of eternity, holding a hieroglyphic device meaning 100,000 years. A pair of cartouches containing Tutankhamen's names flank the god's face, while above him appears a complex writing of the King's throne name.

94. *Gold inlay necklace and pendant with scarabs.*

This example is understandably one of the most baroque pectorals among all the jewelry of Tutankhamen. Made of gold, lapis-lazuli, carnelian, turqoise, and green feldspar, the visual effect is dazzling since the colors unite to bombard the optical senses. To the ancient Egyptians, visual effect was paramount, and glass, at that time a deluxe product, could be used in such elaborate jewelry.

Only after one overcomes the initial optical sensation does one come to realize the wealth of decorative motifs packed into this pectoral. The scarabs within the *wia* barks, flanked by uraei crowned with sun disks and pushing disks, are common enough elements in the jewelry of Tutankhamen. Yet between the scarab and the uraei are a series of *djed*, *ankh*, and *nefer* signs. The sun disk itself is flanked by two uraei. This disk is itself then set into the hieroglyph for "horizon," indicating that the motif represents the rebirth of the sun on the Eastern Horizon at dawn.

The straps themselves are formed by the scarab, *neb* sign, and sun disk—composing the prenomen of Tutankhamen—which alternate with pairs of uraei, each crowned by sun disks and separated by a central column of *nefer* and *ankh* signs. The straps terminate with two figures of the vulture goddess Nekhbet, from whose beaks descend four strings of beads from which the counterpoise, made of two confronted uraei, is suspended.

95. *Pectoral with three scarabs.*
96. *Pectoral with* udjat *eye protected by the vulture and the uraeus.*

This example, as well as Pl. 96, forming part of the eleventh and twelfth layers of objects found on the mummy of Tutankhamen, were two of the five pectorals actually suspended from his neck. Because of their position on the mummy, these pectorals appear to have been more personal and may very well have been worn during Tutankhamen's lifetime.

Plate 95 is similar in its design to Plate 90 but is more simple in its rendition. The main decoration consists of solar scarabs in lapis-lazuli, a semiprecious stone imported into Egypt from Afghanistan; each scarab supports a disk of gold. The floral pendants encountered in Plate 90 reappear. Instead of employing three vertical strokes, as found beneath the scarab in Plate 90 to indicate plurality, the scarab is here repeated three times so that Tutankhamen's prenomen, *Neb-Kheperu-Re*, "Re is the Lord of Forms," is written in a different but nonetheless grammatically correct form. The scarabs are suspended by ten strands of plain and granular gold beads.

At the rear is a second, smaller pectoral acting as a counterpoise by which this piece of jewelry was balanced when worn. The kneeling figure of a bearded man, forming the central motif, is the hieroglyph for *heh*, "millions," which when taken with the *djed* pillar, symbolizing stability, and the *was* scepter, at the far left, symbolizing "dominion," translates: "millions [of years] of stability and dominion." This group is protected by a uraeus wearing the White Crown. In the cartouche above appear the words: "The good god, Neb-Kheperu-Re, Amen-Re, the chosen of Re," a variant of the titulary of Tutankhamen.

Plate 96 was the central pectoral and was found lying over the center of Tutankhamen's thorax. Its three strings are made of alternating faience and gold beads. The clasp, at the rear, is itself shaped like a pectoral in miniature with two hieroglyphs on a base. Stylized representations of the human spinal column—the *djed* pillar—flank a single *tat* amulet, representing a knotted ribbon and associated with the goddess Isis; the *tat* amulet was at times substituted for the *ankh* to indicate "life."

The main motif on this charming pectoral, of gold and inlaid with lapis-lazuli, a pale green stone, and colored glass, is the *udjat* eye. Here, the eye represents the hieroglyph for the verb "to be sound/hale/healthy." The meaning is a wish, "May Tutankhamen be hale." The *udjat* eye is itself protected by the goddess Wadjet of Buto, and by the goddess Nekhbet of Elkab. This significance of this pectoral is not unlike that of the fillet (Pl. 86).

97. *Necklace with blue faience* udjat *eye.*

This blue faience *udjat* eye with a uraeus cobra was part of the jewelry placed around the neck of Tutankhamen at the time of his burial. The amulet hangs from a necklace comprised of cylindrical faience and gold beads, some of which are granulated. The necklace terminates in a pair of gold cups set between a spherical bead of blue-black resin.

Traditionally, the *udjat* eye meant "whole" or "complete," and represented the eye of the falcon god Horus. But the incised inscriptions on this example indicate that it represents the less frequently depicted Eye of Re, the Lord of the Sun. The left Eye of Re was the bark in which the sun god traveled during the day in the form of Khepri, and it is that aspect of the sun mentioned in the inscription when the amulet appears, as it does in the plate, as the left eye. When reversed, however, the charm became the right eye, the sacred vessel of Re-Harakhti, who voyaged through the Underworld during the twelve hours of night. Not surprisingly, the inscription on the "right eye" invokes Re-Harakhti.

The ancient Egyptians also considered the uraeus cobra a manifestation of the Eye of Re, charged with protecting the king from his enemies. The cobra's presence here was probably intended to reinforce the amuletic powers of the *udjat* eye. Together with the tiny looped hieroglyph for "protection" behind the cobra, the composition can be taken to mean, "The forms of the Eye of Re give protection to the King."

98. *Earrings in the shape of falcons with ducks' heads.*

This pair of earrings was found in a wooden box in the shape of a cartouche containing Tutankhamen's nomen. Like today, earrings on men were not an uncommon sight during the Eighteenth Dynasty. It is conjectured that this fashion for Egyptian men was adopted from Western Asia. The mummy of King Tuthmosis IV, who lived about one hundred years before Tutankhamen, is the earliest known royal mummy with pierced ears. From the marks of use on this pair and from the presence of pierced earlobes on the gold mask of Tutankhamen, it is probable that he himself wore earrings, despite the fact that none of the earrings from his tomb were found on the mummy itself. By the Nineteenth Dynasty, however, earrings on men became commonplace.

The motif, of gold inlaid with quartz, calcite, faience, and glass of various colors, is a falcon's body with a duck's head. Such fusion of disparate motifs was quite common (Pl. 88), especially since both the falcon and the duck were associated with Amen-Re. Each talon holds the *shen* sign, symbolizing eternity. A series of pendants in an alternating pattern of blue and gold which terminate in the heads of five cobras complete the design.

99. *Earrings with gold filigree and stone beads.*
100. *Earrings with an effigy of the King between two uraei.*

This pair of earrings (Pl. 99), made of "purple" gold, dark blue glass, and black resin is perhaps the most unusual jewelry found in Tutankhamen's tomb. Almost every other example had, as part of its design, tangible motifs which formed hieroglyphs and contained messages. The total absence of figural representations in this pair of earrings comes, therefore, as quite a surprise. One can only conclude that it was the technique and the material used in these earrings which gave them their intrinsic value. To be sure, glass was used frequently in jewelry found in the tomb. The use of black resin, as an element in jewelry, seems to be restricted to the Eighteenth Dynasty, where it was used in place of amber. The use of iron, a metal which was extremely rare in Tutankhamen's Egypt, was responsible for giving the gold in these earrings their purple hue. It appears, therefore, that the craftsmen fully exploited certain technical avenues, and it was this technical achievement which was valued in these earrings.

Plate 100 represents a second pair of earrings made of gold, carnelian, quartz, and glass, along with colored adhesives. Beneath the cylinders is a circle, at the top of which is a winged falcon. Within the circle is a carnelian representation of Tutankhamen flanked by two uraei, crowned with sun disks. The King wears a Blue Crown and stands on the hieroglyph for *heb*, "festival." Since the Blue Crown was used during the Eighteenth Dynasty as a symbol of coronation or jubilee, one can assume that these earrings commemorate the festival of Tutankhamen's coronation. Six beaded tassels, from which are suspended drop beads in gold and glass, complete each earring.

101. *Royal scepter, used for offerings.*

Scepters of this shape were used by both kings and members of the nobility as insignia of power. Only a pharaoh, however, would be likely to possess such a richly decorated example. The artist who fashioned it created a handle in the form of a slender papyrus plant whose shaft terminates in a fanciful feather pattern comprised of cloisonné inlaid with glass and semiprecious stones. Atop the stem rests a broad papyrus umbel, from which the scepter's convex blade emerges.

One side of this blade features five embossed figures of bulls, all trussed and partially dismembered. Such a depiction recalls periodic sacrifices made at Egyptian temples, and suggests that this scepter was employed in such a ritual. The other side has a blue and gold faience inscription reading: "The Good God, the beloved one, one dazzling of face like the sun disk [Aten] when it shines forth, the Son of Amen, Neb-Kheperu-Re, may he live forever."

Unlike other precious insignia of this type found in the innermost Treasury, this scepter lay in the Annex at the time Howard Carter entered the tomb. The excavator hypothesized that it was part of a complete set of ritual regalia stored in one of the ornate chests deposited in the Annex. It may also have been brought from the Treasury by thieves who penetrated the tomb in antiquity but who had second thoughts about removing the scepter or who were caught in their larcenous act.

102. *Gold filigree ring bracelet with turquoise-type stone.*
103. *Gold ring bracelet with carnelian vulture.*

During the unwrapping of Tutankhamen's mummy, thirteen bracelets were found on his arms, seven on his right and six on his left. Other bracelets were also found elsewhere on the body within the linen bandages and in other parts of the tomb. All of the bracelets were worn as personal adornments by the King during his lifetime.

Plate 102 was the second bracelet from the wrist worn on the left forearm. It is made of two halves: the front, containing the setting for the marbled turquoise-like stone, is decorated with triangles of granulation and spiral filigree, while the back is composed of tubular sections of gold representing bound stems of papyrus and lily flowers which appear at the hinge and the clasp. These floral motifs may be intended to represent the heraldic plants of Upper and Lower Egypt. The two halves are joined at one side by an ingenious hinge, similar in design to that found on a modern door. The clasp at the other side appears to be of the bolt variety, which pulls out of its sockets, thus separating the two halves. The other bracelet (Pl. 103) is similarly hinged and clasped. Like all the bracelets found in the tomb, it has a rather small diameter, indicating the diminutive physical size of Tutankhamen. This bracelet was found next to the elbow, as the first bracelet slipped over the right forearm. It is made of gold with several inlaid motifs. The vulture Nekhbet is inlaid in carnelian; the *udjat* eyes and uraei, crowned with sun disks, are of inlaid hard stones and glass.

This particular example appears to have been a charm bracelet worn to protect the owner from harm. Nekhbet wears the *atef* crown, consisting of the White Crown of Upper Egypt flanked by the two feathers of truth. She clasps *shen* amulets in her talons and is herself protected by the cobras flanking her. The *udjat* eyes in the field to the left and right of Nekhbet represent the hieroglyphs for "health/soundness."

104. *Band bracelet with three lapis-lazuli scarabs.*

The ancient Egyptians saw nature as a series of eternal cycles—the periodic rise and fall of the Nile; the annual planting, growth, and harvesting of grain; the daily rising and setting of the sun. They believed that by associating themselves with a potent image of one of these cycles, they would become identified with it and likewise become eternal. Certainly the daily progress of the sun from horizon to horizon was the most conspicuous and oft-repeated natural cycle. And of all the sun symbols in Egyptian iconography (ram, disk, cobra, etc.), the scarab was the most dynamic, since it depicted the sun at the dramatic moment when it emerged reborn over the eastern horizon.

This bracelet is dominated by a trio of lapis-lazuli scarabs. Next to each is a hieroglyphic assemblage containing four amuletic devices: the *neb* basket; the *nefer* (good) hieroglyph; the uraeus cobra; and a sun disk. The artisan who fashioned these groups used gold, turquoise, and carnelian for their components. Two assemblages of six gold and faience bead strings hold the composition together. One of the two rectangular gold terminals features a locust executed in inlaid stone.

105. *Band bracelet of three scarabs, one white, with clasps showing the King's cartouches.*

Like the previous example, this bracelet features a trio of scarab beetles, two in blue faience and one in greenish white feldspar. Each scarab pushes a carnelian sun disk with its front legs. The two lapis beetles are flanked by rearing uraeus cobras wearing golden disks atop their heads and resting on *neb* baskets. The tails of the two cobras next to the central scarab end in a design recognizable as a twisted bolt of rope. These two signs, plus the sun disk they flank, form the Egyptian word *neheh*, meaning "eternity."

The terminals of the bracelet take the form of cartouches containing the King's name. Each is surmounted by a pair of ostrich plumes and a sun disk.

This bracelet was found with six other examples worn around the right arm of Tutankhamen.

106. *Four bracelets with beads and semiprecious stones.*

Howard Carter found three of the four bracelets illustrated on this plate around the right forearm of Tutankhamen. The fourth (top) was presumably dropped by thieves fleeing the tomb, perhaps when alarmed by approaching guards.

A pinkish red carnelian *udjat* eye forms the primary decorative element of one of these bracelets. A uraeus cobra wearing the Double Crown of Upper and Lower Egypt emerges from the eye, as if protecting it. The back of the gold cloison holding the eye carries an inscription reading: "The Lord of the Two Lands, the Image of Re, Neb-Kheperu-Re, the Ruler of Divine Order, may he be given life like Re for ever and ever." The eye amulet is attached to nine rows of gold, faience, and glass beads threaded between six gold spacers fashioned to imitate beads.

The simple bracelet with a tiny scarab reproduces a magical device found on jewelry and other objects scattered throughout the tomb.

The large bracelet with its blue lapis bezel has no amuletic or religious designs associated with it, suggesting that it was fashioned for purely decorative purposes. Immediately surrounding the bezel is a band of minute bosses applied by a technique called granulation.

THE GOLD OF TUTANKHAMEN

Next comes a running spiral, a design imported from the Near East during the Eighteenth Dynasty.

The final example has a scaraboid bezel surrounded by granulated triangles.

107. *The collar of Nebti, chased sheet gold, with the Nekhbet vulture and the Buto uraeus.*
108. *The collar of Buto, chased sheet gold, with the uraeus.*
109. *The collar of Horus, chased sheet gold, with the falcon.*

During the course of mummification—a process developed to insure the incorruptibility of the flesh in the tomb and thereby provide the soul with a body to which to return after its peregrinations upon the earth—the body was wrapped in successive layers of linen which enclosed, in an ordered sequence, numerous amulets.

These collars, which covered the thorax, were part of a group of thirty-five objects, grouped into seventeen sets and wrapped as thirteen layers within linen bandages. The gold collars themselves extended well below the clavicles and covered the shoulders. Each was suspended from the neck by means of a gold wire and each was posited on the body by means of a *mankhet*, the Egyptian word for counterpoise, which in these examples is in the shape of a floral motif.

Plate 107 is the collar of Nebti, and was the second collar in this group on the body. It was placed over the left side of the body. The animals here represented are the vulture of Elkab, Nekhbet, and the serpent of Buto, Wadjet, as encountered in Plate 86, the fillet. This pair are the hieroglyph for *Nebti*, "The Two Ladies," which formed part of the second of five names used in the canonical titulary of most Egyptian pharaohs. Their function, like that on the fillet, is to protect the king for eternity, as symbolized by the *shenu* signs held in the talons of Nekhbet.

Plate 108 is the collar of Buto, which was found third in this series, positioned to the far left. The figure eight arrangement of the coils of her body is characteristic of her representations in Egyptian art. She is here provided with outstretched wings, consistent with the Egyptian penchant for combining into one form disparate elements. The presence of the wings reinforces the overtones of divinity and otherworldliness ascribed to Wadjet.

Plate 109 is the collar of Horus, which covered Tutankhamen's neck and formed the uppermost layer of this series of collars and amulets. Such collars, according to the rubrics in the *Book of the Dead*, were required to be placed around the deceased's neck or over his breast to effect certain spells necessary for existence in the hereafter.

110. *Collar of cloisonné work terminating in falcon heads.*

Howard Carter found this collar with its tag, or *mankhet*, and three similar examples in the coffin of Tutankhamen. Each was folded and crushed over the King's knees and shins. This example is made of many gold plaques inlaid with colored glass in the manner of cloisonné. No doubt, the red and blue glass imitates prototypes in semiprecious stones such as carnelian, lapis, and turquoise.

The falcon-head terminals refer to the King's role as a mundane avatar of Horus, the falcon god. Originally, such collars were exclusively a royal prerogative, and the famous gold mask which covered the head of Tutankhamen's mummy shows one as part of the design. As time wore on, however, private people also began to wear falcon collars, thereby underscoring the diminution of power and authority of the throne.

111. *Broad "floral" bead collar.*

Certainly one of the least ornate objects from Tutankhamen's tomb, this faience collar lacks any inscription or royal emblem that would link it to a king's burial. No doubt, it imitates in red, green, yellow, blue, and white faience the festal collars of natural materials such as flowers and leaves that were presented to guests attending funerary banquets.

In this well-preserved example, the white beads reproduce the shape of poppy petals; the others take the form of cornflowers. The white faience terminals feature inlaid floral motives. The tassels emanating from these terminals were used to secure the necklace around the wearer's neck.

112. *Collar of the falcon Horus, in cloisonné.*
113. *Collar of the vulture Nekhbet, in cloisonné.*

Like the collars in Plates 107–109, both of these examples had similar functions. They were found on the thorax of Tutankhamen's mummy and are, occasionally, called breastplates. Both are composed of a very large number of separate gold plaques, chased on the reverse, and minutely inlaid with glass imitating turquoise, jasper, and lapis-lazuli. Each separate plaque was then strung together with the others by threading the tiny eyelets at the upper and lower edges of each plaque. The result is a figure which is extremely flexible and which can shimmer when held by the floral-shaped *mankhet*, which serves as the counterpoise.

Plate 112 is a collar of the falcon Horus, composed of some thirty-eight gold plaques tied together by gossamer strands of thread. Of particular note is the border of minute beads strung around the outer edges of the plaques forming the wings.

Plate 113 is a collar of the vulture Nekhbet, which is more elaborate than the example in Plate 112, since this object is composed of 156 segments, each of which is linked to the others by a string passing through eyelets located as in Plate 112.

Each plaque is separated from its neighbor by a minute bead which is itself strung into the system. The details of the head of Nekhbet are finely chased; her beak and eye are inlaid with obsidian, a glassy volcanic stone. In each talon she holds a *shenw* sign which symbolizes eternity.

114. *Scarab pectoral with cloisonné wings.*

This pendant, made of gold which is inlaid with carnelian, turquoise, green feldspar, lapis-lazuli, and calcite, is beautiful in the simplicity of its form and in the directness of its statement. As such it contrasts a great deal with Plate 94, which is extremely baroque in character. The two, when considered together, clearly demonstrate the wide range of taste that was current at the court of Tutankhamen.

The contour of this pendant, in the form of a gently curving heart, frames the winged scarab, *neb* sign, and sun disk, which are arranged along a strong vertical, thereby monopolizing the pendant's focal point. This focal point consists of the three hieroglyphs in the prenomen of Tutankhamen, Neb-Kheperu-Re, "Re is the Lord of Forms." There are no distracting elements in this composition, so that the equation of Tutankhamen with the sun at dawn and the concomitant implication that he, like the sun, will be reborn are emphatically stressed.

115–119. *Five pectorals with images of bird deities.*

The ancient Egyptians were not disturbed by seemingly contradictory explanations of natural phenomena. Thus they saw no incongruity in explaining the sun's daily passage across the firmament as a divine bark ferried across the heavens by a host of godlings, as a scarab beetle pushing a glowing disk above the earth, or a majestic falcon soaring through the skies. This latter image, identified as the primordial sky god Horus and later called Re-Harakhti, is reproduced in this exquisitely executed pendant. The bird's plumage is turquoise, carnelian, and blue glass. He wears a flaming carnelian disk atop his head and carries the *ankh* (life) and *shen* (infinity) hieroglyphs in his talons—ideal attributes for the life-giving, eternal sun. This pectoral was found with a host of other such pieces in a wooden chest deposited in the Treasury.

A nearly identical image was found beneath the twelfth layer of bandages surrounding the body of Tutankhamen (Pl. 118). Here Re-Harakhti confronts the viewer full-face, and the sun disk adorning his head has the addition of a uraeus cobra. Once again, the falcon clutches a pair of *shen* signs.

Not all the avian deities rendered on Tutankhamen's pectorals should be understood as Re-Harakhti. Plates 116, 117, and 119 all depict the vulture goddess Nekhbet, the primordial patroness of Upper Egypt. In each case, Nekhbet's outstretched wings are comprised of feathers fashioned of blue lapis-lazuli; carnelian details highlight the wings of two examples. The pectoral showing Nekhbet wearing the *atef* crown of Osiris (Pl. 116) has the bird's head modeled in the round. This treatment, also visible in Plate 119, is not an Egyptian convention and may indicate the presence of foreign craftsmen at the court of Tutankhamen. The final vulture pectoral (Pl. 119) was worn by the King's mummy on the eleventh or twelfth layer of wrappings. Quite probably the young King wore this piece during his lifetime. The back of the pectoral (not visible in the photo) shows Nekhbet wearing a miniature pendant of her own: two cobras flanking the royal cartouche.

120. *Six gold amulets, five of which are inlaid with glass and semiprecious stones.*

Amulets were artifacts which were essential to the Egyptians. Symbolizing all the divine forces, they were to guard and direct

316

them throughout their lives as well as in the afterlife. Many of these amulets were found in the mummy's wrappings. They are made of gold and symbolize, from the upper left, the Primordial Lotus, the sacred blue lotus, emblem of Nefertum, the lord of the perfumes, god of Memphis; in breathing their heavy aroma, it was believed that the dead would be brought back to life. The *djed* pillar represented by a gold amulet and another one inlaid with blue faience were symbols of stability. At the time of Tutankhamen, the pillar was believed to be the spine of Osiris, and on the gold one, the long inscription refers to the *djed* pillar as "Thy backbone." On the lower part of the plate we find three inlaid amulets. The god Anubis, "He who presides over the embalment rituals" and "He who keeps the secrets" is figured as a seated jackal made of feldspar. In the center, Horus of the Horizon is inlaid with lapis-lazuli. The last figure is made of a piece of blue glass inlaid in its gold frame representing an ibis, symbol of the god Thoth, the god of wisdom who guided the dead through the trials of the Netherworld.

Objects of Royal Life

121. *Religious throne and foot stand.*

This religious throne, at times called "Ecclesiastical" because of its resemblance to the medieval "*cathedra,*" is one of the most elaborate pieces of craftsmanship of the tomb. It was probably used for religious purposes. The seat of the chair with its gilded inlays imitating leopard skins, set in "negative" in an ebony framework, resembles the "folding" stool which is illustrated on Plate 125. The crossed legs are terminated by ducks' heads and are joined by an elaborate openwork representing the sign for the unification of Upper and Lower Egypt, with the lotus and papyrus tied together, the *smatawy* symbol. As in other pieces of furniture of this kind, it is this particular symbol which was damaged by the early robbers of the tomb. The back of the seat is inlaid with semiprecious stones, ivory, and glass paste. It bears hieroglyphic inscriptions giving the king's name as Tutankhaten and Tutankhamen. The falcon Horus is outstretching his wings over these hieroglyphs, holding the feather symbol of Truth, Maat, in his claws. A series of uraei are placed on either side of a larger Aten disk, reminiscent of Amarnian times, on the upper edge of the seat back.

The foot stand, inlaid with blue faience plaques, shows figures of gilded prisoners, symbolizing the demons on which the king would be stamping.
Height of throne: 40 inches.

122. *Cedarwood chair.*

This very elegant chair is made of cedar (or maybe palisander or cilician fir; it has been difficult to decide with precision the kind of redwood used by the Egyptians). Some gilding appears on the winged Aten disk flanked by two uraei on top, as well as on the lion claws terminating the feet of this chair. The seat is slightly curved as it was intended to receive a cushion. The back is extremely finely carved with the kneeling figure of the god Heh of eternity holding the reeds (unnamed years) stemming from tadpoles, which symbolize 100,000 years. Two falcons wearing the double crown, *pschent*, and suspended from a uraeus coiling around a solar disk are perched on top of banners which show the King's titles and refer to Horus. Height: 37³/₄ inches.

123. *The gilded throne.*

This wooden chair is entirely gold plated and set with semiprecious stones, glass paste, and terracotta. On the seat back, contrasting with the stately usage of such a throne, Tutankhamen is depicted in a familiar scene with Ankhesenamen (see Pl. 49). This kind of representation occurred much more frequently during the Amarnian period when actually Queen Nefertiti took an even more active and political role. The arms of the seat are shaped in the form of a winged serpent wearing the double crown, *pschent*, and guarding the name of the King. The two lions of the Eastern and Western Horizon are placed on either side of the seat, and the feet are in the shape of lion paws and mounted on bronze drums. They were originally strengthened by a framework representing the symbol *sma-tawy* of the union of Upper and Lower Egypt, the lotus and papyrus tied together, of which only the central motif remains. The back of the seat shows a papyrus swamp in which ducks are flying. Height: 45 inches.

124. *Child's chair with ebony and ivory inlays.*

The size of this chair leads us to conclude that it was probably intended for a child aged seven to nine. Built out of ebony with inlays of gold and ivory, this chair comprises the by now familiar elements of the craftsmanship of the New Kingdom, lion-legged feet, curved seat, and slightly oblique back. Once again the feet are mounted on short bronze drums and are further supported by open-work, which is also found on the base of some alabaster lamps, and is held together by four bars bearing a floral motif of ivory at each end. The back of the seat is decorated with a very sober geometrical design of alternating ebony and ivory plaques. The armrests are filled with gold sheets showing interlacing branches inside and a recumbent ibex outside. Nothing except the high quality of the craftsmanship recalls a royal commission; therefore we may advance the hypothesis that this chair was made for the child Tutankhamen before he was crowned Pharaoh. Height: 28 inches.

125. *Crosslegged stool with imitation leopard-skin seat.*

This stool was made in imitation of the folding seat across which animal skins were stretched. However, the crossed legs terminated by ducks' heads are firmly held together by a slightly incurved wood seat inlaid with gilded pattern in a "negative" rendering of a leopard skin. This piece of furniture was originally intended to be very realistically completed at each corner by feline paws which were

broken by the early robbers of the tomb. A small gilded tail is hanging from one of the sides. It has been said that this stool was probably the work of Nubians, and as a matter of fact it was also in Nubia that leopards were plentiful at the time of the King.
Height: 13⁹/₁₆ inches.

126, 127. *Ebony bed with lion legs, and detail of bed stand showing the god Bes.*

A couple of beds found in the tomb, along with a traveling bed which folded inwards, are all mounted on feline legs standing on bronze drums. This particular example is carved in ebony and covered with a string mesh painted white. The openwork of the headboard is divided into three panels representing the god Bes, protecting the family against the evil spirits. Plate 127 shows one of these panels depicting three figures of the god Bes crowned with feathers; the kilt worn by the lion-headed human figure in full-face in the center as well as the crowns and manes borne by all three lions are gilded. Their lips and tongues are made of ivory. The two lions in profile are resting on *sa* signs of protection. A gilded hieroglyphic strip bearing the two names of the king and the customary invocations are placed on the ebony framework which supports the three panels.

128. *Headrest of lapis-lazuli blue glass.*

Four headrests were found in Tutankhamen's tomb, along with one small model the size of an amulet made out of iron which had been placed under the head of the mummy in its wrappings. This headrest of lapis-lazuli glass paste was made of two parts joined together in the middle. This joint was concealed behind a narrow gold stripe decorated with geometrical cloisonné inlays of glass. A hieroglyphic cartouche appears on the base giving the name of the King.

129. *Headrest ornamented with heads of the god Bes.*

This painted ivory headrest was made in the shape of a folding stool, with two heads of the god Bes on either side and feet in the shape of ducks' heads. The ivory is painted dark green, brown, and black. On the upper side of this headrest, instead of the lions' manes is a lotus flower design silhouetted against a black background.
Height: 8 inches.

130. *Symbolical ivory headrest with the god Shu as support.*

This unique ivory headrest represents the god Shu (air) according to the legend, supporting the celestial vault in order to hold it separated from the earth. The symbol *sa* for protection is carved around his shoulders and thinly underlined in blue—as is his hair and the kilt he is wearing. The two lions carved on either side represent either the mountains Manu and Baku or the lions Routy that guarded the Eastern and Western Horizons. These lions are very different from each other; one is young, the other old. Their tails are outstretched along their sides as on Tutankhamen's lions from the Temple of Soleb now in the British Museum, as opposed to the traditional coiled tail. On the back of the figure of Shu, a hieroglyphic band refers to the King's title, Neb-Kheperu-Re, as son of Amen. Headrests were perhaps used by the ancient Egyptians during their lifetime, and they were essential to the rites of rebirth as described throughout an entire chapter in the *Book of the Dead*, Chapter 166. The dead man was considered like a sick person asleep, and it was essential for his head to be lifted up towards the skies. The god Ptah would then overthrow his enemies, and thus like Horus, son of Isis, the dead man's head would slowly soar to heaven and acknowledge its own eternal rebirth.

Height: $6^7/_8$ inches.

131. *Chest in the form of a shrine, with gold plaques and blue faience inlays.*

This funerary chest was made in the shape of the Sanctuary of the South, *Per-Wer*, with its sloping roof, as the second and third great gilded shrines of the Burial Chamber. It is made of wood subsequently gilded and decorated with blue faience panels, and was probably fastened as for the portable redwood chest by a cord passed around the two faience knobs on the lid and on the narrow side of the chest which bore the hieroglyphic cartouche of Tutankhamen. On the narrow sides, the blue faience panels contain a gilded decoration composed of the two official cartouches of the King, with his birth name Tutankhamen, and his coronation name, Neb-Kheperu-Re, set between two kneeling figures of Heh, symbolizing eternity. He is holding reeds (symbolizing years without number) that soar up from tadpoles, which symbolize 100,000 years. On the other panels, which run across the length of the chest, the two gilded cartouches of the King alternate with two uraei facing each other and surmounted by solar disks. This chest was found in the great Antechamber of the tomb, piled up along with other chests on the lion-headed funerary bed. C.B.

132. *Coffer with gilded openwork decoration.*

This wood coffer was decorated with a framework of ivory stripes bearing the five titles of Tutankhamen as well as his name and Ankhesenamen's, painted in black hieroglyphs. A delicately gilded openwork is inserted between the narrow bands of ivory framework: it presents a series of *ankh* signs (i.e., life) flanked on either side by the *was* sign of dominion growing from a basket which itself symbolizes "All." The chest was intended to be fastened by a rope passed around two wooden knobs, one on the lid and the other on one of the sides. The feet of this chest are capped in silver. The interior was divided into sixteen compartments, probably meant for precious vessels that disappeared during the early violations of the tomb.

Height: $16^3/_4$ inches.

133. *Painted alabaster coffer.*

This painted alabaster coffer was fastened by two knobs made of obsidian. Two bouquets, consisting of a papyrus flower set between lotus lilies, poppies, cornflowers, and mandrakes are painted on the lid. They frame a hieroglyphic band giving the King's name and

titles. The lower part of the coffer is decorated with colored geometric patterns. The two cartouches are of the King as Tutankhamen and as Neb-Kheperu-Re, along with Ankhesenamen's cartouche figure under the lower knob. In this coffer, which was found in the Antechamber, there was an ivory pomegranate, some pieces of linen, animal hair, and two balls of human hair wrapped in linen.
Height: 13 inches.

134. *Chest with ivory inlays.*

This wooden chest is also in the shape of the great Sanctuary of the South, *Per-Wer*. The sides are entirely veneered with great ivory plaques, while the upper rim in the shape of a cornice is gilded. The feet are mounted on small bronze pieces. This chest was found in a remarkable state of preservation, and depicts hunting scenes and wild fauna painted on the box amid a jungle-like profusion of various flowers and plants. On one end of the chest, the King is seated with Ankhesenamen at his feet; she is holding a lotus in one hand and an arrow, which she is ready to give him as he aims at ducks and fishes hidden in the luxurious vegetation, which forms the decorative pattern of the chest. This is one of the rare examples where, following the Amarnian custom, the Queen figures with the King, but once again, unlike Nefertiti, who in Akhenaten's case seemed to share the exercise of power, Ankhesenamen is only associated with leisurely and intimate activities. Wild animals are painted on the other three sides, galloping through the woods: a piebald bull, a Nubian ibex attacked by the King's lion, and so forth. These scenes were probably meant to represent the Edenic setting of Tutankhamen's afterlife. The lovely quality of the rendering, whether it concerns the animals or the vegetation surrounding them, suggests a foreign influence. The wild animals, the luxuriant vegetation, the King and Queen seen together in a garden (see Pl. 48), all these scenes recall the art of the people of Assur, which had maintained many commercial, if not even colonial, ties with Egypt for many years.
Length: $28^5/_6$ inches.

135. *Wood cabinet on legs with decorative openwork.*

This is the only chest of the funerary equipment which is set on high legs, and thus closely resembles eighteenth-century European cabinetwork. Its entire framework, including its legs, is made of ebony with panels of cedar (?) inserted between the ebony strips framing the box. The lid is mounted on the chest with bronze hinges. Two gilded knobs were tied together with a string or rope to close the chest. The one on the chest bears the King's birth name Tutankhamen, the one on the lid shows his throne name, Neb-Kheperu-Re. Narrow strips of hieroglyphic inscriptions are disposed around the chest in such a way that their meaning would be instantly legible, just as on the semicircular box with the *sma-tawy* sign (Pl. 136). They all refer, in the usual bombastic terms, to the King's accomplishments, and associate the King with the pre-Amarnian Ennead: he is the beloved of Amen-Re, King of the Gods, while Aten has regained his regular place in the pantheon of ancient gods. The

lower part of the chest is decorated with an open gilded framework showing series of *ankh* life signs stemming from the basket, sign for "All," between two *was* scepters of dominion. This chest was found in the Annex, robbed of its original contents which had been replaced by four headrests.
Height: 27 inches.

136. *Semicircular box with royal gold cartouche over* sma-tawy *symbol.*

This semicircular box was made of a frame of light-colored wood veneered with ebony and redwood. It was meant to be carried by four bronze rings, of which three remain attached, and its use has not been discovered. A hieroglyphic inscription hastily painted on the lid refers to the *khetkhet* of the King, giving life, preservation, and death: its meaning is still entirely sibylline. An elaborate system of attaching the lid to the box with a batten fitting in a concave channel allowed the lid to stay locked once shut. The knob placed on the box itself probably belonged originally to another box as it bears under the cartouche of Tutankhamen the name Neferneferuaten, throne name of Smenkhare. But the knobs placed on the lid bear no trace of erasure. This chest is decorated on the bow-shaped side with the *sma-tawy* sign of the union of Upper and Lower Egypt, symbolized by the knotted papyrus and lotus surmounted by three cartouches. The central cartouche gives the birth name of the King in its Theban version Tutankhamen; at its right, over the lotus flower, figures the cartouche with the King's coronation name, Neb-Kheperu-Re; both these cartouches are crowned by a solar disk held by two ostrich feathers. On the left, over the papyrus which is always associated with femininity, the cartouche of Ankhesenamen is represented, surmounted by the straight plumes sometimes worn by queens, which also recall in some ways those of the god Amen. Hieroglyphic bands running vertically and horizontally around the box were meant to be read together and thus were placed this way; they refer to the King with the customary emphasis.
Height: 11 inches; length: 14 inches.

137. *Alabaster chalice in the form of a lotus flower.*

Placed immediately at the entrance of the Antechamber, this alabaster chalice was made in the shape of a white lotus plant in contrast to the blue lotus, from which the sovereigns after Amenhotep III drank the nectar poured by their queens. It represents a plant in the water with a large open flower composed of sixteen striped petals. On either side, stemming from the "underwater" pedestal, three smaller buds support the figure of the god Heh, symbolizing a million years. A hieroglyphic cartouche painted black, right in the middle of the central flower, gives the birth name and throne name of the King, beloved of Amen-Re, Lord of the Thrones of the Double Country, Lord of the Heaven. The inscribed band running around the rim of the cup gives the five complete titles of the King. From the central *ankh* sign this text reads, interpreted by Carter, as a series of wishes "that you may live millions of years, O you who have not ceased to love Thebes, seated while turning your face in the North wind, your eyes contemplating felicity." It is from the

dark of the primordial water that the white lily of Heliopolis had grown, over which the sun had risen. The garden of Eden (of the painted ivory chest, Pl. 134) on the Island of Flame had been the birthplace of the gods and each year religious mysteries were celebrated there. This cup therefore celebrates the apparition of the god on the lotus, the rebirth of the dead as the red flow of the Nile giving life to Egypt. It was meant to contain the wine that Hathor had drunk, thus saving mankind.
Height: 7 inches.

138. *Alabaster unguent container in the form of a ceremonial boat.*

One of the most elaborate perfume containers from the tomb is this ibex-headed ship mounted on a chest-like base painted with a mosaic of lotus and geometrical elements. The painted ship is terminated at the bow and stern by two miniature ibex figures, each with a gilded collar and bearing the real horns of a young ibex. The boat carries in its center a sarcophagus-shaped cabin probably meant to hold flowers or unguents. It is sheltered by an awning canopy held by small painted and gilded columns terminating in double capitals composed of lotus and papyrus motifs. On either side of this canopy two miniature statues of naked women steer the ship: a young woman clutching a lotus flower against her breast is kneeling on the prow, while her "duenna," an older woman, holds a steering pole. It has been advanced that the young kneeling princess at the prow might be one of Ankhesenamen's sisters.
Height: 26 inches.

139. *Triple alabaster lamp in the shape of a lotus plant.*

This triple alabaster lamp was made in the shape of a lotus flower growing out of a pond with its leaves floating on the surface of the water. A larger, open flower grows from the central stem, coupled by two smaller half-open buds. The Egyptians filled this cup with vegetable oil in which a wick made of flax fibers was put. The curving delicacy of this alabaster lamp may remind the modern viewer of the excesses of *art nouveau* which in a way find their counterpart in the work of the Amarnian period.
Height: 11 inches.

140. *Perfume vase with Hapi deities holding papyrus and lotus plants.*

This perfume vase was found between the first and second shrines. It is made of four pieces of alabaster, and symbolizes the Nile fertilizing the two lands of Upper Egypt and Lower Egypt, honoring the King and Queen, whose names appear on the painted inscription on the vase. The base is formed of openwork, representing on the long side two falcons—Horus holding the cartouche of the King showing his birth name on one side and his throne name, Neb-Kheperu-Re, on the other—between two dominion signs, *was*, and perched on the hieroglyph sign, *neb*, for gold. On the narrow sides, the vulture Nekhbet wearing the *atef* crown is also holding Tutankhamen's cartouche between its wings. Two Hapi deities with pendulous breasts—one crowned with the lilies of Upper Egypt, the other

with the papyri of Lower Egypt representing the fertile Nile—clutch a *sma-tawy* symbol made of lotus and papyrus plants tied together, symbolizing the Union of the Two Lands. The vulture wearing the ostrich feather crown surrounding a sun disk is placed on top of the vase, while two gilded uraei wearing on one side the crown of Upper Egypt, and on the other the tiara of Lower Egypt are resting on reeds held by each of the Hapi deities.
Height: 27$^1/_2$ inches.

141. *Alabaster unguent jar with a lid in the shape of a recumbent lion.*

Between the first and the second shrines, Carter found this unguent vase carved out of a single piece of alabaster. The recumbent lion placed on the lid has the cartouche of Neb-Kheperu-Re, coronation name of the King, painted on its back. Once again, the lion's crossed paws, the outstretched tail, and the protruding tongue painted red, reminiscent of the god Bes, are a departure from the Ancient Egyptian tradition of representing stylized lions and sphinxes symbolizing the King. On the vase itself, scenes are painted red, green, and blue, showing lions and dogs, fighting bulls and an ibex. The vase is resting on a crossbar base, terminating in the heads of two African prisoners, adorned with earrings, and of two Assyrians. Two lotiform columns are placed on each side of the base surmounted by heads of the lion god, Bes.
Height: 10$^3/_4$ inches.

142. *Alabaster flask with decorative inlays.*

This alabaster flask is decorated with sober elegance: three bands of inlaid glass circle the neck of the flask as if they were a garland of blue lotus petals. A small residue of oil found in this flask has not been identified.
Height: 9$^1/_2$ inches.

143. *Unguent jar in the form of a standing lion.*

This alabaster unguent jar is carved in the shape of a standing lion, the god Bes. His left paw rests on the sign for protection while he is raising the right one. His right hind paw is placed slightly forward, a position which differs from the convention of standing figures of men with the left leg forward. The lion's tongue and teeth are made of ivory. The mouth of the vase on the lion's head is carved in the shape of a crown placed on a circular base with a checkered decoration. On this crown, lotus petals alternate with papyri and rosettes. The two cartouches of the King, along with Ankhesenamen's, are inscribed on the chest of the lion. Bes is standing on a base decorated with a checkered pattern with lotus petals and mandrakes. The legs of the pedestal are joined by a simple openwork design of alabaster which we find also on several other vases.
Height: 23$^5/_8$ inches.

144. *Silver vase in the shape of a pomegranate.*

This silver pomegranate vase is decorated with leaf patterns and lotus flowers on the upper part, and cornflowers and leaves on the body of the vase. Pomegranates came from Palestine and had retained in ancient Egyptian their Semitic name; the fruit had probably been brought back during the campaigns of the earlier kings. Height: 5¹/₄ inches.

145. *Lid of an alabaster jar showing a bird on its nest.*

This young duck which seems to have just come out of its egg in this alabaster nest was carved of wood and painted. It is surrounded by four wooden eggs and placed in this bowl, which is fixed to a flat alabaster disk, and this in turn served as the cover for another fine alabaster bowl.
Diameter: 5¹/₃ inches.

146. *Ostrich feather fan with ivory handle.*

The King's ostrich fan was made out of painted ivory on which the double cartouche of the King had been inscribed. The shape of the handle minimized the motion of the hand and imitates a papyrus stalk and corolla. The handle itself terminates in a papyrus form, which is circled at its base by gold rings and is painted green, blue, and red.

147. *Ceremonial flabellum with colored glass inlays; the royal cartouches protected by vultures.*

On this ceremonial flabellum made of wood and covered with a gold sheet, two winged vultures representing Nekhbet are placed on either side of the King's double hieroglyphic cartouche. One is wearing the crown of Upper Egypt while the other is adorned with the tiara of Lower Egypt. The *shen* sign of eternity is placed between their wings along with the animal-headed scepter *was* sign of dominion. Both vultures and cartouches are set upon the hieroglyph for gold. Holes were made on the circular edge of the flabellum for the ostrich feathers. This fan is mounted on a long gilded wooden stick, inlaid at the top end with a geometric decoration shaped as a papyrus flower and engraved with the prophylactic signs of life and eternity. The gentle motion of the flabellum was designed to restore the breath of life to the king as well as creating the fresh breeze needed in the afterlife. The classical elegance of this piece of craftsmanship recalls the tradition of the goldsmiths of the Middle Kingdom, like other objects in this tomb. While some flowing and mannerist objects relate more to the Amarnian style, others such as these come closer to the classical Egyptian canons of aesthetics.

148, 149. *Three ceremonial canes showing the adversaries of Egypt.*

Three figures of Egypt's hereditary enemies are carved on the work of these ceremonial canes, which were supposed to be cast down, symbolizing perhaps the dragging of the prisoners in the dust, thus protecting the realm's frontiers.

The first cane is entirely gilded but for the painted feet, hands, and head of a Semitic-looking prisoner whose face is very realistically carved and painted: red hair and beard, black pupils set within the white corneas of his eyes. The second cane, on the bottom left, is covered with a different kind of gilding composed of an alloy comprising more copper: it shows an African prisoner with head, feet, and hands, carved out of ebony. The cane on the right is also painted and terminated by the head of an Asiatic, probably an Assyrian, inlaid with ivory, whose eyes, beard, and hair are painted. There also the racial traits of the prisoner are clearly stressed.

150, 151.   *Gold sandals, and wooden sandals with gilded inner soles showing figures of captives.*

These gold sandals were placed over the mummy's feet and toes, capped in their gold sheaths. The second pair is made out of wood overlaid with green leather, bark, and gilding. A group of African and Assyrian captives are depicted on each inner sole placed between four bows painted at each end of the sandal. They represent the nine traditional enemies of Egypt on which the Pharaoh had to tread. The outer soles of these sandals are covered with white stucco.

152.   *Left to right: ivory smoother for papyrus, Princess Meritaten's palette, and ivory and gold palette with brushes.*

This ivory burnisher was probably meant as a funerary model of the wooden instrument which originally served to smooth out papyrus sheets. It is made of two parts: the handle is terminated by a painted papyrus flower, while the upper part bears a hieroglyphic inscription containing the cartouches of the King's birth name on one side and of his coronation name on the other, and it is dedicated to the gods Thoth, patron of scribes, and Amen-Re.

The little ivory palette shows six small holes which still conserve traces of white, yellow, red, blue, and black pigments. As a writer's palette contained only black and red pigments, this palette was made for painting. The slot in the middle was for the brushes, which were actually made out of rushes, the extremities of which were chewed to make the writing point. The double inscription which runs horizontally and vertically on the palette tells us that this object belonged to Meritaten, born from the Great Royal Spouse, Neferneferuaten-Nefertiti, who in marrying Smenkhare had become Tutankhamen's sister-in-law as well as niece. The other inscription referring to Thoth, god of writing and wisdom, tells us that this palette allowed the dead to regain his power once equipped with the secrets of Thoth. Placed between the paws of the great black Anubis (see Pl. 59), this object was not only the ex-voto the princess had used as a child to write and paint, but it was also an essential instrument in the ritual of Tutankhamen's rebirth.
Length: 8⁵/₈ inches.

The second palette, also made of ivory but much larger, was used solely for writing and as such still shows remains of the little black and red cakes, the traditional inks used by the scribes. In the central slot, seven rushes, or *calami*, from the name of the reed growing in the Nile, were found. One of its edges is capped with a gold sheet, and the palette bears the cartouches of Tutankhamen and an epithet

"beloved of the Gods Atum, Amen-Re, and Thoth."
Length: 12 inches.

153. *Ebony and ivory gaming table and cabinet.*

There were four gaming boards in Tutankhamen's tomb and playing these games must have been one of the King's favorite pastimes. Chapter 17 of the *Book of the Dead* refers to a game called *senet*, which was one of the occupations of the dead in the afterlife. Another later religious text refers to *senet* as the game the deceased had to play against a divine opponent which would thus decide his fate.

This elaborate checkered box is placed on an ebony stand composed of a sledge surmounted by four feline legs with golden claws resting on gold drums. The gilded tail of the feline appears at one end of the stand. The ebony box is placed on this stand and is inscribed all around with a gilded hieroglyphic band, wishing the King prosperity and referring to his different epithets. Two game boards are placed on each side. The one which is hidden underneath in this plate is the *tjau* (thieves) game with twenty-four squares, of which three are inscribed. On the top, as is shown in this plate, is the *senet* game with five inscribed squares. It seems that the aim of the game was to reach the square inscribed with three signs along with happiness and beauty. Cones and knuckle bones were used as playing pieces. Two pairs of casting sticks were found, one shaped as human figures, the other as fox heads, all four made of ebony and ivory. It seems that the game was played like the game of goose, although here these sticks replaced dice. All these pieces were kept inside the box, which opened from the side.
Length: $18^1/_8$ inches.

154. *Detail of beaded hassock.*

A great deal of woven basketwork was found in the tomb. This hassock was made of rushwork and lined with linen. It was covered with a beadwork which has retained all of its fresh colors: here a prisoner seems to be floating near lotus and papyrus reeds; he is depicted between circles of different geometric patterns which form a rosette motif.

155. *Mirror case in the shape of a kneeling figure representing the symbol of eternity.*

One of the two mirror cases found in the tomb (the other in the shape of an *ankh* life sign), this painted wood case is in the shape of the god Heh: the kneeling figure is holding two gilded reeds evoking the years without number stemming from gilded tadpoles (sign for 100,000 years), which are themselves resting on the rings of eternal life. Heh is wearing an unusually long beard, and on either side of his head are placed the two royal cartouches of the King. The mirror case stands above his head, and on it is carved the figure of a winged scarab, pushing the solar disk forward. This funerary mirror case was certainly intended to preserve the face of the King in his eternal youth, as demonstrated by the symbols carved on the case.
Height: about $10^5/_8$ inches.

Index